TOYOTA
SUPPLY CHAIN
MANAGEMENT

A STRATEGIC APPROACH
TO THE PRINCIPLES OF
TOYOTA'S RENOWNED SYSTEM

ANANTH V. IYER
SRIDHAR SESHADRI
ROY VASHER

Mc
Graw
Hill

New York Chicago San Francisco Lisbon London Madrid Mexico City
Milan New Delhi San Juan Seoul Singapore Sydney Toronto

1 2 3 4 5 6 7 8 9 0   DOC/DOC   0 1 5 4 3 2 1 0 9

ISBN 978-0-07-161549-5

MHID 0-07-161549-0

This publication is designed to provide accurate and authoritative information in regard to the subject matter covered. It is sold with the understanding that neither the author nor the publisher is engaged in rendering legal, accounting, futures/securities trading, or other professional service. If legal advice or other expert assistance is required, the services of a competent professional person should be sought.

—*From a Declaration of Principles jointly adopted by a Committee of the American Bar Association and a Committee of Publishers*

McGraw-Hill books are available at special quantity discounts to use as premiums and sales promotions, or for use in corporate training programs. To contact a representative, please visit the Contact US pages at www.mhprofessional.com.

This book is printed on acid-free paper.

To my wife Vidhya and daughters Apsara and Rani,
and in memory of my parents
Thank you

Ananth

To my wife Shubha, daughters Padmavati and Sharada,
and all my family
Thank you

Sridhar

To my wife Audrey; daughters Jody and Neely; my mother Emma,
who at the time of this writing is 105; and all my family
All my love

Roy

Contents

Foreword

For decades, Toyota's success in the marketplace has been admired by business practitioners and executives alike. The automaker is the envy of others within the automobile industry, but the company is also considered to be the symbol of excellence in business in general. The firm has been the focus of research in academia.

The power of Toyota has been attributed to its two distinct core values: the Toyota Way and the Toyota Production System (TPS). The Toyota Way has created a culture of respect for individuals, promoting innovation and fostering cooperation. TPS has been the engine under which lean manufacturing, kanbans, quality systems, just-in-time, and continuous improvement practices have been developed. Together, they have been the pillars for the foundation upon which Toyota has become so successful.

But the Toyota Way and TPS are just foundational pillars. There is another concrete secret to the success of Toyota: the way the company runs its supply chain. The Toyota Way and TPS of course have been part of how Toyota has developed its supply chain principles and how the company has applied such principles to work with its suppliers, dealers, and manufacturers. Based on these principles, Toyota has coordinated the plans across the supply chain—and it has executed them well. Supply chain management excellence is the ultimate way in which Toyota has built its superior efficiency in operations.

I am delighted to see this book about Toyota's supply chain management written by two leading academics and an experienced Toyota executive. This book reveals the powerful way that Toyota runs its supply chain, and it shows vividly how the Toyota Way and TPS have been ingrained in the processes used by Toyota to run its supply chain. I submit that reading about Toyota Way and TPS is only a starting point for really learning the innovativeness and effectiveness of Toyota's operations. The current book completes the picture.

While TPS is the central theme of how Toyota runs its factories, the scope of supply chain management is much greater. It spans suppliers to Toyota as well as possibly the suppliers' suppliers, the distribution channel, the dealers, and ultimately, the consumers. The coordination, planning, and control of this extensive network are a daunting task. The current book well describes how Toyota has been very smart in examining three dimensions of supply chain management: geography, product, and time. This book gives us a treatment on how Toyota has designed and operated supply chains to adapt to these three dimensions. For example, the needs for the Japanese and U.S. markets, the Camry versus the Lexus, and at different points in time of the product life cycle, are different, and so different supply chain processes are needed.

I would urge the reader going through this book to keep two perspectives in mind. First, it describes in great details how Toyota runs its supply chain. As a result, there are many innovative ideas that Toyota uses, and many best practices described. So the reader can pick up a lot of useful tips and revelations. Second, the structure of the book is extremely helpful to organize your thoughts and evaluations of your own supply chain. The chapters that follow cover the whole spectrum of what constitutes comprehensive supply chain management. So, going through the chapters gives you a framework to follow. In that sense, even if you extract the Toyota content out of the chapters, the book is a good guideline to develop sound supply chain management practices.

One of the most useful conceptual frameworks in this book is the v4L construct. We see how Toyota manages its supply chain to ensure that the 4v's—variety, velocity, variability, and visibility—can be controlled. In every chapter, for every supply chain operation, the authors describe how this can be done. Again, seeing how Toyota has done it is valuable and informative. But I also think that the reader can benefit from seeing how the authors developed the thought process behind what Toyota did to accomplish the objectives of gaining control of the 4v's. That knowledge by itself is highly educational.

For anyone who wants to learn the true secret of Toyota's operational excellence, this book is a must-read. In addition, while learning about Toyota's supply chain management, we also are given a journey of sound supply chain management in general.

In my personal research, I have come across Toyota's supply chain management practices and have been very impressed by how thorough and innovative the company has been since its inception in the 1930s. I must congratulate the authors of this book, as they have done the most comprehensive, insightful, and penetrating treatment of this subject.

Hau L. Lee
Thoma Professor of Operations, Information, and Technology
Graduate School of Business, Stanford University
Stanford, CA

Acknowledgments

The authors express their appreciation to the management of Toyota Motor Engineering & Manufacturing North America, Inc., for providing access to their executives for interviews as well as for the tour of the Georgetown manufacturing facility. Nancy Banks, manager external affairs, was extremely helpful in coordinating the interviews and arranging for the plant tour. Nancy also spent countless hours reviewing drafts of the book and providing excellent feedback.

The interviews with Toyota executives provided deep insights into Toyota's management of the supply chain. We would like to thank all of the interviewees for taking precious time out of their busy schedules to speak with us. Gene Tabor and Jamey Lykins, general managers in Toyota's Purchasing Division, discussed how Toyota's purchasing relationship with suppliers plays an important role to ensure a strong partnership with suppliers at all levels. David Burbidge, vice president of Production Control, provided an excellent overview of Production Control's role in managing the supply chain. Mike Botkin, general manager of Logistics, shared with us his expertise of Toyota's Logistics operation.

In addition, the interviews with executives from Toyota's partners enlightened us on how the extended supply chain supports Toyota's management philosophy. Jeffrey Smith, vice president and general manager for Toyota Business Unit Johnson Controls, Inc., has several years of working with Toyota around the world and was able to provide the supplier perspective. Gary Dodd, former president of Tire & Wheel Assembly, also discussed the supplier's role and explained the process of becoming a new Toyota supplier. To round out the supply chain we spoke with Steve Gates, dealer principal, Toyota South in Richmond, Kentucky, to obtain an understanding of the dealer operations in the Toyota environment. Steve is also a member of Toyota's dealer council, so he was able to provide a comprehensive view not only of the dealer's operation but also the Toyota dealer network. Achim Paechtner, former senior manager of Toyota of Europe, provided a framework of how Toyota and other automobile companies operate in Europe. Achim's understanding of the European markets was extremely helpful.

We thank the Toyota Motor Corporation for endowing the Term Professorship at the Stern School of Business without which Sridhar Seshadri, the first Toyota Motor Term professor, would never have met Roy Vasher and this joint project would never have been undertaken. Ananth Iyer acknowledges the support of the Krannert School of Management at Purdue University whose Fall DCMME Manufacturing Conference, where Roy was a speaker in 2007, provided a forum for the authors to meet face-to-face for the first time.

We thank Mayank Agarwal, MBA student at the Stern School of Business for his extensive research into the automobile business. The research was used in this book to confirm the benefits of Toyota's supply chain management. The final manuscript would not be complete without the assistance of Leslie Culpepper, who helped copyedit this manuscript.

Introduction

Toyota uses unique processes to effectively manage and operate the supply chain. These processes span the supply chain and have enabled Toyota to deliver remarkably consistent performance over decades. The authors, a retired Toyota senior executive with hands-on experience and two senior academics, have pooled their combined experience to both describe existing processes as well as understand why they work. By combining the insights of a practitioner with almost 20 years of Toyota's execution and management experience and two academics with decades of research experience, we hope to provide a unique presentation of the topic that can influence supply chain practices at auto and nonmanufacturing companies.

The fundamental thesis of this book is that understanding process details, as well as the logic associated with their success, will enable adoption of these ideas in both manufacturing and service contexts. The material in the pages that follow provides insights into how Toyota uses learning (L) processes to implement practices and principles, both within Toyota's cross-functional organizations as well as with Toyota's partners (including suppliers and dealers)—in short, across the extended supply chain. *We show how integrated and synchronized processes enable careful balancing of variety, velocity, variability, and visibility (4v's) across the supply chain.* Learning is linked to the 4v's to form the v4L framework. We will describe the v4L framework in more detail in Chapter 1.

In keeping with the "how-to" approach to these complex topics, most chapters provide illustrative examples that both explain details as well as illuminate the logic behind the processes. The choice of topics is meant to focus on essential tactical and operational differences in the way Toyota manages its supply chain. Chapter 1 describes the v4L framework and the Toyota learning principles. Chapter 2 provides a comprehensive overview of processes that are part of the overall supply chain. That, in turn, is followed by topics in the sequence of activities in a supply chain. First, there's "Mix Planning" (Chapter 3) to support production stability and how this is translated into "Sales and Operations Planning" (Chapter 4). We then cover how sales requests are supported by "Production Scheduling and Operations" (Chapter 5), "Parts Ordering" (Chapter 6), and "Managing Suppliers" (Chapter 7). The inbound and outbound "Logistics" processes are described next (Chapter 8), followed by "Dealer and Demand Fulfillment" (Chapter 9) and dealer-related processes, which will complete the supply chain coverage. Finally, Chapter 10 covers how Toyota handles "Crisis Management."

The detailed discussion of Toyota's supply chain processes will be followed by chapters on "The Toyota Way of Managing Supply Chains" (Chapter 11) and how that has been used to design and improve each of these steps, and "How to Apply Toyota Way Principles to Nonautomotive Supply Chains" (Chapter 12). We have also included a chapter titled "The Beer Game and the Toyota Supply Chain" (Chapter 13), which describes the well-known bullwhip effect in supply chains and examines how following Toyota's integration of processes across the supply chain enables reduction of the bullwhip effect. Two "Reflections" chapters conclude the book: Chapter 14 examines the reflections of supply chain participants; Chapter 15 reflects on the Toyota experience in general and considers potential future innovations in the automotive supply chain.

Although there are several excellent books that describe the Toyota production system, as well as a few that cover principles used in the Toyota supply chain, we believe there is a benefit to understanding process details in order to execute processes consistent with the principles. The sources of material for this book include firsthand experience with applying these processes at Toyota, direct interviews with Toyota-experienced managers and suppliers, existing books on Toyota's processes, academic research, surveys, and empirical case studies.

Chapter 1

Toyota Learning Principles and the v4L Framework

Toyota is well known for its approach to problem solving and continuous improvement. Articles by practitioners, researchers, and participants have made the tools and techniques of continuous improvement familiar to every business executive. For example, phrases such as *andon, heijunka,* and *kanban* have become part of the day-to-day vocabulary of managers. In an insightful commentary on these tools and techniques, Jeffrey Liker writes that Toyota's success goes beyond these tools and techniques to what he calls "The Toyota Way."[1]

Liker presents the Toyota Way as an all-encompassing method for designing and managing processes. Every student of Toyota also knows that the Toyota Way is unique, not only in its approach to problem solving but also in perpetuating its way of thinking across different types of operations, organizations (including suppliers, logistics providers, and dealers), and worldwide locations. Underlying the success of Toyota is the company's approach to scientifically examining problems, solving them, learning from the experience, and passing on that knowledge to others.

Toyota is a global auto company with many products and markets. The company encompasses markets across the globe with different characteristics (e.g., the United States, Europe, and Japan) that warrant different supply chain configurations. In addition, differences among the Toyota, Lexus, and Scion vehicles warrant different supply chain processes. Although common processes underpin these supply chains, variations across these supply chains provide additional insights. We believe that an understanding of how all these supply chains coexist in one company provides an excellent learning opportunity for a practicing supply chain manager to apply the v4L framework to his or her work.

v4L Framework

Performance at Toyota is evaluated with equal weight given to both the process used to derive performance and the results achieved. This process focus aims to generate a balance of key supply chain parameters—variety of products offered, velocity of product flow, variability of outcomes against forecast, and visibility of processes to enable learning. The learning follows a carefully documented process that promotes continuous improvement. At the end of every chapter a reflection section will be included that links the chapter to the v4L framework: balancing variety, velocity, variability, and visibility across the supply chain. One way for managers to understand Toyota's concepts is to first ask how their company's supply chain achieves this balance. Often, variety is chosen with a focus on marketing benefits with scant attention to supply chain implications, velocity, variability, and the like. This off-optimal choice of variety can have severe repercussions across the supply chain, which is often difficult to untangle. A careful choice of v4L parameters enables superior supply chain performance at Toyota.

Learning (L) Principles

Toyota has mastered the art of learning and believes that the principles to attain mastery are universal. Moreover, Toyota has spread these ideas throughout its supply chain in its leadership role. We shall review these ideas in later chapters and provide a summary of methods that makes learning a practical and ongoing process at every level and every task in Toyota. Toyota's way of making learning happen not only conforms to the theory of learning (as we mention in Chapter 11) but can be simply explained (as is often the case with things that are very hard to accomplish!). The following are the main principles:

- *Create awareness.* Unless problems are seen, they will not be solved. Systems need to be in place to report ideas, problems, deviations, and potential issues to a direct team leader with no delay.
- *Establish capability.* Unless someone is capable of solving a problem that might arise within the system boundaries set for him or her, that person will be unable to contribute to the problem-solving process and will be unable to recognize the need for specialized help.
- *Make action protocols.* Actions have to be taken within a set of constraints, and they must conform to certain standards. Doing so will help in the identification of the relation between action and results. It will aid in the codification of the knowledge for future use, with the same language and format used as well as similar content.
- *Generate system-level awareness.* As experience with solving problems is obtained, greater awareness of other areas that might be affected

by actions or that might impact one's own performance needs to be created.

■ *Produce the ability to teach.* As system-level awareness and experience accumulate, the capability to teach others about these methods needs to be in place.

v4L Principles

The v4L learning principles are combined across all Toyota supply chain management processes to systematically focus on the v4L balance:

■ *Variety* is carefully chosen to balance market demands and operational efficiency. Awareness of the impact of variety on the market demand and on manufacturing and supply chain costs enables all the entities across the supply chain to be considered when decisions regarding variety are being made. In one sense, variety represents a crucial supply chain design choice that has an impact across all supply chain participants. A key issue when variety is being chosen is the need to have feedback loops to ensure that the selected variety represents the best response to current market conditions. As we will discuss in each of the chapters, this is where the learning features of Toyota's process enable the constant loop of Plan, Do, Check, and Act (PDCA).

■ *Velocity* of supply chain flows is the next key concept, and it manifests itself in all processes across the supply chain. A focus on maintaining a steady flow throughout the system enables capacity planning to be synchronized across the supply chain. The detailed process descriptions in the following chapters will highlight how a rate-based approach serves as a linchpin for the planning processes across the system.

■ *Variability* of orders or deliveries across the supply chain is minimized by how the individual processes are executed. Reducing variability enables all of the supply chain flows to operate with low levels of inventory. It also enables quality improvement processes to operate without interruption, thus enabling continuous cost reductions and quality improvements. Notice that variety, velocity, and variability all interact to stabilize supply chain performance.

■ *Visibility* of all processes is ensured with use of the right metrics and the requirement that a consensus be reached before plans are changed. At Toyota, performance metrics have a 50 percent weight for results and a 50 percent weight for process compliance. In other words, the goal is to reward not only short-term successes but also ensure that the correct processes are followed. Such an approach ensures that bottlenecks are visible and responses immediate, changes are deliberate, velocity is maintained, variety is synchronized to demand, and variability is minimized. Visibility enables continuous learning and feedback, thus guaranteeing that execution of processes remains synchronized with market realities.

We suggest that v4L highlight the intricate balance of all supply chain processes. How each of them is balanced by vehicle type or geography is a business choice that reflects Toyota's competitiveness in that market. The choice of the v4L and the actions required to implement these choices are guided by the learning principles. All companies should be asking themselves how their current choices reflect the impact of the v4L. A way to remember this concept is to ask, is the supply chain's v4L engine at my company appropriately tuned for competitive performance?

Endnote

1. Jeffrey K. Liker, *The Toyota Way*. New York: McGraw-Hill, 2004.

Chapter 2

Comprehensive Overview of Supply Chain

The Toyota Production System (TPS) is the benchmark used throughout the world as the foundation for "lean" thinking. At Toyota, the TPS practices and principles extend well beyond the factory walls to include the extended supply chain and require some crucial choices to ensure supply chain efficiency. This chapter explains how Toyota plans and operates its supply chains globally. But first, a brief look at the extended global automobile supply chain is in order, which will enable you to understand the processes described in the following chapters.

The automotive supply chain is very complex and consists of many processes that, when linked together, form a supply chain from the customer back to the various tiers of suppliers. The physical processes consist of the production of parts at the suppliers, transportation of these parts to the assembly plant of the original equipment manufacturer (OEM), assembly of parts into a completed vehicle, distribution of completed vehicles to dealers, and finally delivery to a customer. In addition to the physical processes, there are both pre-production and day-to-day operational support processes. To fully understand these processes, some background on the auto industry is necessary. The following questions need to be answered:

- What is the product?
- Who are the customers?
- What are the distribution models?

What Is the Product?

A car or a truck can be described with its specifications. Each OEM uses a slightly different terminology to define a vehicle's specifications. Toyota uses a

Table 2-1. Vehicle Specifications Hierarchy

Make	Model	Body	Grade	Options	Accessories
Toyota	Camry	Sedan	LE	Sunroof	Spoiler
		Sedan	XLE	Navigation	Floor mats
	Tundra	Crew cab		XM Radio	Tow hitch
		Double cab		Sunroof	Bed liner
Lexus	ES350	Sedan		Navigation	Floor mats

hierarchical method of vehicle specifications. The typical hierarchy of the vehicle specifications is shown in Table 2-1. The following are some examples of vehicle specifications:

- *Make*. Toyota, Lexus
- *Models*. Camry, Avalon, Tundra, Sienna, etc.
- *Body style*. Four-door sedan, two-door coupe, convertible, crew cab, double cab, etc.
- *Grade*. XLE, LE, SE, etc. When a grade is selected, it usually includes several standard equipment items. Typically the higher-grade vehicles include many standard items. Sometimes when the grade is selected, the engine and transmission combination is included as standard equipment.
- *Engine*. Six-cylinder, four-cylinder, etc.
- *Transmission*. Automatic, five-speed, etc.
- *Factory options*. Engine, transmission, sunroof, air-conditioning, navigation, radio, power windows, etc.
- *Accessories*. These items are like options, but they can be installed in the factory or added after the vehicle is built. Examples are spoiler, tow hitch, roof rack, and pinstripes.

In addition to the above specifications, exterior and interior colors must be included to complete the vehicle build specifications:

- *Exterior color*. The outside color is usually one color; however, it could be two-toned.
- *Interior trim/color*. The interior colors (e.g., black leather and gray cloth) are usually coordinated with exterior ones, but not all interior colors always will be available with all exterior colors.

So each vehicle is built with a unique set of specifications called a "build combination." If all possible build combinations were produced, then the total build combinations for a model would be in the millions. This variety would make managing the supply chain an extremely complex and costly process; therefore, many automotive companies limit the number of build combinations offered in each market area. Toyota has been extremely successful in balancing the combinations that are made and sold by sales area. For example, one approach used at Toyota to reduce the build combinations is to include many standard equipment options based on the model and grade that is selected. The methodology on how to choose profitable levels of variety to be offered across market areas is explained in Chapter 3.

Who Are the Customers?

Automobile companies have several categories of customers that need to be considered. The following is a list of the types of customers and a brief description of each:

- *Retail consumers.* The retail segment is the largest segment of customers, and it is also the one in which the automotive companies make the most profits. Although not all retail customers are the same, as yet there are not clear classifications for groups of customers. Figure 2-1 illustrates how various customer types can be plotted along a continuum: at one end is the serious buyer and at the other is the serious shopper.
  - The serious buyer is a person who needs a vehicle within a short time frame. This type of buyer shops for price and value and will compromise on vehicle specifications. Some reasons that this type of buyer is in the market for a vehicle are that a vehicle needs replacement because of an accident, the current vehicle needs major repair, or the lease is expiring. This type of customer wants to walk into a dealership and drive out with a new vehicle.
  - The serious shopper is a person who has done homework and knows exactly what he or she wants. This type of shopper has researched several vehicle models and options prior to visiting the dealership and then proceeds to the dealer with the complete vehicle specification in

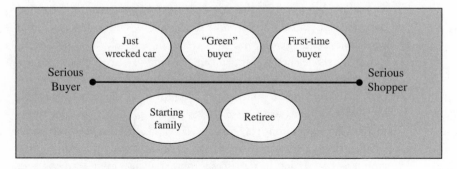

Figure 2-1. Customer continuum

hand. Because the serious shopper is very particular about the vehicle he or she wants, this customer will shop around or perhaps wait until a vehicle can be ordered "fresh from the factory." Examples of the serious shopper are a consumer who is young, a first-time buyer, and a car enthusiast.

  ○ The area on the continuum from the serious buyer to the serious shopper is by far where most customers can be found. Indeed, most customers who walk into a dealership have not made up their minds on the exact vehicle specification or even if they are ready to buy a vehicle.

■ *Employees/suppliers:*

  ○ *Employees.* Automotive companies allow employees, relatives, and (in some cases) friends to purchase a limited number of vehicles per year at a substantial discount. The employees must receive prior approval before proceeding to a dealer to make a purchase or place an order. The purchase price is calculated automatically based on the discount allowed. The dealer may also receive some rebate to ensure that the dealer margin is maintained.

  ○ *Suppliers.* Automotive companies may offer selected employees of suppliers a vehicle purchase program. This arrangement is similar to the employee purchase program in that the purchaser must get prior approval before proceeding to a dealer to purchase a vehicle. The purchase price is calculated automatically based on the discount allowed. The dealer may also receive some rebate to guarantee that the dealer margin is maintained.

■ *Fleet:*

  ○ *Rental companies.* The rental companies (Hertz, Avis, Enterprise, etc.) negotiate a contract with each automobile company for annual volume of each model. The detailed specifications of each monthly vehicle order are submitted in advance, and the vehicles are scheduled for production based on the delivery schedule requested by the rental companies. Because space at most rental facilities is limited, the rental companies need to minimize the overlap of new vehicles arriving and the used vehicles being shipped out for auction or resale.

  ○ *Commercial fleet.* These are private companies that provide a company car for selected employees who require a vehicle to perform their job or for certain executives as a perk. Examples are senior management, sales representatives, taxi drivers, and delivery persons. These smaller fleet customers may negotiate a deal with the automotive company or a dealer. In some cases there may be a long-term contract with multiple automotive companies to provide specific models for a company vehicle program. The company may offer employees an option to select from a list of vehicles with specified options from multiple automotive companies. Then, either based on a lease period or on mileage, the employee will order a replacement vehicle.

o   *Government entities.* All levels of government—federal, state, and local—purchase vehicles from the automotive companies. Contracts are usually negotiated with the automotive companies to provide vehicles over a period of time. In many cases, special orders may need to be placed for vehicles with unique equipment such as police cars and fire trucks.

Clearly, streamlining the supply chain requires an understanding of the customer types and relative size and profitability of each segment. The following are some examples that show how the customer types affect the supply chain:

■   At Toyota plants in Japan, a large percentage of the production orders are exported to countries all around the world. So these order requirements are fixed and scheduled at least one month in advance for production. Toyota's advantage is that it can allow its domestic dealers in Japan to change a greater percentage of orders closer to production because the export orders do not change. The export orders create a buffer to absorb the domestic changes in orders.

■   At Dell, about 85 percent of the orders are for corporate customers. Corporate orders are forecast in advance and can be scheduled based on the lead time for each corporate customer. The retail orders coming through the Internet can be fulfilled quickly even if demand is highly volatile, because the corporate orders can be shifted slightly to absorb the variability in retail customer demand.

■   At Ford, when Hertz was a wholly owned subsidiary, at least 40 percent of some models were sold to Hertz. This arrangement enabled Ford to use the Hertz volume to fill in the valleys in demand during the year when retail sales were slow.

Thus, customer types and order characteristics can be used to build a more flexible supply chain.

What Are the Distribution Models?

The term "distribution model" defines the method used to distribute vehicles from the assembly plant to the dealers. There are many variations in the distribution model within the automotive industry. At Toyota, the distribution model is different for various regions around the world. For example, the United States, Europe, and Japan all have different models, and in some cases the models vary within a regional area. Lee, Peleg, and Whang explain that just as Toyota has a set of central core values but allows individual divisions to customize to local conditions, when it comes to supplying to different geographies, different products, or at different times in the product life cycle, "the company adapts the design and control of its demand chain so that it has the right demand chain for the right product, in the right place, and at the right time."[1] In the United States, there are three distribution models:

- *North American production.* In this model, vehicles are produced at the North American assembly plants and shipped to North American dealers. Once vehicles are released from the plant, they are moved to a marshaling yard. The function of the marshaling yard is to prepare the vehicles for shipment. Vehicles are shipped via train and truck to the dealerships. If vehicles are shipped by train, then they must be transferred to trucks at a railhead near the dealership. If vehicles are shipped by truck, then they will be delivered directly to the dealership. While the vehicles are in the marshaling yard, some accessories can be added, a final quality assurance check performed, prep performed on selected vehicles, and the price label affixed to the side window. "Prep" is a term that describes the tasks that are normally performed at the dealer just prior to customer delivery. The total time it takes to distribute a vehicle once it leaves the assembly plant can range from two days to three weeks, depending on how far the dealer is located from the factory. In this distribution model, vehicles are typically allocated and assigned to dealers two to four weeks prior to production. The vehicle inventory is stored at the dealerships.

- *Overseas production distributed in North America.* With this distribution model, vehicles produced in Japan are shipped via large vessels to ports in North America and then transported to dealerships. The port provides functions similar to the marshaling yards'; however, typically there are several accessories that are installed at the port to enable the dealers to customize the vehicles closer to delivery. It takes three to five weeks to ship the vehicles from Japan to North American ports. It can take another two days to one week to transport to dealers via truck. The reason why this delivery time is shorter than the time it takes to transport vehicles from the North American factories is that vehicles arriving from Japan are shipped to a port that is located geographically close to dealers. The ports are located in cities such as Portland, Oregon; Long Beach, California; Houston, Texas; Jacksonville, Florida; and Newark, New Jersey. The vehicles are normally allocated and assigned to dealers while they are in transit from Japan to the port; however, they must be allocated to a regional area prior to being loaded onto the ships. That step is necessary because vehicles destined for the East Coast will be loaded onto different ships than ones destined for the West Coast. As with the North American model, vehicle inventory in this production model is stored at the dealerships.

- *Scion model.* Scion cars are produced in Japan and distributed in North America in a manner similar to the distribution model described previously; however, there are some significant differences that provide the dealers with much greater flexibility to customize the Scion cars for customers. The first difference is that Scion cars are shipped to the ports with only basic equipment installed at the factory and in limited colors. The second difference is that Scions are allocated but not shipped to the dealers until the dealer makes a request. That arrangement allows the dealer to select a base model and color, and then add accessories to customize it to meet the customer requirements. Most vehicle inventory is held at the port, which allows flexibility for customization. That adaptability is consistent with the key strategy behind Toyota's introduction of the Scion, namely, to keep a customer for life.[2] As stated previously, the vehicle inventory is stored at the port with the exception of a limited number of vehicles located at dealers for display.

- *European distribution model.* In Europe, the distribution model is very different from North America, because most dealers are located in urban areas and do not have room for vehicle stock. Therefore, once vehicles are released from the plant, they move to a marshaling yard. The function of the marshaling yard is only to stage the vehicles for shipment. Vehicles are shipped primarily by truck to a consolidation point called a "hub." Generally there is at least one hub for each country; however, smaller countries may share a hub, and large countries may have multiple hubs. The hub serves to hold the vehicle inventory until a dealer signs a contract with a customer. At that time, an order is sent to the hub for a specific vehicle. Also, the dealer can request additional accessories to be installed at the hub prior to shipment. The transit time from a hub to the dealer averages one week. In Europe, most vehicle inventory is stored at the hub, not at the dealerships.

- *Japanese distribution model.* In Japan, the distribution model is similar to that for Europe because most dealer retail outlets have very small storage lots. The difference is that in Japan each dealer has a consolidation center where the vehicle inventory is stored until one of the dealer retail outlets sells a vehicle. At that time an order is sent to the consolidation center and the vehicle is shipped to the dealer retail outlet. Again, as in Europe, most vehicle inventory is kept at the consolidation center, not at the dealerships.

Supply Chain Overview

The supply chain has both physical components as well as operational and planning processes.

Physical Flows

The physical flow of the supply chain is shown in Figure 2-2. Parts are produced by suppliers and transported by inbound logistics to the assembly plant. At the assembly plant, the vehicle begins in the body shop, moves to the paint shop, then to assembly, and finally to inspection. Once the vehicle is produced, it is transported to the dealerships via outbound logistics. On paper this process looks very simple; however, it is complex because a vehicle is very large and bulky, it is assembled from thousands of parts that are produced by hundreds of suppliers, and there are thousands of vehicle combinations that could be produced.

Suppliers Suppliers provide thousands of parts and components that go into the vehicle. These parts and components are received via the inbound logistics network from hundreds of tier 1 suppliers. Tier 1 consists of the first-level suppliers that make parts and ship directly to the assembly plants. Because suppliers also have suppliers, and those suppliers have suppliers, the supply chain contains several levels that are referred to as tier 1, tier 2, tier 3, and so on. So you can imagine how complex the inbound supply chain is for an automobile assembly plant. In addition, because suppliers are located in various geographic areas, the time for parts to arrive from each supplier to the assembly plant can vary greatly. Local suppliers may be only one or two days away from the assembly plant, whereas suppliers located overseas may require several weeks of transportation time.

Inbound Logistics After parts are produced by the suppliers, they are shipped to the assembly plants. The process to ship these parts from the many suppliers to each assembly plant is referred to as "inbound logistics." At Toyota, parts are delivered in two ways. Overseas parts coming from Japan are shipped via vessel

Suppliers	Inbound	Factory				Outbound	Dealers
	Logistics	Body	Paint	Assembly	Inspection	Logistics	

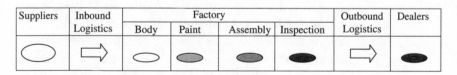

Figure 2-2. Physical flow

and then by railcar to the assembly plant. Once the railcar arrives at the assembly plant rail yard, the container is offloaded onto a truck and driven to the assembly dock.

Local parts produced in North America are shipped by truck using a dedicated logistics partner. Toyota takes complete responsibility for pickup and transportation of parts from the suppliers to the plants, because Toyota's just-in-time parts inventory practice requires extreme reliability of inbound logistics. Toyota organizes the suppliers into clusters based on geographic proximity. The truck routes are designed for parts to be picked up from multiple suppliers and delivered to a regional cross-dock. To improve efficiency, the same truck will pick up parts not only from multiple suppliers but also from each supplier destined for different Toyota plants.

Once trucks arrive at the cross-dock, the parts are unloaded and staged for each assembly plant. They are then loaded onto trucks that take parts directly to each plant. Trucks are unloaded at the plant based on the progress of production. If the plant is operating on schedule, the trucks will wait only a few hours in the plant yard. After the parts are unloaded, the truck is reloaded with the corresponding empty returnable containers. These returnable containers flow in reverse through the cross-dock and back to the supplier to be reused for a future shipment.

Production   Vehicles are produced at the final assembly plant from the parts provided by hundreds of suppliers. A typical assembly plant will have one or more separate lines on which vehicles are assembled. The plant is subdivided into shops. The vehicle is born in the body shop where the frame and body are formed. The body parts are stamped in the stamping shop by presses. The body shop is where numerous robots are used to weld the body parts together. Once the body is assembled, then the vehicle moves to the paint shop and its exterior is painted.

After the vehicle is painted, it moves down the line into final assembly. At that point most of the supplier-provided parts are installed to make a finished vehicle. Each part is assigned a line location so that parts can be delivered from the dock to a line address based on a bar code label affixed to the parts container by the supplier. After the vehicle is assembled, fuel is added and the vehicle is driven off the assembly line. But at that point the process is not yet complete because the vehicle still needs to go through several quality control steps along with final inspection. Once the vehicle completes the final inspection, it is released from the factory for shipment to the dealer.

Outbound Logistics   Vehicles that are produced at an assembly plant must be transported to each dealer. This process is commonly referred to as "outbound logistics." In the United States, vehicles are transported by two modes: railcar and truck. Because of the long distances that vehicles must travel, about 75 percent of the vehicles travel via railcar and are then loaded onto trucks for delivery to the dealers. The remaining 25 percent are delivered by truck to dealers that are located within two to three days' drive from the factory. In Europe, most vehicles are shipped by truck; however, sometimes ships must be used when there is a large waterway that must be crossed.

Just outside the assembly plant, there is a large yard that is used to stage the vehicles prior to shipment. At Toyota, these yards are referred to as "marshaling yards." In the United States, these yards perform three functions. Team members install accessories, perform final quality assurance, and stage vehicles for shipment. Once the vehicle is ready for shipment, it is driven to either the railcar staging area or the truck staging area.

For railcar shipments, there are two types of railcars: bi-level and tri-level. "Bi-level" means vehicles are loaded onto two levels within the railcar, and "tri-level" means vehicles are loaded onto three levels. The capacity of a bi-level railcar is 9 to 10 vehicles; a tri-level, 14 to 15 vehicles. Therefore, vehicles are staged in lanes according to the capacity of the railcar and the destination.

Vehicles shipped by truck are identified by the dealer and parked in a truck staging area. The trucking company is responsible for selecting the vehicles to be loaded onto each truck based on the route plan for that truck. The trucking companies have a delivery performance objective to deliver all vehicles within two days. To ensure that both the trucking and rail companies have adequate capacity to ship vehicles, the assembly plant needs to provide a day-to-day forecast of volume by destination.

Dealers   Dealers play a key role in the supply chain because they are the face of Toyota to the customer. They are responsible for selling the vehicles produced by the manufacturer to the retail customers. In addition to selling vehicles, dealers have an extremely important influence on customer satisfaction. Independent customer surveys such as the "J.D. Power survey"[3] measure customer satisfaction in various categories. The two prime categories are (1) initial vehicle quality and (2) customer satisfaction regarding the selling process. Customers that score the selling process low also tend to give lower scores on the initial quality survey. A high J.D. Power score can be a valuable marketing tool for an automobile manufacturer. Therefore, it is critical not only that the vehicle quality itself be high but also that the customer buying experience be positive—or at least not negative. Two reasons that the Lexus vehicles always score high in the J.D. Power survey are that the vehicles are assembled with extreme attention to detail and that the customer is also pampered by the dealer.

It is imperative that a dealer invest sufficiently in a facility so that it can operate efficiently and at the same time meet or exceed its sales objectives. A key factor in a lean supply chain is the optimum level of dealer stock. It is also critical that a dealer have an adequate mix of stock so that most of the customers can be persuaded to buy from stock and the dealer does not end up with too many aged stock units. (Mix planning is discussed in Chapter 3.)

Vehicles are shipped to dealers from the assembly plants or from the port of entry. They are delivered by truck. The delivery time window will vary by dealer depending on dealer location and operating hours. Most dealers will accept vehicles only during business hours; however, a dealer may not want to be interrupted during very busy times. Therefore, the trucking company must understand the dealer's delivery time windows and schedule its deliveries accordingly. Most trucks will deliver a load of vehicles to multiple dealers, so the loading sequence must be planned based on the delivery route.

One of the key responsibilities of the salesperson is to guide customer demand. Toyota's sales model is designed so that a high percentage of vehicles is sold from a relatively low level of dealer stock. The objective is to stock 20 percent of build combinations that represent 80 percent of the sales for each market area. Some of the techniques that a dealer uses to achieve this end are to advertise and promote only the popular models and display these models in the showroom or in an area that is easy for the customer to see.

Once a vehicle is sold, the dealer must "prep" the vehicle for customer delivery. That usually means the dealer has to install wheel covers, wash and clean the vehicle, fill the tank with fuel, and inspect the vehicle to ensure that there are no defects. In addition, the dealer needs to prepare appropriate documents. At the time of delivery, the dealer will instruct the customer on how to operate various features of the vehicle, complete the paperwork, accept payment or arrange financing, and in some cases take possession of the trade-in vehicle.

After the vehicle is delivered, the dealer submits a sales transaction to the manufacturer, which will relieve the stock, provide the dealer with credit for the sale, and start the customer warranty date.

Various operational processes are necessary to operate the supply chain; Figure 2-3 provides another view of the transformation process that takes place from parts produced by suppliers to vehicles ready for sale at dealers.

What is the difference between the supply chain of most car manufacturers and of Toyota? Visualize the Toyota supply chain operation as a giant Swiss clock. The plant is the main mechanism of the clock. When a clock is opened to expose all of its working mechanisms, there are various-sized movements that are all moving at different speeds but are integrated precisely to ensure that the correct date and time are displayed on the face. This continuous motion repeats itself at numerous intervals: seconds, minutes, hours, days, months, and so on.

Company	Transformation Flow
Suppliers	
Inbound Logistics	
OEM	
Outbound Logistics	
Dealers	

Figure 2-3. Transformation from parts to vehicles

Similarly, inside the Toyota plants, vehicles move down the main assembly line at a constant speed—or "takt time." Feeder lines are also moving key sub-assemblies to various stations along the main line, where the correct engine or other subassembly arrives just-in-time to be installed in the exact vehicle that requires that subassembly. In another area of the plant, for example, seats are arriving by truck from a sequenced supplier to be installed in the vehicles, again based on the exact match. In the staging yard just outside the plant, trucks loaded with parts produced by hundreds of suppliers are arriving and are unloaded based on the vehicle sequence and progress of the vehicles moving down the main line. Looking back through the supply chain, the cross-docks and truck milk routes are all operating on repeatable cycles to support the main line's need for parts. Also, all tier 1 suppliers and their suppliers are operating on a schedule to produce parts based on the scheduled pick-up time.

Thus, Toyota's supply chain functions like a finely tuned Swiss clock. It is synchronized and integrated to perform as a lean supply chain. Nevertheless, it produces sufficient variety and at a sufficient velocity to satisfy demanding customers.

Operational Processes

Several operational processes must be performed on a periodic basis to guarantee that the physical supply chain is operating efficiently and effectively. These processes integrate and synchronize the operational processes with the physical processes to ensure a lean supply chain. The key processes are as follows:

- Mix planning
- Sales ordering/forecasting
- Production scheduling
- Dealer allocation
- Parts ordering/forecasting
- Inbound logistics planning

For some perspective of what these processes entail, a thorough explanation of Toyota's practices and principles follows. The detailed processes and the logic used to execute these processes will be described in Chapters 3 through 9.

Mix Planning   Mix planning is the process of limiting the number of build combinations that are ordered for stock in each market area. As mentioned earlier, "build combination" is a term that defines the unique set of specifications for a vehicle. For mix planning purposes, vehicle specifications are divided into three categories: factory-installed options, color, and accessories that can be installed after a vehicle is built. Mix planning is initially performed on an annual basis prior to new model launch and can be adjusted monthly to reflect changes in demand and/or seasonal trends. For the United States market, the mix planning is done at the region level to ensure that the vehicles ordered for stock closely meet the needs of the geographic area. For example, sport utility vehicles (SUVs) ordered for dealers located in the northern states would almost always be equipped with four-wheel drive, whereas SUVs ordered for southern states would be ordered with two-wheel drive. Another example is vehicles ordered for Arizona being painted with light colors (certainly not black!) because of the heat.

In Europe, the mix planning is done country by country because many of the countries have unique requirements. For example, the United Kingdom requires right-hand-drive vehicles whereas the countries on the Continent require left-hand-drive. Also, there are various regulations in different countries, significant climate differences from Norway to Spain, and substantial economic differences between Western and Eastern Europe.

Sales Ordering/Forecasting   One of the functions of the sales division is to provide a monthly production order and forecast. That is in the form of a rolling three-month plan with the first production month categorized as a firm order and the next two months as a forecast. The firm order requires the sales division to commit to the total volume of units for the month, whereas for the forecast months the volume can change. The content of the order month, however, can change in terms of number of vehicles up to one to two weeks prior to production. The process starts with the sales and production divisions first agreeing to a planned volume of units or vehicles that are going to be produced each month. Sales divisions determine their request by analyzing recent sales and stock levels. Sales divisions will also consider marketing promotions and seasonality changes. Both sales and production divisions collaborate to agree on the total planned vehicle volume for each of the next three months. The total vehicle volume is further broken down by vehicle model and by plant. Next, sales divisions allocate the total volume by model to each region based on sales performance. Then each region uses the mix plan along with the recent sales trends to create the quantity of each build combination for each month for each vehicle model. The mix plan or target is compared to the actual mix of sales and the actual mix of stock to determine which build combinations need to be ordered to maintain the target level of mix for stock. In addition, the regions may need to make adjustments for any special dealer requests and also need to consider any special promotions or seasonal trends; for example, sunroofs and convertibles sell better in spring and summer.

Once the forecast is made and the order is completed by each regional office, it is sent to the sales divisional headquarters. There it is checked before it is forwarded to the production divisional headquarters to create a production schedule.

Production Scheduling   Production scheduling is the process of taking the monthly order and forecast from sales and assigning a production date and sequence to each vehicle. The objective is to create a production schedule that is leveled across each day of each production month using the *heijunka principle*.

Heijunka is a Japanese term that is defined as "smoothing." The concept is to assign each vehicle option a smoothing weight based on its importance to manufacturing. For example, engines will get a higher weight than color, because if they were not evenly scheduled over the month and there were a change in production of engines, that would have a greater negative impact on manufacturing.

The term "production month" is different from "calendar month." For each calendar year, a production calendar is created. There will always be 52 or 53 production weeks in a year. A week is assigned to a month, based on Monday's date. For example, if January 31 falls on Monday, then that complete week is considered January production. February production would start with the February 7 week and end with the February 28 week. The only exception to this rule is the week that includes January 1. The week that contains the January 1 production day will always be week 1, even if January 1 does not begin on a Monday, which means it may contain some December days. Each production month will contain an even four or five weeks.

After the production plan is complete, it is sent back to sales with a scheduled build date for each vehicle. A copy is also sent to the parts ordering group at each assembly plant.

Dealer Allocation   Dealer allocation is the responsibility of the sales regions. The dealer allocation process is usually performed twice each month for two weeks of production at a time. That occurs four to five weeks prior to the scheduled build dates for the vehicles that are being allocated.

Prior to the allocation process, dealers can update their profile with specific guidelines on the type of vehicles they either want—or in some cases do not want—to be allocated. For example, dealers in northern cities may want a cold weather kit, and dealers in Arizona may not want dark-colored cars. This dealer profile is important because each region covers a large geographic area of several states that may have different climates and demographics.

The allocation process is executed by each region for its dealers. The allocation quantity for each vehicle model is based on a "fair-share method" (sometimes referred to as "turn and earn") to guarantee that each dealer is treated fairly. The concept involves basing the allocation on how well each dealer is selling its previous allocation compared to all other dealers. Another benefit of this method is that it ensures that the inventory is rebalanced across all dealers.

After the vehicles are allocated, they are assigned to the dealer and will be visible to the dealer as pipeline orders. A pipeline order is a vehicle that is in the scheduled pipeline and will be built during the week identified with each vehicle. Each vehicle has a full set of specifications, including color. Therefore, the vehicle will be built as is unless the dealer submits a change request.

Parts Ordering/Forecasting   The parts ordering process is actually two different processes: one for local parts and another for overseas parts. The local process requires that the vehicles scheduled for each day be placed in the exact sequence that they would be built on the assembly line. The next step, after each vehicle is scheduled by day, is to sequence the vehicles into the ideal sequence in which they would be assembled. The concept used is to consider the impact of the schedule on the factory team members and equipment. It is important to sequence the vehicles so that vehicles that contain high workload or process complexity are not scheduled back to back.

Once the vehicles are aligned in sequence for each day, parts calculation is performed for each vehicle. Then the parts installation time stamp is applied to each part for each vehicle. One time stamp calculation follows:

- Vehicle number 500 of the day is scheduled to line-off the end of the assembly line at 1 p.m.

- Part A is installed at a workstation 2 hours prior to line-off.
- Part B is installed 2 hours and 30 minutes prior to line-off.
- Part A would have a time stamp of 11 a.m. (1 p.m.–2 hours).
- Part B would have a time stamp of 10:30 a.m. (1 p.m.–2:30 hours).

Next each part's lead time from the supplier to the lineside is determined. That will determine at what day and time the supplier will need to ship the part to arrive at the lineside just-in-time. Other factors, such as lot size, shipping frequency, and adjustments, need to be considered as well when the parts order is calculated.

Adjustments are made in two ways. One way is for a vehicle specification to be changed by a dealer after parts have already been ordered from some suppliers. This occurs when a supplier's lead time is longer than the freeze point for the assembly plant. A freeze point is the last day prior to production on which changes can be made to vehicle specifications. The plant's freeze point is based on the 80 percent rule (i.e., the point is selected so that 80 percent of the suppliers have a lead time shorter than the freeze point). In other words, if the freeze point specification is five days, then 80 percent of the suppliers' deliveries should take less than five days. The freeze point will vary by plant but will range from 5 to 10 days. This still leaves 20 percent of the suppliers that are outside the freeze; thus, there is a need to make adjustments based on the dealer's changes. That is done by comparing the parts calculated each day to the previous day's calculation, and if there is a difference and the part has already been ordered, an adjustment is made on the next order. A second adjustment is made by comparing the actual usage for each production day and the planned usage. The purpose of this adjustment is to catch any scrap or misused parts.

The order is transmitted to the suppliers daily. In addition to the daily order, a weekly forecast is sent to the supplier as a prenotice for the next 12 weeks. It is extremely important for the suppliers to wait for the daily order to prepare the shipments. (The supplier's role is discussed in Chapter 7.)

Logistics Planning   Once the parts forecast is completed for the next production month, a determination needs to be made about the most efficient routes for the logistics partner to pick up the parts from all suppliers. A sophisticated software program is needed to simulate the various route options. Some of the inputs needed and constraints are locations of each supplier, quantity of parts by supplier by pick-up time, location of cross-docks, location of assembly plants, and cost per mile. Assurances need to be made that all delivery times for parts will be met and the cost of operating the fleet of trucks optimized. This process may take numerous simulations before a route plan can be finalized.

Relationship of Processes to Physical Flow

Figure 2-4 illustrates how these operational processes are integrated and synchronized to support the transformation flow of the physical parts and vehicles.

Planning Processes

The final processes necessary to complete the picture of the comprehensive supply chain are performed one to three years prior to actual production. These processes are as follows:

1. Product planning and design
2. Plant design for capacity and flexibility
3. Package design for logistics
4. Purchasing
5. Annual sales and operations planning

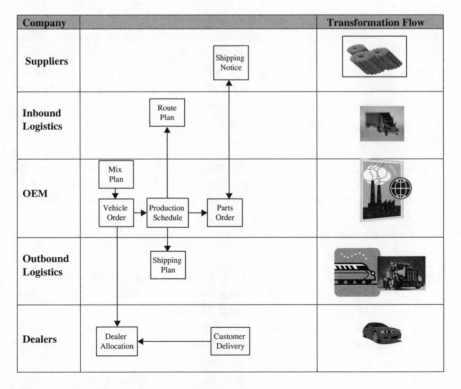

Figure 2-4. Transformation processes

Product Planning and Design   Vehicle design starts about 36 months prior to production and is completed about 18 months prior to production. During the design phase the physical design and functional design are completed, in addition to all parts and components. The designers and engineers must collaborate with product planning, sales and marketing, purchasing, and manufacturing on the new vehicle design. In addition, many of the suppliers collaborate with the engineers on selected components.

One of the factors to be considered during the vehicle design is the impact on the supply chain. For example, the more parts that can be shared by multiple vehicles, the greater the efficiency, as there will be fewer part numbers and a higher volume of parts produced per part number. The result will be improved economies of scale and the ability to source high-volume parts to multiple suppliers.

Another example is to reduce the number of parts that is directly associated with an option or color. That arrangement will increase the dealer's flexibility to change options or colors, because fewer parts will be impacted.

Plant Design for Capacity and Flexibility   At Toyota, most final assembly plants are designed to produce multiple vehicle models on multiple assembly lines. That design provides flexibility to shift production volume from a slow-selling model to a faster-selling model to ensure that each plant maintains a stable production volume. In the event that the total volume needs to be adjusted either up or down, then the average time allowed between vehicles that come off assembly (the "takt" time), can be adjusted to increase or slow down the line speed. Line speed adjustment can be planned and implemented with one to two months lead time. In effect, this type of flexibility allows Toyota to change production capacity to meet market demand quickly.

Package Design for Logistics   Inbound logistics must also be lean to support Toyota's supply chain. Therefore, when parts packaging is designed, careful consideration must be taken to make sure that parts can be moved efficiently through the logistics network. In addition, Toyota has a strong "green" policy, so almost all packaging uses returnable containers. The following are some of the major packaging considerations:

- *Don't "ship air."* Ensure that parts can be arranged in the container so that cubic space utilization is optimized. For example, a part shaped like a hockey stick cannot be packaged efficiently.
- *Stackable.* Design containers so that they can be stacked with many other parts containers and can be interlocked so containers will not shift during transit.
- *Lot size.* Order parts in small lots with frequent shipments.
- *Quality.* Guarantee that parts will not be damaged because of movement during shipment.

Purchasing   Purchasing is responsible for parts and component sourcing and must work closely with engineering and quality. Purchasing considers many factors when selecting suppliers such as supplier capability and capacity, current supplier base, price, location, local content targets, and minority supplier objectives.

In addition to these more obvious criteria, purchasing should also consider the impact on the supply chain. Again, the focus should be on understanding the relationships of options and colors to parts. One way to enable flexibility to change options closer to production is to purchase these option-related parts from suppliers located close to the assembly plant. Managing suppliers requires Toyota to choose how to operate the assembly plant to stabilize supplier orders. That role requires implementation of all of the processes described earlier. But it also requires leveraging the benefit of order stability to provide a competitive product to the customer.

Annual Sales and Operations Planning   Sales and manufacturing must collaborate on the annual plan for all vehicles sold and produced within a market (e.g., North America or Europe). That process can be a very contentious one because manufacturing and sales goals naturally conflict. The manufacturing objective is to operate all plants at full capacity with stable volume and to minimize interruption during model changeover. The sales objective is to maintain flexibility in order to change production volume as market demand shifts and to avoid producing too many vehicles of old models when a new model is scheduled to be introduced. One common objective is to maximize profits; however, that is easier said than done. (This topic will be discussed in detail in Chapter 4.)

Reflection Points

Toyota has effectively implemented the Toyota Production System across the extended supply chain and has demonstrated its capability to be a learning organization by the following:

- Viewing the supply chain as a very broad and comprehensive set of processes that must be designed to function cohesively
- Promoting cross-functional teamwork to ensure that all internal and external parties are collaborating to kaizen both processes and operations
- Streamlining the supply chain to be synchronized and integrated so that it functions like a fine-quality Swiss clock

Although there are many examples of the v4L principles in this chapter, we will wait and highlight them at the end of each of the chapters that discuss them in detail.

Endnotes

1. Hau Lee, Barchi Peleg, and Seungjin Whang, "Toyota: Demand Chain Management," Case GS-42, Stanford Graduate School of Business, Stanford University, Stanford, CA, 2005, p. 18.
2. The thinking goes something like this: A twenty-something person starts out purchasing a Scion, then gets married and moves up to a Camry, then starts a family and adds a sports utility vehicle or van, and then as an empty nester moves up to a Lexus.
3. J.D. Power and Associates Ratings, www.jpower.com/autos/car-ratings/, October 11, 2008.

Chapter 3

Mix Planning

Mix planning is an important process for companies that manufacture and distribute products to retailers in multiple market areas. For vehicle manufacturers, this decision is extremely important because of the complexity of a vehicle. This complexity creates millions of possible vehicle build combinations or variants. The objective of mix planning is to reduce the variants of each vehicle manufactured by several orders of magnitude, from millions to hundreds.

Mix planning is a process that is undertaken during major model change preparation. It can also be adjusted annually during minor model change and to a lesser degree during the model year. The model change mix planning is completed about 12 months prior to new model introduction, to enable the following to happen:

- Marketing strategies for each region to be synchronized with product offerings
- Manufacturing to fill the supply chain pipeline with parts
- Sales regions to order vehicles to have in stock in time for new model introduction

Mix planning at Toyota deals with choosing the specific mix of vehicles that will be offered at sales regions across the country. The goal of mix planning is to carefully manage dealer-level product demand so as to enable stable production at the manufacturing plant. That also translates into stable orders to suppliers. In other words, the aim of mix planning is "to nip some of the demand variability in the bud" through careful planning. The associated upstream stability because of mix planning permits a focus on improved quality, cost reduction using kaizen, and ultimately higher value to customers that enables higher customer satisfaction and retention.

Studies suggest that Toyota cars offer approximately $2,500 in additional value to the customer compared with competing midpriced, high-volume cars.

That additional value translates directly into a higher resale value that customers receive for their Toyota cars compared to most manufacturers in the auto industry. We attribute this higher value to variety reduction, variability control, improved visibility across the chain, and higher velocity. Thus, in order for the v4L strategy to be viable it must generate significant value enhancement to all players. We will cover this topic in later chapters, but first we focus on how Toyota does mix planning.

Mix Planning Objective

Mix planning at Toyota means that the planned variety offered in a sales area is chosen carefully to be primarily the 20 percent of product range that represents around 80 percent of the demand in that region. Thus, planned offerings in a region are frequently a small subset of all available product types or even of all product types offered in the national market. That simple decision enables synchronization of all activities in a region, from TV advertisements focusing on the specific colors and options available in a region to newspaper and periodical pictures and dealer brochures, all suggesting offerings that synchronize with the product available at the dealer. In addition, the smaller range means that most dealers carry similar products, thus both enabling customers to decide where to buy the car and keeping dealer margins competitive. Availability of the same set of products among dealers increases retail availability without the need for high levels of dealer stocks. Similarly, a focus on offerings with high-demand velocity also decreases dealer inventories and thus increases inventory turns. That is one of the reasons that Toyota's average incentive cost per vehicle is typically about $1,000 compared to the $3,000 average for the industry as shown in Table 3-1.

A key risk to be managed in the selection of a subset of items is that that supply has to remain synchronized with current demand trends. Also, there is a

Table 3-1. Incentives Offered by Six Automakers

Automaker	June 2007	June 2006
Chrysler Group	$3,962	$4,045
Ford	$3,187	$3,648
General Motors	$2,830	$3,135
Honda	$1,397	$770
Nissan	$2,218	$2,677
Toyota	$1,308	$961

Source: Edmunds.com. Reference www.autoobserver.com/2007/07/june-sales-gm-hits-all-time-low-market-share.html (downloaded on 7/10/08).

natural tendency for the sales organization to attempt to justify why more is better. In other words, it is tempted to keep adding variants because doing so will help create incremental sales. That effort requires the need for thorough analysis of selling trends by product type and features, as well as monitoring of competitor offerings, in order to determine the optimum mix of variants. The key is that it is easier to add complexity or variants after the vehicle is introduced than it is to remove them. Therefore, it is important to start out by erring on the lean side and if necessary adjusting variants on a periodic basis after several months of sales history and trends can be evaluated. This method of adjusting mix during the monthly ordering process will be discussed in Chapter 4.

Complexity Reduction

Before mix planning can be undertaken, the product complexity needs to be reduced. That effort requires collaboration among design, sales and marketing, and manufacturing groups. The following is a summary of some methods that are used to achieve complexity reduction.

Product Planning, Design, Sourcing

- Look for opportunities to use common parts across products (i.e., share radios). This step focuses on studies that suggest that over 80 percent of manufacturing costs are fixed at the design stage.[1] So, preventing designers from adding variety when none is warranted is the first step. In addition, part commonality permits higher inventory turns for original parts as well as spare parts, production flexibility for suppliers and the assembly plant, and economies of scale in purchasing, design, and production.
- Consider making high-volume options standard (e.g., if air-conditioning is sold in 95 percent of all vehicles, it should be made a standard feature). Such a step focuses on trading off the forecasting difficulties when choices are left to consumers against the enhanced value perceived when customers are offered standard features. For example, antilock brakes and other standard safety features may not be valued by customers if offered as separate choices but may well enhance the product preference if offered as standard. In addition, the forecasting of individual variants is often more difficult than forecasting the total demand for a product. This gain in forecasting accuracy as well as improvement in perceived value may well offset the lower margins because some features are discounted to customers who may not want them.
- Eliminate options that do not sell well (e.g., if ashtrays are only ordered in 5 percent of vehicles, eliminate them as an option). This approach

focuses on simplifying designs even at the cost of losing some customers in order to make demand more predictable.

- Minimize parts that vary by option and color—for example, does the window washer nozzle on the hood have to match the color, or can it be black? In our example, supplier-part orders for the window washer nozzle will be kept standard even if customer vehicles vary by color. Because the same supplier component may be used in many car types, it is a great example of assembly postponement applied to stabilize supply while providing variety.

- Attempt to source optional parts to local suppliers to shorten lead time. Such an approach focuses on decreasing safety stock by lowering lead time for difficult-to-forecast parts. In addition, because the forecast error for some options may be higher than for standard equipment, the lead time impact on safety stock inventory for optional parts is higher than for standard equipment parts. Thus, a more responsive supplier for option parts may well generate lower overall costs compared to an efficient long lead time supplier.

- Design accessories that can be installed after the vehicle leaves the factory at a hub or at a dealer to minimize impact on the factory and supply chain. Such a practice moves some accessorizing tasks to the point of sale or close to the point of sale and permits last-minute customization for the customer. It is particularly relevant for cars like the Scion. The Scion is produced in Japan with almost no options or accessories. The vehicles are then kept in stock at the ports until the dealers submit an order, at which time the accessories are installed and the vehicle is shipped to the dealer.

Marketing

- Limit product offering for a market area. Vehicles sold in Europe and the United States should each offer a subset of products that best reflects local demand (e.g., manual transmission may be offered in Europe as an option but not in the United States). Such synchronization of products offered to local preferences makes demand levels more predictable and thus improves supply chain performance. In addition, such an approach increases the chance that demand can be satisfied directly from dealer stock, thus decreasing retail customer lead time.

- Combine related options into packages (e.g., the safety package may include side airbag, stability control, and auto window wiper). Bundling of features permits the market segment as a whole to be targeted rather than individual feature choice. This process balances "up-selling" whereby customers end up choosing more than they actually need, with stability on the supply side. In addition, by converting products into, perhaps, three offerings (economy, deluxe, and luxury), with associated option bundles, customer choice is simplified and the number of variants sold at retail reduced.

- Consider making high-volume options standard, not offering low-selling options, or both.

Mix Planning by Sales Region

After the complexity reduction activities outlined previously have been completed, the next step is for each sales division to work closely with its sales region to determine which subset of the vehicle mix will be the high-volume sellers in each region. This step is necessary because each sales region may have different demand characteristics. The following are some of the guidelines that are to be considered:

- Limit stockkeeping units (SKUs). Determine which build combinations will be stocked by a sales region. A sales region within a sales company's territory could be the southern region of the United States or Italy within Europe.
- Analyze past sales, competition offerings, and local regulations to predict demand for future sales.
- Use the 80/20 rule. The 80/20 rule identifies the SKUs that account for 80 percent of the sales. This should be about 20 percent of the possible SKUs.
- Stock high-volume SKUs. Dealer stock should include only the 20 percent of the SKUs that represent 80 percent of the volume.
- Target marketing campaigns to support mix planning by region. Synchronizing offerings with marketing plans permits customer preferences to be "guided" whenever feasible. For example, featuring the same subset of colors and features in print ads, TV ads, dealer showrooms, and dealer inventory increases the chances that customers will choose from the available colors and features and thus reduces the customers lost because of unavailability of special colors featured but not offered.
- Manage demand. Provide guidance to dealers on ways to respond to demand for vehicles that are not in stock:
  - The salesperson can gently persuade the customer to change his mind and take one of the vehicles in stock. This is called "guided selling." However, this technique could result in negative customer

satisfaction. (Note: it is not necessary to sell a vehicle to every customer; sometimes it is better to lose a sale than to have an unhappy customer.)
○ Locate a trade with another dealer.
○ Request an order change from the factory. (This process will be explained in Chapter 9.)

Mix Planning Details

This example shows how the mix planning process is performed by the Toyota sales company:

1. Determine the volume of vehicles that is expected to be sold by region. For this example, assume that 10,000 cars—specifically, Camrys—are to be distributed across four different regions. The percentage sold in each region reflects the share of the national volume; this is shown in Table 3-2. With this market share, the volume by region is also calculated to ensure that the aggregate mix will be weighted accurately.
2. Next break the planned volume into the volume of sales by vehicle model. This planned mix reflects marketing plans, production volumes, supplier commitments, expected competition and price points, demographics, and so on. Table 3-3 shows such an example.

Table 3-2. Allocation Total Volume of All Camrys by Region

Camry Allocation	Regions				Total
	West	East	South	North	
Market Share	25.0%	30.0%	25.0%	20.0%	100.0%
Monthly Volume	2,500	3,000	2,500	2,000	10,000

Table 3-3. Sales and Production Model Mix of Camrys

Model	Volume	Percent
CE	1,000	10%
LE	5,000	50%
SE	1,500	15%
XLE	1,500	15%
Hybrid	1,000	10%
Total	10,000	100%

Table 3-4. Distribution of Model Mix by Region

Model	West	East	North	South	Total
CE	200	250	250	300	1,000
LE	1,400	1,600	1,150	850	5,000
SE	250	500	350	400	1,500
XLE	350	450	500	200	1,500
Hybrid	300	200	250	250	1,000
Total	2,500	3,000	2,500	2,000	10,000

Table 3-5. Model Variants Offered

Model	B/C No.*	VSC	Sunroof	Spoiler	Nav
CE	CE-01	X			
CE	CE-02				
LE	LE-01	X	X		
LE	LE-02		X		
LE	LE-03	X	X		
SE	SE-01	X	X	X	
SE	SE-02	X	X	X	X
XLE	XLE-01				X
XLE	XLE-02	X			X
Hybrid	HB-01		X		
Hybrid	HB-02				

*B/C No. = build combination number.

3. Use data from each region to break up the total vehicle volume for a region into a composition by model. That data should be derived through collaboration between the sales headquarters and each regional manager. Table 3-4 shows this breakdown by model by region.

4. Take each car model and decide on the number of different variants that will be offered and the specific features of each variant. An example is shown in Table 3-5. This is the most difficult part of the process, because it is extremely challenging for the marketing staff to limit the number of variants. Note that this example is an oversimplification. In normal cases, there will be hundreds of build combinations that must be considered. That is where the 80/20 rule will be applied. The result will be to select about 20 percent of the variants that will represent 80 percent of the volume.

Table 3-6. Mix of Model Variants by Region

Model	B/C No.*	Mix of Each Model by Region			
		West	East	South	North
CE	CE-01	0%	0%	70%	20%
CE	CE-02	100%	100%	30%	80%
LE	LE-01	50%	0%	50%	0%
LE	LE-02	50%	0%	0%	70%
LE	LE-03	0%	100%	50%	30%
SE	SE-01	100%		50%	30%
SE	SE-02		100%	50%	70%
XLE	XLE-01	80%		20%	30%
XLE	XLE-02	20%	100%	80%	70%
Hybrid	HB-01	100%	40%	20%	30%
Hybrid	HB-02	0%	60%	80%	70%

*B/C No. = build combination number.

5. Decide on which of these variants will be sold in each region, and determine the mix of variants by region (Table 3-6). The mix by region will then be used to calculate the volume of each variant by region during the monthly ordering process. (This process will be discussed in detail in Chapter 4.) Note that in this example not all regions will decide to order stock for all variants that were preselected by the sales division for the entire national market. However, they will still be able to make daily order changes or submit special orders for variants that appear on the national list.
6. Finally, take each of these quantities and decide the colors that will be offered in each region and thus the specific quantities by color of each of these variants that is expected to be shipped to each region.

Toyota processes reduce complexity and limit the mix sold within sales regions. The metrics for mix planning are the number of build combinations by region or country by model. Next we will examine how a mathematical model can be used to evaluate various mix planning strategies.

A Simulation Model

Although Toyota's success may be proof that the 80/20 rule is valid, another issue that deserves focus is the empirical observation that SKUs that have lower sales volume have higher demand variability. In addition, the identity of these SKUs might not be the same from region to region. Thus, staying with the top 80 percent limits the variability seen by the plant; it also reduces inventories at the dealer. That reduces cost, improves forecasting, and further contributes to reducing variability. Moreover, it focuses selling effort on a small set of models and thus can drive demand in the right direction.

Given these different possible reasons for mix planning, we will focus on one such reason to understand details. The Appendix will provide a specific example; here we refer to the learning points from that example. Increasing product variety potentially attracts new customer segments to purchase the product and may thus increase the mean demand for the product. This increase in customer segments, however, may make the specific composition of demand for products in a period less predictable. Such a decrease in predictability may be understood (intuitively) as arising from the inability to predict the demand process for each customer segment. So the benefit associated with attracting more customers to the product has to be balanced with the increased forecast error for individual products offered. In such a context, it may be better to offer a narrower range with more predictability. A more limited, more predictable demand stream may then enable a stable supply chain to be created, which offers the opportunity to increase customer value associated with a product.

A key question is, how much of the demand can be retained when variety is decreased? If, instead of 50 percent of the potential being captured, the demand drops to 30 percent, then it is worth considering how profitable this lowered variety is relative to increased variety.

What is the fundamental message of this model? Increasing product variety may increase demand forecast error because of difficulties in forecasting demand. It is the difficulty in understanding the composition of customer demand that creates significant forecast error—that is, it is easier to forecast aggregate demand but quite difficult to forecast the variety. Thus, careful targeting of customers and choice of product offerings can stabilize the system if the demand is not affected significantly. The trade-off between stability and sales volume has to be made prior to determination of the mix planning strategy.

Non-Toyota Examples of Mix Planning

A paper by Chan and Mauborgne on the "Blue Ocean Strategy"[2] describes the process of pursuing differentiation and low cost. They describe a company that "generates cost savings by reducing factors that an industry traditionally competes on. Buyer value is lifted by raising or creating elements the industry never offered. Over time, costs are reduced further as scale economies kick in, as sales volumes increase due to superior value provided." An example that is provided focuses on the choices by Casella Wines, an Australian wine company that entered the U.S. wine industry in 2001, when the industry had over 1,600 wine choices in the market.

Unlike existing strategies, Casella decided to focus on simplicity and on attracting new customers who were not traditional wine drinkers in the United

States. The company thus decided to use one bottle type for red and one for white wines and offer only two types of each wine, simplify packaging, eliminate promotions, and go after nonwine drinkers with a fruity flavor. It eliminated all technical jargon from wine bottles and used simple, bright colors. Retail employees were encouraged by its ease of description to recommend it to customers. By eliminating a lot of the wine reputation–building costs faced by traditional wine companies, Casella focused on new tastes that made it easy to purchase, while simultaneously lowering production costs. At the same time, Casella managed to charge more than budget wines while growing the market significantly. The narrowing of choices and simultaneous raising of satisfaction permitted a significant increase in the volume sold and enabled the company to emerge as the fastest-growing brand in U.S. wine history, surpassing the wines of France and Italy. In 2004, the company sold more than 11.2 million cases in the United States.

In the book *Conquering Complexity in Your Business*,[3] Michael George and Stephen Wilson discuss the impact of adding low-volume, less predictable offerings mixed with higher-volume products. If the low-volume products have greater variability relative to the mean, while the high-volume products have a lower variability relative to the mean, then offering all the products when their manufacture involves setups can decrease production cycle time efficiency for all products. Process cycle efficiency thus drops for all offerings when low-volume offerings are added in the presence of setup costs. George and Wilson suggest the need to identify the requisite level of variety that will optimize profitability by trading off the cost impact with revenue consequences of different levels of variety.

Titleist is the world's leading golf ball manufacturer. The key to becoming a successful golf ball manufacturer is to achieve remarkable consistency in the plastic polymer used around the ball. Because all balls of the same type have to maintain equal performance to enable competition to focus on golfer ability, the company strives to carefully control quality. At the same time, there is the need to offer golf balls for a range of golfer preferences. The company thus has an appropriate range of golf balls but constantly works to keep the range as narrow as possible and still fulfill needs of golfers of all skill levels as the world's leading golf ball manufacturer.[4] Narrow variety, consistent quality, and economies of scale through appropriate pricing for performance all combine to enable Titleist to maintain its position as the leading golf ball manufacturer.

Reflection Points

How does increased variety hurt a company? When variety is increased while customer service must be maintained, the forecasting of demand and the adjustment of the supply chain become key issues. At the same time, greater variety permits products to appeal to a larger set of market segments whose preferences are now met by the new SKUs. If this new segment can be predicted and incorporated into existing processes, there is an opportunity to increase profitability. However, if the new market segments introduce fickle consumers and confuse existing customer segments, then adding SKUs may increase forecast error substantially, thus significantly increasing supply costs.

Toyota has demonstrated its strength as a learning organization by continuously refining its capability to manage vehicle complexity and the model mix sold in each sales region and by spreading these processes across the global organization. Specific examples are linked to the v4L:

- *Variety* is selected by region to represent the popular mix demanded at a point in time. That permits wide availability of offerings among dealers for customers and thus keeps dealer markups low.
- *Velocity* of sales is maintained by choosing to order for stock a few variants in each region. Those variants account for over 80 percent of the demanded offerings. That improves inventory turns at dealers and reduces days of inventory in the dealer lot.
- *Variability* of sales is decreased by synchronizing sales and operations planning to focus on a few variants by region. Those choices are adjusted in response to observed sales. Thus, supplier and production quantities are stable in the aggregate.
- *Visibility* of the planning process across sales and operations enables buying at the regional level. The push system of allocating cars to dealers enables fast turns and thus low dealer inventories.

The thesis of the chapter is that optimal choice of the v4L enables Toyota to increase value. The learning methods of Toyota are applied throughout the process to enable value creation, specifically:

- *Create awareness.* The quantification of variability makes planners aware if they are not meeting the 80/20 guideline. In some instances, Toyota prefers to wait and see if the trends are permanent; for example, Toyota studies trends to see if mix changes are permanent.
- *Establish capability.* Limiting variability where it occurs—at the dock in the case of the Scion, or at the design stage when it comes to limiting variety—makes the system more capable of handling variation.
- *Make action protocols.* The quantification of the variety and the careful sequencing of planning steps, some top-down and some bottom-up, enables coordination.
- *Generate system-level awareness.* The goal of mix planning is system-level optimization, where the system includes the customer and the entire supply chain.

Endnotes

1. D. E. Whitney, "Manufacturing by Design," *Harvard Business Review*, vol. 66, no. 4 (1988), pp. 83–91.
2. Renee A. Mauborgne and W. Chan Kim, "Blue Ocean Strategy," *Harvard Business Review*, October 1, 2004.
3. Michael L. George and Stephen A. Wilson, *Conquering Complexity in Your Business*. New York: McGraw-Hill, 2004, p. 80.
4. *Conquering Complexity*, p. 37.

Chapter 4

Sales and Operations Planning

S
ales and operations planning (S&OP) is a critical component of the supply chain planning process. It is linked upstream to the mix planning process and downstream to the production scheduling process. The goal of S&OP is to generate a production plan that balances demand and supply in a profitable way. The end point of this process is an order for vehicles with full specifications that will be scheduled for production (see Chapter 5).

To understand the Toyota approach to sales and operations planning, an understanding of which entity in the supply chain submits the vehicle order is necessary. Simply put, it is not the dealers. At Toyota, the regional offices submit the vehicle orders once each month. Toyota uses a monthly allocation process to allocate the vehicles planned for production to each dealer—in other words, it uses a top-down approach. Many other automobile companies create production plans from the bottom up; that is, they collect the orders submitted by dealers and then create a production plan. There are pros and cons to both approaches; however, the top-down approach works well for Toyota because it enables Toyota to ensure that the resulting production plan is stable.

Sales and operations planning processes at Toyota are performed in two stages: annual planning and monthly ordering.

Annual Planning

The objective of the annual planning process is to establish a rolling three-year sales and production forecast. The process is repeated semiannually so that the forecast is updated based on the latest market and economic conditions. The annual forecast is used throughout the company to project profits, establish capital and operating budgets, evaluate plant and supplier capacity requirements, conduct annual price reviews with suppliers, and influence marketing strategies.

Annual Planning Process

The annual planning process is a collaborative process between the sales and manufacturing divisions. The responsibilities of sales are to grasp the market and economic conditions, predict competitive product plans and strategies, and understand new product launches and marketing plans to create a sales forecast for each model for each month and year. Manufacturing's responsibilities are to determine the operating capacity for each model and each plant, evaluate various model mix scenarios, and identify peaks and valleys in the production calendar that are created by model changeover schedules.

The process is executed over a period of several weeks twice a year. There is a push-pull momentum: sales submits its request for each model by month and year, while manufacturing simultaneously attempts to mix and match the model volumes across the plants. Collaboration is required because typically the sales request is different from manufacturing's capabilities and/or objectives.

Typical sales objectives are to remain flexible to respond quickly to market changes and to limit the use of incentives to sell vehicles. Some of manufacturing's key objectives are to operate at full capacity and to produce high-profit vehicles. Because most plants produce multiple models and many models are produced at multiple plants, numerous scenarios must be considered. Some significant conflicts may need to be resolved, which results in the push-pull momentum, or the give-and-take exchange, between sales and manufacturing. The collaboration process focuses on adjusting the variables that can be used to bridge the gap. Some of these adjustments to the sales and operations plan are as follows:

- Sales can plan to use incentives selectively to create demand for slow-selling models and for models that are scheduled for a major model changeover.
- Sales can adjust marketing strategies to promote selected models. For example, special-edition models may be created to enhance a model's marketability. This strategy is used mostly during the later years of a model's life. (Note: Most automobile models are produced for about five years before there is a major model change.)
- Manufacturing can upgrade facilities to increase capacity for selected models.
- Manufacturing can adjust the speed or takt time of the assembly line at a plant to increase or decrease production.
- Manufacturing can vary the model mix within a plant.
- Manufacturing can vary the planned overtime by plant (e.g., schedule overtime on Saturdays).

One example of collaboration between sales and manufacturing that generated significant benefits occurred at the Toyota plant located in Fremont, California. The California plant could produce only 20 percent of the Corolla models with sunroofs. The Corolla model was also produced at another Toyota plant near Toronto, Canada, that did not have this constraint.

The demand from the West Coast for Corollas with sunroofs was very high. Unfortunately, the California plant could not produce enough vehicles with sunroofs to meet the demand, so some of those vehicles destined for the West Coast had to be produced at the plant in Canada. The result was an extremely negative impact on vehicle distribution. The vehicle distribution group preferred to ship the Corollas produced in California to dealers west of the Mississippi and the Corollas produced in Canada to the dealers east of the Mississippi. The reasons are obvious: logistics costs are lower and the time to get the cars from the plant to the dealers is shorter because of the geographic proximity of dealer locations to the assembly plant.

The dealers located in the West were requesting over 40 percent of the Corollas equipped with sunroofs. The consequence of the inability of the California plant to produce Corollas with sunroofs to meet this high demand was that many cars produced in Canada were shipped across the country to the West Coast and an equal number of Corollas without sunroofs were built in California and shipped back East. At each annual planning meeting, people from the sales group would argue that this situation was unacceptable and request the California plant to install additional equipment to eliminate this constraint. The plant management was very cost conscious and would not agree to invest the millions of dollars required to install the equipment. The stalemate continued for several years until there was a detailed analysis done to calculate the profit impact on both sales and the plant. It was determined that Corollas that were ordered with sunroofs normally were equipped with other higher-profit options. Thus, the profit margin of the Corollas without sunroofs was significantly less than that of those with sunroofs. It was determined that by increasing the mix of cars with sunroofs built in California from 20 percent to 40 percent, to respond to sales demand, the plant would recover its multi-million-dollar investment in a few months. When the plant manager realized this missed profit opportunity, he quickly agreed to install the necessary equipment.

Another example of the types of decisions that are made during the annual planning process is found in a July 2008 Toyota press release:[1]

July 10, 2008—Erlanger, KY—Toyota is responding to changes in consumer demand and improving the production efficiency and stability of its North American operations by adjusting production mix at three plants. The changes include the addition of the Prius hybrid sedan to its North American lineup. The changes are as follows:

- *The Prius will be built at a plant under construction in Blue Springs, Miss. Production is scheduled to begin in late 2010. Prius, which will join the Kentucky-built Camry Hybrid as the second Toyota hybrid built in North America, enables Toyota to better respond to increased consumer demand for hybrid vehicles.*

- *The Highlander mid-size SUV, originally scheduled to be built in Mississippi, will now be manufactured in Princeton, Ind., beginning in fall 2009.*

- *Production of the Tundra full-size pick-up truck, currently built in Indiana and Texas, will be consolidated at the San Antonio plant in spring 2009.*

This is an excellent example of how Toyota has the agility to make major changes in its production schedules in a relatively short time frame.

Component Planning

After several weeks of discussions and analysis, the annual plan is finalized by model by plant. Then the focus shifts to determining the ratio of key components of vehicles. For example, engines, transmissions, and similar options may have a capacity constraint at the supplier level. One of the complications of planning component volumes is that most components are used by multiple models across multiple plants worldwide. Again, there is a need to run several scenarios to determine how to best balance component plant production plans with the various assembly plants. As you can imagine, this is like trying to solve a giant Rubik's Cube.

Creating Buy-In

Another important point is that the sales and operations planning process cannot be resolved simply by inputting variables into a computer and getting a mathematically accurate result. Certainly, computers play an important role in calculating the various scenarios; however, the human interaction that takes place over the hours, days, and weeks not only improves the quality of the annual plan but also builds an overall consensus among sales and manufacturing groups that reinforces teamwork. This creates an environment to achieve success by motivating all parties to work together to ensure that the annual plan is a commitment for both the sales and manufacturing organizations. Such collaboration is not the normal process in different functional disciplines. They tend to stick to their viewpoint—not because they somehow benefit from doing so, but because they do not see the viewpoint of others. In such cases, there is much more reliance on computer results than on human interaction. So Toyota prefers a combination approach. That is part of the Toyota Way, in which the human-machine combination is often assumed to produce the best possible result.

It is interesting to observe how many Toyota Way principles are demonstrated during the annual planning process. Teamwork and mutual respect are key principles used throughout the planning process. Moreover, the process through which the annual plan is reviewed and updated semiannually is a good example of how Toyota practices one of the key Toyota Way principles: Plan, Do, Check, and Act (PDCA). The plan is developed and is used as a basis for day-to-day operations. Then it is checked after six months, and action is taken to adjust the plan and/or make changes in plant or supplier capacity. This results in a closed-loop control that is repeated over and over again. PDCA is also applied to the planning process itself.

After each annual planning cycle, a reflection report is prepared to evaluate the process. This report highlights what went right and what needs improvement. The items that need improvement are analyzed further to identify root causes and countermeasures that should be implemented.

Capacity Planning

Capacity planning consists of two aspects: the internal plant capacity review and the supplier capacity review.

Internal Capacity Planning

Each assembly plant conducts a periodic review of its production capacity. The purpose is to calculate the upper and lower limits of its operations rate for each product. The capacity planning activities are performed on an annual (or, in some cases, a semiannual) basis. However, most major investments to the facilities are usually implemented during the next major model change. For assembly plants, the products are the various vehicle models that are produced on each assembly line. For component or unit plants, the products are the components such as engines and transmissions. Using the annual plan volumes as a forecast, each production facility will consider the variables that impact capacity. A key constraint is how much the operations rate varies by assembly plant. The following are some of the variables that impact the operations rate and thus can be adjusted:

- *Direct labor and the flexibility to add workers—or reduce the workforce— and thus, adjust the production rate.* Because Toyota strives to avoid layoffs of Toyota employees, most Toyota plants employ some percentage of temporary workers to support the normal production level. If production needs to slow down because of slow demand, then temporary workers can be reduced. On the other hand, if production needs to be increased, then, most likely, temporary workers would be added initially. If the increase appears to be permanent, then some temporary workers would be converted to full-time employees.

■ *Facility and equipment.* Each process must be analyzed to determine the weakest link in the production process. In other words, even if one could add unlimited numbers of workers, there will be some equipment that would not be able to produce at a higher rate. It could be a machine that is used to install a sunroof, perhaps an additional paint booth might need to be installed, and so on.

Supplier Capacity

So that potential weak links in the supply chain can be identified, supplier capacity as well as internal capabilities must be evaluated. Because this is a joint responsibility, purchasing and production control need to work with each supplier to identify any constraints that could restrict the supply of a part. Although most companies focus attention on the upper limit of each supplier's capacity, it is also important for a supplier to highlight any planned production cutback that would severely impact its ability to operate. Thus, a result of this capacity planning study is for Toyota to document the upper and lower range of production for each part and supplier.

Proactive steps can be initiated to solve the capacity issue. For example, a supplier could be added if production volume for a part were increasing rapidly. Such a step would provide Toyota with a backup situation in the event its primary supplier has a problem. But there are other reasons that Toyota would consider developing a dual source for some parts. Some of these considerations are risks because of location of suppliers that could restrict supply (e.g., poor weather or the potential for flooding or earthquakes) or the financial stability of the supplier. Thus capacity planning provides a perspective of overall production rate that can be executed across the supply chain.

Monthly Order

At Toyota there is a monthly global process to receive the sales orders from each sales company from around the world. That is translated into a production plan for each assembly plant as well as for each Toyota unit plant. Toyota's culture emphasizes a process that does not rely only on sophisticated computer systems. Although Toyota certainly utilizes numerous computer systems that process data and crunch the numbers, the results provided by the computers are reviewed and discussed by a cross-functional team of sales and manufacturing managers. The process is an iterative one that ultimately generates a three-month rolling production plan for all Toyota assembly and unit plants worldwide. A joint focus by both sales and manufacturing on the monthly order ensures that all perspectives are balanced and the logic for the decision is clarified.

Production Calendar

One prerequisite to creating the production plan is to determine the number of production workdays in a production month. One of the reasons that a production month is not the same as a calendar month is because some of the processes within manufacturing are based on a weekly cycle. The concept of a production month was implemented so that each month would consist of either four or five complete weeks. Each year, a production calendar is created based on the following rules:

1. Each week is assigned a sequential number from 1 to 53.
2. Week number 1 is always the week that includes the first production day of the year. For example, if January 1 is on Wednesday and January 2 is the first workday, then the week will be designated production week 1. Note: In this case, this week will actually include two days of December. Although this breaks the next rule, it is not considered an issue because in the auto industry in the United States the last week of the year is a non-production week.
3. The month into which each Monday falls is used to determine which weeks are classified into a production month except for January. For example, if April 30 is a Monday, then the entire week is included in the April production month.

Because there are 52.2 weeks in a normal 365-day year, there will be some years that contain 53 weeks. The production calendar is published prior to the beginning of the calendar year and includes the production week classification as well as company holidays observed by each plant. Use of a production calendar prevents confusion regarding planning across calendar months and preserves the weekly planning process.

Production Planning Process

Once the production calendar is published, it can be used to create a monthly production order for each plant. The monthly order process is a global process managed by Toyota Motor Corporation (TMC) in Japan. Each manufacturing assembly plant creates a preliminary operations plan that shows the quantity of each model that will be produced, including critical options such as engines and transmissions. In addition, each unit plant creates an operations plan that shows how many engines, transmissions, and other options it can produce.

An example of an operations plan is shown in Table 4-1. In this example, one week of a month is shown; however, the complete plan would show all weeks in each of the three months that make up the rolling three-month plan. The key components of this plan are as follows:

- *Standard work hours.* In this example, Monday is a holiday, so work hours are zero. For all other days, standard work hours are 16, because most plants work two 8-hour production shifts.
- *Overtime.* Normally there is some limited amount of overtime that is prescheduled. In this example, it is two hours (or one hour per shift) per day. Day-to-day adjustments to the overtime are made just prior to the start of each shift based on operational conditions at the plant.
- *Takt time.* Takt time is a term that refers to the speed of the assembly line. This unit of measure is the amount of time it takes a vehicle to move from one station to the next. In this example, a takt time of 60 seconds means that workers assigned to each station along the line have 60 seconds to complete their work. The rate of vehicles

Table 4-1. Sample Operations Plan

Item	Days					
Date	1	2	3	4	5	Total
Week Day	Mon	Tue	Wed	Thu	Fri	Week
Work Hours						
Standard hours	0	16	16	16	16	64
Overtime hours	0	2	2	2	0	6
Subtotal	0	18	18	18	16	70
Operations						
Takt time (sec)	0	60	60	60	60	
Operations rate	0	95%	95%	95%	95%	
Production						
Vehicles per hour	0	57	57	57	57	
Vehicles per day	0	1,026	1,026	1,026	912	3,990
Model 1 ratio	0	40%	40%	40%	40%	
Model 1 volume	0	410	410	410	365	1,595
Model 2 ratio	0	60%	60%	60%	60%	
Model 2 volume	0	616	616	616	547	2,395

completed and driven off the line is one per minute or one every 60 seconds.

- *Operations rate.* The percentage of the time that the assembly line is running at the normal production rate is the operations rate. That is usually set at *less* than 100 percent in a Toyota plant, because Toyota emphasizes quality first. So all workers are encouraged to stop the line if any problem occurs so that problems can be corrected before the vehicle gets produced. That measure also ensures that problems that may affect multiple vehicles are identified and corrected early. The operations rate is reduced by the time required to fix the problem. Thus, if the takt time is 60 seconds, 1 percent of the production is interrupted by a line stoppage, and it takes 5 minutes (300 seconds) to fix the problem, then the expected operations rate = $60/(60 + 0.01 \times 300) = 60/63 = 95.2\%$.

- *Vehicles per hour.* This is calculated as seconds in an hour (360) divided by takt time in seconds (60) times the operations rate.

- *Vehicles per day.* This is calculated as total work hours per day times the number of vehicles per hour.

- *Model ratio.* Most Toyota assembly plants produce multiple vehicle models. Therefore, the ratio of each model as a percent of the total of all models must be determined to create a production volume by model.

- *Model volume.* This is calculated as model ratio times the production volume.

As you can see from the sample operations plan (Table 4-1), all of the components are variables that can be manipulated to create what-if scenarios that can be evaluated during the negotiation process. These metrics, or key performance indicators (KPIs), are also used on a day-to-day basis to monitor the plant operations.

The monthly planning process requires input from all sales and manufacturing operations worldwide. Each sales company submits its request for production of each model by month. This information is transmitted to TMC in a file that contains a record for each vehicle, including full specifications. Although the sales request contains the full vehicle specifications, this initial planning step considers volumes only by model and key components such as engines. The total worldwide demand is compared to the proposed operations plan for each plant. Table 4-2 shows a sample of how vehicle and engine volumes by month are summarized by the global regions.

The next step is to balance the sales request with the production operations proposal to determine the optimum sales and operations plan. Then the production volume and model mix for each plant is allocated to each of the global sales regions.

Table 4-2. Worldwide Sales Request

	Month			Month + 1			Month + 2		
	Total	6 Cyl.	4 Cyl.	Total	6 Cyl.	4 Cyl.	Total	6 Cyl.	4 Cyl.
				United States					
Model 1	20,000	8,000	12,000	19,500	7,950	11,550	20,100	8,020	12,080
Model 2	15,000	0	15,000	16,000	0	16,000	15,500	0	15,500
Model 3	8,000	3,500	4,500	19,500	7,950	11,550	20,100	8,020	12,080
Model 4	10,000	10,000	0	11,000	11,000	0	10,000	10,000	0
Model 5	12,000	8,000	4,000	19,500	7,950	11,550	20,100	8,020	12,080
				Europe					
Model 1	5,000	1,000	4,000	5,200	1,100	4,100	4,800	1,000	3,800
Model 2	2,000	0	2,000	2,100	0	2,100	2,200	0	2,200
Model 3	8,000	3,500	4,500	9,500	3,000	6,500	9,000	8,020	980
Model 4	0	0	0	0	0	0	0	0	0
Model 5	12,000	8,000	4,000	19,500	7,950	11,550	20,100	8,020	12,080

Global/Regional Allocation

Each of the sales companies receives a share of the production for each model and each assembly plant from TMC for each of the rolling three months. Thus, each sales company (for example, Toyota Motor Sales, USA) must submit a monthly order and two months of forecast. The order month is designated as "N." The first forecast month is "N + 1" and the second is "N + 2." So, if July is the order month "N," then August is "N + 1," and September is "N + 2." Some references classify these months as PPR1, PPR2, and PPR3, where PPR stands for "production plan requirements."

Each sales company then subdivides its volume into an allocation for its regions and/or countries. For example, in the United States, the allocation is broken down into 12 regions, and in Europe it is allocated across more than 25 countries. The volume by region by model will vary based on performance versus sales objectives for each region.

Next we will examine how each region can manipulate the content of its allocated vehicles to match its regional mix.

Final Sales Order Preparation

The headquarters for each sales company will aggregate the order of each of its regions and transmit that information to TMC. During the aggregation process, the sales headquarters must do a final check to see to it that the total order complies with TMC's guidelines.

The following paragraphs show a scenario that a region would follow to generate its monthly order and forecast. (A sample of only one region's data is used, for purposes of keeping the illustration simple.) The first step is to analyze the current stock situation in the region. That is done by counting all stock by build combination as well as by color. (In this scenario, color is used as an example; however, the same process is done for each build combination.) Stock is classified as dealer stock or pipeline stock: dealer stock is owned by the dealer and either is physically at the dealer or will arrive within two to three days; pipeline stock is further divided into in-transit and allocated stock. In-transit stock is completed vehicles that are at the plant and/or in-transit to the dealers. Allocated stock is production that has been scheduled for a region but has not been built.

For this example, we have assumed that the quantity of each of these categories is equal to one month. Obviously, that figure will vary depending on many factors such as recent demand, in-transit time, and allocation point.

Table 4-3 shows how stock is calculated across the pipeline by each build combination and color. Then the mix of stock is calculated. This example is just showing colors; however, these processes need to be repeated for each build combination and color across all models.

Next the stock mix is compared to the target mix. As discussed in Chapter 3, the target mix is determined prior to new model introduction and may be adjusted periodically if market conditions change. The variance of the actual stock quantity compared to the quantity computed using the target mix ratio is used to make an order adjustment. Those calculations are shown in Table 4-4.

Next the three-month order and forecast is calculated based on the target mix, as shown in Table 4-5.

Finally, the order adjustment is used to adjust each month's quantity to rebalance the actual total stock to equal the target mix. Note that the adjustment is applied over a three-month period to avoid overreacting to changes in demand

Table 4-3. Stock Analysis

	Pipeline				
Colors	Dealer Stock	In-Transit	Allocated	Total Stock	Stock Mix
Red	150	125	150	425	14%
Black	200	225	190	615	21%
White	250	275	300	825	28%
Silver	350	300	275	925	31%
Green	50	75	85	210	7%
Total	1,000	1,000	1,000	3,000	100%

Table 4-4. Mix Analysis

Colors	Total Stock	Stock Mix	Target Mix	Target Stock	Order Adj.
Red	425	14%	15%	450	25
Black	615	21%	20%	600	−15
White	825	28%	30%	900	75
Silver	925	31%	25%	750	−175
Green	210	7%	10%	300	90
Total	3,000	100%	100%	3,000	0

Table 4-5. Baseline Three-Month Order and Forecast

Colors	Target Mix	Order (N)	Forecast (N+1)	Forecast (N+2)	Total
Red	15%	150	150	150	450
Black	20%	200	200	200	600
White	30%	300	300	300	900
Silver	25%	250	250	250	750
Green	10%	100	100	100	300
Total	100%	1,000	1,000	1,000	3,000

Table 4-6. Final Three-Month Order and Forecast

Colors	Order Adj.	Order (N)	Forecast (N+1)	Forecast (N+2)	Total
Red	25	158	158	159	475
Black	−15	195	195	195	585
White	75	325	325	325	975
Silver	−175	192	192	191	575
Green	90	130	130	130	390
Total	0	1,000	1,000	1,000	3,000

(Table 4-6). However, if the regional manager has some additional information that would indicate a more sudden change, he or she may make a decision to override this calculation.

These processes are then repeated for each package or build combination. As was discussed in Chapter 3, each region will limit the number of build combinations ordered for stock to the high-volume sellers. Table 4-7 shows how the total number of units may be distributed across the four packages for the three-month period.

Table 4-7. Mix by Package

Build Combination	Total
Package 1	700
Package 2	500
Package 3	1,500
Package 4	300
Total	3,000

Table 4-8. Mix by Package and Color Combination

Build Combination	Colors					Total
	Red	Black	White	Silver	Green	
Package 1	125	150	200	150	75	700
Package 2	100	150	100	100	50	500
Package 3	200	210	625	250	215	1,500
Package 4	50	75	50	75	50	300
Total	475	585	975	575	390	3,000

The order can now be completed by combining the color quantities with the quantities for each package, as shown in Table 4-8. That step is necessary because manufacturing requires the complete vehicle specification to determine the production schedule and eventually the part orders. Shown in Table 4-8 is the final composition of the orders. Each of the four packages is ordered with five different colors.

The process just described assumes that there are no unusual conditions that would affect the regional order. Although such normal circumstances may occur on some models for some months, most of the time external conditions will require that the order be modified. Some of these conditions are special fleet orders, seasonal trends, and special sales promotions.

Special Conditions

Fleet orders can occur at two levels. The national fleet accounts are managed by the sales headquarters. Each month, allocation to all of the regions is reduced by the amount of the national fleet orders. The fleet order is then submitted by the fleet department. In addition to these national fleet orders, each region may have local fleet orders. So the region would subtract the number of vehicles from its allocated amount and create special orders based on the unique fleet requirements.

Seasonal trends can also create a need to modify the mix of the order. Therefore, the targeted mix would change in a stair step manner to reflect projected seasonal changes. For example, convertibles and sunroofs sell better in spring and summer months. Also, lighter colors are preferred in hotter weather.

Special sales promotions also can require that the order be modified. For example, air-conditioning may be included for free if you purchase a car with a sunroof. Obviously, that would require the normal mix calculation to be overridden to ensure that an adequate supply of cars with sunroofs and air-conditioning is ordered.

The point is that a computer system can be programmed to calculate the monthly order if there are no external factors. However, the process requires human intervention to evaluate the computer-generated order and make necessary adjustments. That usually requires multiple iterations before the order is finalized.

A computer making trade-offs might ignore some subtle constraints such as option combinations that are questionable. Human interaction certainly could have helped in the case reported in the *Economist* on January 31, 2002 (story told by Hau Lee): "In the mid-1990s, [Volvo] the Swedish car manufacturer found itself with excessive stocks of green cars. To move them along, the sales and marketing departments began offering attractive special deals, so green cars started to sell. But nobody had told the manufacturing department about the promotions. It noted the increase in sales, read it as a sign that consumers had started to like green, and ramped up production."

Sales Aggregation and Adjustment

Once each region has created its order, it is transmitted to the sales headquarters where it is aggregated to produce a national order to be sent to TMC. The order is checked to ensure that each region has ordered the correct number for each model. Next the order contents must be checked against the manufacturing constraints to ensure that there are not any constraints that are exceeded. For example, there are several controlled specifications such as engines, transmissions, and wheels that may have upper and lower limits. These limits are based on capacity restrictions at Toyota unit plants and key suppliers. In the event that one or more constraints are exceeded, the order can be modified by prorating the adjustment across all regions or, if necessary, manually making adjustments to selected regions.

Keep in mind that even though each region order consists of a package and a color mix that sells best in its particular region, the national aggregate mix will normally be more evenly distributed. In addition, any change from month to month will be muted. Table 4-9 shows how a very different mix of build

Table 4-9. Aggregate Order by Region by Package

Build Combination	East	North	South	West	Total	Mix
Package 1	700	1,500	500	700	3,400	23%
Package 2	500	1,000	2,000	1,000	4,500	30%
Package 3	1,500	1,000	800	1,000	4,300	29%
Package 4	300	1,500	700	300	2,800	19%
Total	3,000	5,000	4,000	3,000	15,000	100%

combinations by sample of four regions will, when aggregated, create a more even mix of build combinations at a national level.

Once the sales order is completed, it is forwarded onto TMC in Japan. TMC aggregates all orders from all sales companies worldwide. Then the sales requests are compared with the production operations plans submitted by each manufacturing plant. High-level meetings attended by sales and production people are held to resolve the differences between sales requests and production operations plans. The result is that some last-minute adjustments will be made to ensure that the optimum production order is submitted. That collaboration process is similar to the annual planning process, with one big exception: the time frame to complete the negotiations is extremely tight. During the annual planning process, the elapsed time to resolve differences is measured in days or weeks, whereas during the monthly process the order must be finalized within one or two days.

One metric to measure accuracy of the forecast is to compare the final order to the previous forecast and measure percent of change or forecast accuracy for each option. If there are any extreme changes, they should be investigated because they may be an indication of an order error.

How Does Toyota's Method Compare to Other Planning Methods?

In many firms, the sales and operations planning process focuses on materials planning constrained by capacity. Detailed accounts of different processes adopted by firms can be obtained from standard books, such as that of Vollmann, Berry, Whybark, and Jacobs.[2] In manufacturing planning and control literature, the coordination between sales and production takes place via the "production planning" process. In addition, some firms might use distribution or sales requirements planning to send shipments from the plant to different regions or warehouses. As Vollmann and others point out, the modern term for such coordination is "sales and operations planning (S&OP)." That process begins with a sales forecast for some predetermined horizon, say 12 to 18 months.

Increase and decrease in inventory levels as well as resources are planned during this process. Limits are placed on the amount of possible increase within, say, three months and for the period three months and beyond. Typically, these plans are reviewed and revised on a monthly basis. In traditional production planning literature, this step is also called "aggregate production planning." The plans are made for groups of similar products, called families, therefore said to be aggregated. The costs considered in production planning are the costs of carrying inventory and changing workforce level, as well as the cost of overtime. As with the Toyota process, the goal is to determine overall sales rates, production rates, aggregate inventories, and backlogs.

As can be discerned from the description, a significant amount of coordination needs to be carried out through meetings. In fact, many writers have emphasized the need for organizational change for successful implementation of S&OP. Therefore, in recent years, the lack of coordination has been explicitly addressed by the introduction of a high-level sales and operations planning process called the "executive S&OP." SAP,[3] for example, offers two blends of S&OP: SAP SOP for executive S&OP and SCM for near-term S&OP. Moreover, the S&OP is said to be the business process for coordinating supply, demand, and financial plans. As Wallace and Stahl[4] have stated, "The term 'Sales & Operations Planning' traditionally referred to a decision-making process for balancing demand and supply in aggregate. This is an executive-centered activity." They go on to say that in recent years the term S&OP has been broadened to include detailed planning at the product and customer order level. It is also somewhat clear from the description given previously that the planning process in other firms is not constrained by "overall" guidelines beyond profit maximization or cost minimization. In Toyota, these "overall" guidelines also control the overall process, namely, paying attention to stability, careful planning before reacting, and measurement of forecast accuracy and consensus building before making changes. These guidelines emphasize the need to consider the impact beyond the immediate functional or firm boundary. In our opinion, such explicit guidelines differentiate the S&OP process at Toyota from that of other firms. Moreover, the performance of the plan and the planning process itself are measured against carefully selected metrics; they are not left to vague or conflicting interpretation.

Reflection Points

Can a firm that does not mass-produce adopt the Toyota S&OP principles? The main principles adopted by Toyota are straightforward and summarized under the v4L framework:

- *Variety* of cars sold is managed by keeping the national aggregate mix of packages and colors stable across time.

- *Velocity* of sales in a region is adjusted to match feasible production rates (takt time) at plants. Capacity planning estimates define the upper and lower production rates across the supply chain.
- *Variability* of production is managed by freezing sales commitments over specified periods. Variability of sales is managed by adjusting sales incentives to deliver planned sales.
- *Visibility* is ensured by tightly linking sales and operations plans, developing them collaboratively with buy-in, and deploying them across the system.

The key learning principles used are as follows:

- *Create awareness.* Deviations from plans are made immediately evident by the use of key metrics. For example, if one of the constraints is exceeded, that fact is highlighted by one of the computer checks and forwarded to a planner to investigate.
- *Make action protocols.* Methods for taking corrective action are clearly documented. For example, in case of a mismatch between operations and sales plan, the sequence of actions is to first clearly identify the gap and then to consider the potential countermeasures, gain consensus on corrective action, and implement changes.
- *Generate system-level awareness.* Systemwide considerations are of the utmost importance. They are made through face-to-face interactions and discussions. Even computer-generated plans are carefully discussed. Weak links in the supply chain are identified and limits placed on variations at each stage of the chain.
- *Practice PDCA*—Plan, Do, Check, and Act—for the planning process itself is a method of taking corrective actions when a new problem is encountered. Changes in the planning process are made using the scientific principle.

Endnotes

1. Toyota press release, July 10, 2008.
2. Thomas E. Vollmann, William L. Berry, D. Clay Whybark, and F. Robert Jacobs, *Manufacturing Planning and Control Systems for Supply Chain Management*, 5th ed. New York: McGraw-Hill/Irwin, 2004.
3. SAP is one of the largest software firms in the world that provides integrated inter-enterprise software solutions for all types of industries.
4. T. F. Wallace and B. Stahl, *Sales & Operations Planning: The Executive's Guide.* Cincinnati, OH: T. F. Wallace & Co., 2006.

Chapter 5

Production Scheduling and Operations

Production scheduling requires close coordination between sales and plant operations. In this chapter, we will explain how the production schedule is used to provide consistent and continuous flow of materials and vehicles throughout the supply chain. In Chapter 4 we described how information is gathered, both top-down and bottom-up, to create a three-month order and forecast. Once a three-month order and forecast are received from the sales divisions, the next step is to create a production schedule for the assembly plants. Before a production schedule can be determined, we need to understand how vehicles flow through the assembly plant.

Assembly Plant Operations

A typical Toyota assembly plant is highly integrated. Figure 5-1 shows how a vehicle flows through a Toyota plant.

Under one assembly plant roof you will find all of the following:

- *Stamping shop.* The stamping shop is where the body parts for a vehicle are stamped out of huge coils of steel. Large stamping presses are arranged in a row connected by conveyors. At the start of one row of presses, sheets of steel are cut from the coil and fed into the first press. After the first press stamps the basic shape of the body part (for example, the hood or the door panel), it is routed to the next press, where the press may create a curved shape. From there, it is passed to a press that punches holes, until finally the finished part rolls off of the press line. Once a press line is configured to stamp a specific body part, it will run for a period of time until an adequate quantity of parts is produced. Typically, the inventory of stamped parts to supply the body shop will be

55

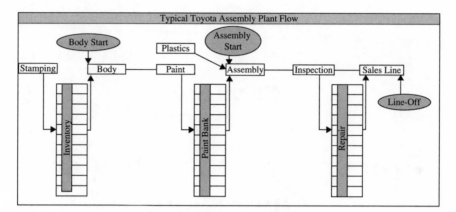

Figure 5-1. Toyota assembly plant process

enough to generate only a few hours of production. The reason that the stamping line is run in batches is because dies must be changed within the presses to reconfigure the line to stamp a different part. But because Toyota plants can change dies in a few minutes, several different parts can be stamped on each press line each day. Many writers have pointed out the practicality of Toyota's practice of running batches through this operation, including Monden.[1] Toyota forsakes the one-for-one ideal with the batch operation, when appropriate. However, unlike many batch operations, very little is left to randomness. For example, typical press operations might waste several blanks before getting the first part right, which is counted as setup time and cost. In Toyota, that waste is avoided by making sure that the presses are maintained and function at a high level of precision. The next step in the process is the body shop.

- *Body shop.* The body shop is where a vehicle is born—where it gets its identity. At body start, each vehicle gets a unique body number and is assigned a Vehicle Identification Number (VIN). The vehicles are started in the planned line-off sequence, which is based on the production schedule and sequence. From this point on, each vehicle is processed individually throughout the production process. The body number is used to track the vehicle and look up the vehicle specifications so that the exact body style is welded together to form the completed body shell. The body shop is highly automated; most of the work is performed by robots that are programmed to weld each of the vehicle panels together to form the body shell. Toyota has made particular innovations in the body shop by using robots with the flexibility to build different types of body parts. From the body shop, the vehicle shell is moved by conveyor into the paint shop. Improvements in robot flexibility have enabled an increase in the body shop process flow at Toyota. Note that at Toyota plants, there is no body shell bank or in-process inventory between the body shop and the paint shop. That is another innovation based on building vehicles one by one in a planned sequence.

■ *Paint shop*. Color is applied to the vehicle at the paint shop. The shop consists of multiple paint booths that use robots to spray-paint the body shells coming from the body shop. As the vehicle body shells enter the paint shop, they are dipped in a solution that covers the body with a protective coating. Then they are organized by color and sent to one of the paint booths. Because of environmental considerations, vehicles are painted in small batches of the same color. That approach reduces the amount of pollutants dispersed into the air, as it limits the number of times the paint nozzles must be flushed (which happens each time the color is changed). Also, some colors will require multiple coats, which will result in the vehicles getting out of the planned line-off sequence. Therefore, vehicles are moved to a paint bank prior to going into the assembly shop. A radio frequency tag is affixed to the vehicle in the paint shop with the unique body number encoded. That tag enables each vehicle to be tracked throughout the assembly process, which is important because each vehicle's specifications are used to identify parts that need to be installed on the vehicle as it moves along the line. The tag is attached at this step because it would be damaged by the paint ovens if it were affixed prior to the paint shop. The next step is to select vehicles from the paint bank to begin assembly.

■ *Assembly shop*. The assembly shop is the most labor-intensive shop. Most of the parts are installed by hand by team members working in small teams. Each team is responsible for the work performed during one process cycle at one workstation. The vehicles thus move from one station to the next at takt time intervals. Recall that takt time is the time it takes one vehicle to be completed or lined off the assembly line. At the assembly start position, a team member selects vehicles from the paint bank to start in the assembly shop. Although a computer is used to suggest the start sequence, a team member actually makes the final decision on which vehicle to start next. There are several objectives that must be considered in making this decision, among which are the following:

○ Keep vehicles in the original planned line-off sequence. Each vehicle has a planned line-off date and time stamp that can be used to pick the oldest first.

○ Avoid starting vehicles back to back that have high workload impact on assembly team members. For example, sunroofs may require extra work in one or more processes.

○ Maintain the ratio of models on the assembly line. For example, if the line is producing two models and the ratio is 45 percent and 55 percent, then this mix should be maintained.

As the vehicles move down the assembly line, the team members receive their instructions (on manifests) about which parts to install on each vehicle. These manifests are generated by the assembly line control system via a scanner that reads the radio frequency tag. The approximate number of steps in assembling a car is 353. Out of these steps, fewer than 10 use parts from sequence suppliers. In addition, sequence parts suppliers receive an electronic transmission that advises them of the exact line-off sequence. The information enables them to build the parts (e.g., seats) based on the exact specifications of each vehicle and ship them in the exact sequence to be installed on the line. Although, most sequenced parts are provided by external suppliers, some sequenced parts, such as plastic shop parts, are produced in-house.

- *Plastic shop.* Although the plastic shop is not part of the in-line process of the assembly plant, it provides key components that must be synchronized with the assembly process, and it functions as an internal sequenced supplier. An injection molding process is used to create plastic parts such as instrument panels and bumpers. Because these parts are colored, they need to be sequenced to match the vehicle colors. As happens with sequenced suppliers, these plastic parts arrive at the assembly line on dollies in the exact sequence of the vehicles in which they are to be installed.

Now to return to the production line direct flow and examine the inspection process:

- *Inspection.* After the vehicle is completed and comes off the main assembly line, it is driven to the inspection line. The primary purpose of this inspection is to conduct functionality tests on such components as the engine, transmission, brakes, and air bags. Next, cars are subject to water-pressure testing to ensure that the vehicle is leak proof. All teams involved in the assembly process are instructed to stop the line in the event a defect is detected or a problem identified. Thus it is not necessary for Toyota to perform rigorous inspection after a vehicle is completed. If a vehicle is identified as having a defect, then it will be diverted to a repair area so that the defect can be corrected before it leaves the plant. The final step before the vehicle leaves the plant is the sales line.

- *Sales line.* The point at which a vehicle's ownership is transferred from the manufacturing division to the sales division is the sales line. As the vehicle passes an imaginary point on the line, the manufacturing team member scans the vehicle into the plant computer system to change the status to "sold," and the sales team member scans the vehicle into the sales computer to change the status to "bought." That point is also where many of the so-called throw-ins are placed in the car trunk or glove box; those items would include floor mats, wheel covers, and manuals. Once the vehicle is lined off and bought by the sales division, the assembly process is complete. The total time it takes a vehicle to move from body start to line-off obviously will vary by plant. However, it usually takes about two calendar days, or three to four production shifts.

Another way to grasp an understanding of the production process is to take a tour of one of the Toyota plants. During the writing of this book, Ananth Iyer and Roy Vasher went on a guided tour of the Toyota Motor Manufacturing Kentucky (TMMK) plant in Georgetown, Kentucky. Ananth Iyer captured the following notes during the tour:

The Toyota factory at Georgetown, Kentucky, covers over 1,300 acres of land and employs about 7,000 team members. There are another 1,500 to 2,000 people employed by vendors working on-site, such as food service, day-care workers, etc.

The starting point at the plant is coils of steel delivered about every 30 minutes, each coil weighs up to 24 tons. Toyota has 19 press lines and 33 presses. Eight-hundred-ton presses operating at 80 strokes per minute create blanks. An example of how Toyota is continuing to kaizen its operations is that a new stamping line is being installed that is expected to save over 32 percent in energy costs and replace two existing lines.

The blanks are transferred by robots to a press that converts parts to requisite shapes. There are over 1,300 dies on site. These components are transferred to a flow rack and conveyed to body weld. The body weld operation takes 274 sheet metal parts and welds them to form a shell. There are over 700 robots that perform more than 4,400 welds to create a shell. Team members rotate tasks every two hours so that they use a different muscle group for their work and reduce monotony.

Of the 20 hours it takes to make a car, around 9 hours are spent in the paint shop. Every 55 seconds of takt time a car is completed. The plants at Georgetown produce nearly 2,000 vehicles every day. Production in the line is in a mixed sequence and varies by color, across Camry, Solara, and Avalon. The paint shop has 20 different colors of paint, but the most popular colors in September 2008 were silver for the Camry and bright red for the Solara. In addition, one in every four Camry models produced is a hybrid.

When the car leaves the paint shop and arrives for assembly, sequenced suppliers receive notification to deliver their parts in the exact sequence that cars are produced. In addition, the doors are removed to permit easy access and to prevent damage to the doors. The door components are assembled sep-arately. The exact door of a body rejoins the car at the end of the line. Assembly line associates operate in teams and use the andon cord (an andon is similar to the cord on a train that when pulled sends a signal) to shut down the line when a problem is detected. The team leader helps fix problems immediately, but if a problem is not fixed within a cycle time, the line is stopped.

The TMMK plant has andon cords pulled over 5,000 times each day. Each area has a different song pattern. Our trip itself saw many different line interruptions. The immediate attention to problems guarantees that quality is built in during production for every car. But it also means that adhering to the production plan is difficult. The role of inventory at the paint shop and at other points along the line is to enable the system to recover from disrup-tions that may change the assembly sequence.

All along the plant there were "blue walls" with information regarding the daily production, productivity, and so on. The data enable managers to "walk the wall" and get a quick read of the plant's operating performance.

The plant and its carefully planned and deliberate pace and methodical execution of tasks have provided a glimpse of a microcosm of the Toyota supply chain in operation.

Now to examine how the production schedule and sequence are created. Some of the metrics to monitor production are first-run ratio (the percentage of vehicles that go through the line and are completed on the first pass without being pulled off the line), actual sequence versus planned sequence, and actual line-off time versus planned line-off time.

Production Scheduling

The production schedule is created once a month from the sales order and fore-cast. As discussed in Chapter 4, sales divisions submit a rolling three-month order and forecast each month. The Production Control division must create a daily production plan to execute the agreed-upon schedule.

Scheduling Inputs

For the purpose of this discussion, assume that the next production month "N" is being scheduled. The "N" month is considered a firm order commitment, and "N + 1" and "N + 2" are considered preliminary forecasts. The difference between the firm orders versus the forecast is that once the firm order is submit-ted from sales to manufacturing, the volume of vehicles by model by plant is frozen. In other words, sales divisions have committed to buying these units, and manufacturing has agreed to produce them. Nevertheless, the content of the vehicle specifications can be changed up to about a week prior to line-off.

The forecast for months $N + 1$ and $N + 2$ do not prevent changes in volume or content. However, because of the 80/20 rule of mix planning described in Chapter 3, the actual variation in individual options from month to month will be somewhat muted when calculated on a daily rate basis.

Another input necessary to create the production schedule is the production calendar and the operations plan for each plant. As discussed in Chapter 4, the production calendar consists of four or five weeks for each month; however, the holiday schedule will vary by plant. For example, Thanksgiving is celebrated in Canada during October and during November in the United States. Each plant also uses a different operating plan that quantifies the number of vehicles to be built on each production day. The quantity per day may even vary by day of the week. For example, planned overtime may be two hours per day from Monday to Thursday and zero hours on Friday. Such flexibility demonstrates that Toyota makes extra effort to accommodate the quality of life of team members.

The final input that is required is the constraints. Those constraints could be a limit on the type of engine that can be built on one of the assembly lines or that certain colors can be built only on one line. Another constraint could be a ramp-up or ramp-down of a specific option. That occurs when a new option or color is introduced as a running change in midmonth. The constraints are established by each plant each month and reviewed by the production planners to ascertain that they are necessary and reasonable. Feasible production schedules have to satisfy these constraints.

Scheduling Process

The first step in creating the production schedule is to use the sales order and forecast data to create individual records for each vehicle and assign a unique reference number. That step is necessary because each vehicle has to be assigned to a production slot. Though eventually the Vehicle Identification Number (VIN) can be used to identify a unique vehicle, the VIN is not assigned until the vehicle is started in the body shop. Therefore, a Unique Reference Number (URN) is assigned to identify vehicles prior to production line-off.

A heijunka process is used to schedule the vehicles by day, by line, by plant. Heijunka (or smoothing) is a technique to avoid supply chain congestion, workload imbalance, inventory batching, and the like. The software that includes the heijunka logic is proprietary, so the details will not be described. However, the concept of heijunka is to create a level, or smooth, production plan. This concept of heijunka is also called "mixed-model production." The benefit of heijunka within the plant is to smooth capacity requirements and balance use of resources. The concept extends beyond the shop floor. By smoothing the flow of dependent parts, Toyota makes sure that its parts suppliers also see a level load. In fact, it ensures a level load for parts even from Japan or from distant suppliers by restricting the day-to-day variation to between +5 percent and –5 percent of the supplier's order.

Usually some sales orders have specific build dates requested, so those orders need to be scheduled first. One such example is fleet orders. The large rental companies such as Hertz, Avis, and National require that their monthly shipments arrive during a specified time period each month. Because of the limited space at most of their rental locations, they attempt to stagger their new vehicle arrivals and the shipments of the used vehicles. Therefore, these orders need to be scheduled based on a date range such as the first week of a month. Another example is an individual special customer order that needs to be prioritized. Such orders are usually scheduled early in the month so the customer will receive his or her vehicle as soon as possible.

Next, the remaining orders are grouped by build combinations and spread throughout the month so that the number of identical orders will be evenly distributed across the month. Then the sum of each option for each day is checked against the constraints. That will result in a need to shuffle some orders around to ascertain whether the constraints are met. As you can imagine, doing so is like trying to solve a Rubik's Cube, because as you move one type of order to resolve a constraint on one option, it will create a constraint violation of another option. To avoid an endless loop when trying to obtain the perfect heijunka for each option, a priority weighting is assigned to each option to determine its ranking. Priority weighting is similar to rate-based planning; for example, demand can be imagined as a rate, production as a rate, and supply as a rate. Constraints on capacity are limitations on rates of different important supplies. If those rates do not match, then there will be creation of inventories or back orders.

In addition to options, the destination of vehicles is also considered as one of the heijunka factors because it is important to have an even flow of vehicles to each region. Thus, the analogy of rates is carried forward to rates in different directions. The goal of heijunka is to balance these rates.

Once the heijunka process is completed, then each order is assigned the scheduled production day. The production day is deemed to mean the scheduled line-off day (i.e., the day that production of the vehicle is completed). This production schedule is then sent back to the sales division to advise its members of each vehicle's Unique Reference Number. The production schedule is also sent to each plant to make the actual production sequence.

A metric to measure the stability of the production plan is to measure the smoothness of the heijunka by option.

Production Sequence

Each plant must determine the exact production sequence within each production day. The sequence is determined by the operational conditions within each plant. Some of these conditions are color batching, workload associated with specific labor-intensive options, and heijunka of the major options within a day. Similar to the heijunka logic, this logic is proprietary and is considered a black box. The daily production plan is the input, and the output is a production sequence for each day. This production sequence is used by the plant to create the parts orders. It is also used as input to the assembly line control system so that vehicles are started in the correct sequence.

Sample Production Plan

Assume that Table 5-1 contains a list of vehicles that are to be scheduled to create a production plan. For this simple exercise, there are only three options for each vehicle (i.e., grade, engine cylinder, and color). The grade can be either LE or XLE. Engine is either a four- or six-cylinder. Color has three choices: red, black, and blue.

The objective is to create a production schedule for these 10 vehicles over a five-day period and to achieve a level quantity of each option. The ideal schedule would contain an equal number of each grade, engine, and color per day. But as you can see, achieving that would be impossible because the sum of each option is not divisible by 5. For example, there are six LE grades and four XLE grades.

Table 5-1. Sample Set of Vehicles

Input Sequence			
No.	Grade	Engine	Color
1	LE	4 Cyl.	Red
2	XLE	6 Cyl.	Black
3	LE	4 Cyl.	Blue
4	LE	6 Cyl.	Blue
5	LE	4 Cyl.	Blue
6	LE	6 Cyl.	Blue
7	LE	6 Cyl.	Red
8	XLE	4 Cyl.	Black
9	XLE	4 Cyl.	Red
10	XLE	4 Cyl.	Black

Table 5-2. Scheduling Template

| | Daily Schedule | | | | | | | | | |
	Day 1		Day 2		Day 3		Day 4		Day 5	
Grade LE XLE	1	2	1	2	1	2	1	2	1	2
Engine 4 Cyl. 6 Cyl.	1	2	1	2	1	2	1	2	1	2
Color Red Black Blue	1	2	1	2	1	2	1	2	1	2

Table 5-2 is a sample template that illustrates how the schedule results will be shown by option by day.

The first step is to group the vehicles by unique build combinations. As you can see from Table 5-3, there are two vehicles that are in group A. They both are LE, four cylinders, and blue. In this example there are seven groups. It is important to identify how many vehicles have the same build combination, because if you spread the groups across the production days, you will automatically smooth several options.

Table 5-3. Grouplike Build Combinations

| | Group | | | |
No.	Grade	Engine	Color	Group
3	LE	4 Cyl.	Blue	A
5	LE	4 Cyl.	Blue	A
1	LE	4 Cyl.	Red	B
4	LE	6 Cyl.	Blue	C
6	LE	6 Cyl.	Blue	C
7	LE	6 Cyl.	Red	D
8	XLE	4 Cyl.	Black	E
10	XLE	4 Cyl.	Black	E
9	XLE	4 Cyl.	Red	F
2	XLE	6 Cyl.	Black	G

The next step is to sort the vehicles from the most important priority to the least important priority. Priority is assigned to the specifications that are most important to the plant production flow. Doing so will enable the scheduling process to start with the first vehicle and schedule the vehicles in sequence day by day. In our example, the highest priority is "grade," followed by "engine." Table 5-4 shows the result of this sorting process.

Table 5-5 shows the result of scheduling vehicles based on the most important option: grade. That schedule is obtained by distributing the orders from the

Table 5-4. Vehicles Sorted by Highest Priority Specification

	Sort by First Priority			
No.	**Grade**	**Engine**	**Color**	**Group**
3	LE	4 Cyl.	Blue	A
5	LE	4 Cyl.	Blue	A
1	LE	4 Cyl.	Red	B
4	LE	6 Cyl.	Blue	C
6	LE	6 Cyl.	Blue	C
7	LE	6 Cyl.	Red	D
8	XLE	4 Cyl.	Black	E
10	XLE	4 Cyl.	Black	E
9	XLE	4 Cyl.	Red	F
2	XLE	6 Cyl.	Black	G

Table 5-5. Results of First Scheduling Pass

	First Pass									
	Day 1		**Day 2**		**Day 3**		**Day 4**		**Day 5**	
Grade	1	2	1	2	1	2	1	2	1	2
LE	A3	D7	A5		B1		C4		C6	
XLE			E8		E10		F9			G2
Engine	1	2	1	2	1	2	1	2	1	2
4 Cyl.	A3		A5	E8	B1	E10		F9		
6 Cyl.		D7					C4		C6	G2
Color	1	2	1	2	1	2	1	2	1	2
Red		D7			B1			F9		
Black			E8		E10					G2
Blue	A3		A5				C4		C6	

Table 5-6. Results of Second Scheduling Pass

	Second Pass									
	Day 1		Day 2		Day 3		Day 4		Day 5	
Grade	1	2	1	2	1	2	1	2	1	2
LE	A3	D7	A5		B1		C4		C6	
XLE				E8		G2		F9		E10
Engine	1	2	1	2	1	2	1	2	1	2
4 Cyl.	A3		A5	E8	B1					E10
6 Cyl.		D7				G2	C4		C6	
Color	1	2	1	2	1	2	1	2	1	2
Red		D7			B1			F9		
Black				E8		G2				E10
Blue	A3		A5				C4		C6	

list uniformly across the days of the week. As the table reveals, the result is not perfect, because there are six LE grades to be scheduled over a five-day period. When the number is uneven, then the goal would be to make the best fit. In that case, there will be two LE vehicles scheduled on the first day. Now if we look at the second-priority option (engine), there is an uneven schedule on days 2, 3, and 5. On days 2 and 3, there are two 4-cylinder engines scheduled on both days. On day 5, there are two 6-cylinder engines scheduled.

The next step is to attempt to rebalance the vehicles based on making a smoother engine distribution without breaking the smoothness of the grade. In our example, that could be accomplished by swapping vehicles E10 and G2. The results of the second pass are shown in Table 5-6.

The final step is to create the production schedule for each vehicle by assigning the production day and production slot sequence to each vehicle. Table 5-7 shows the final schedule of each vehicle. The output is then used by the sales division to allocate vehicles to dealers. In addition, the output is used by the assembly plants to create the parts order.

In our simple example, it has been fairly easy to manipulate the vehicles to arrive at a smooth schedule for all options. That task is much more complex when there are thousands of vehicles to schedule with hundreds of build combinations.

Why Is Heijunka Important?

As illustrated previously, heijunka is one of the foundational processes that has enabled Toyota's extended supply chain to operate as if it is an extension of the

Table 5-7. Final Scheduling Sequence

		Output Sequence			
No.	Grade	Engine	Color	Day	Slot
3	LE	4 Cyl.	Blue	1	1
7	LE	6 Cyl.	Red	1	2
5	LE	4 Cyl.	Blue	2	1
8	XLE	4 Cyl.	Black	2	2
1	LE	4 Cyl.	Red	3	1
2	XLE	6 Cyl.	Black	3	2
4	LE	6 Cyl.	Blue	4	1
9	XLE	4 Cyl.	Red	4	2
6	LE	6 Cyl.	Blue	5	1
10	XLE	4 Cyl.	Black	5	2

TPS. There have been many books written about TPS and how it is synonymous with "lean production." What Toyota does by establishing a smooth production schedule using heijunka is to ensure that its own assembly plants are operating in an efficient and effective manner while at the same time extending stability throughout the supply chain.

Toyota understands that the cost of sales includes the total cost of operating the supply chain, not just Toyota's internal production costs. Let's consider how heijunka can positively impact all elements of the supply chain, including the various tiers of suppliers, inbound logistics, assembly operations, and outbound logistics, as well as dealers.

Multiple tiers of suppliers exist (this tier structure will be discussed in greater detail in Chapter 7). Tier 1 suppliers receive their orders directly from the OEM and are responsible for producing parts based on the pickup schedule provided by Toyota. Tier 2 suppliers are the tier 1's direct suppliers and receive their orders from the tier 1 suppliers; they must produce parts or materials based on the tier 1 supplier schedule. This process continues backward throughout the network of suppliers. Now assume that the orders from the OEM have not been level for each daily order. For example, on day 1, the tier 1 supplier received an order for 1,000 parts; on day 2, the order was 500; and on day 3, the order was 2,500. Next, the tier 1 supplier broke down these orders into their component parts and sent the order to the tier 2 supplier. In this example, if there were four parts per order, then the tier 2 supplier would receive an order of 4,000, 2,000, and 10,000. Now let's assume that the tier 1 supplier's daily production capacity is 1,000 and the tier 2 supplier's daily capacity is 5,000. One of two things could happen: either each supplier would stock extra inventory to enable it to fulfill the demand or it would ship short and create a back order until it could catch up. That would create a "bullwhip effect" (as examined in Chapter 13) and lead to inefficient operations at all tiers of suppliers, especially if these variations could not be forecasted in advance. Thus, even with the best intentions, the variance of orders would exceed the variance of demand (the bullwhip effect) unless efforts were made to dampen the effect. Even though suppliers adjust and attempt to respond to these dramatic changes in demand, the inefficiencies result in higher operating costs, which are passed along to the OEM.

Now let's consider Toyota's orders based on the production schedule using heijunka. As we discussed earlier in this chapter, it is not possible to create a perfect heijunka for all parts; however, a good heijunka result would be a variation of between +5 percent and −5 percent. If Toyota's average parts order were 1,000, then the expected daily order to the tier 1 supplier would be between 950 and 1,050 parts. Therefore, the tier 1 order to the tier 2 supplier, based on four parts per order, would range from 3,800 to 4,200 parts. In that case, because the variation in daily orders would be very small, the suppliers could adjust their daily production by varying the level of overtime instead of maintaining high levels of safety stock or risk shipping short.

The next segment of the supply chain is inbound logistics. Heijunka plays an important role in smoothing the daily shipments from tier 1 suppliers to the Toyota assembly plants. Toyota uses third-party logistics partners to manage and operate a fleet of trucks that picks up parts on a daily basis and delivers them to multiple assembly plants. Heijunka of the parts volume for each supplier in the network ensures a consistent flow of parts through the logistics network. That maximizes transportation efficiency by facilitating a high utilization of trucks and drivers every day.

Once the parts arrive at the assembly plants, they come under the control of the internal logistics group. Internal logistics is responsible for moving parts from the dock to the line side just-in-time. Kanbans are used to signal when the parts are needed for each line side station. Again, heijunka ensures a smooth flow of parts within the plant. That enables the forklift drivers to operate in an orderly manner on a regular internal route schedule.

Once the vehicles are produced, they are ready for shipment to dealers. Vehicles are transported by various methods including ship, rail, and truck. In the United States, however, most vehicles are transported by rail to a regional railhead. After the vehicles arrive at a railhead and are unloaded, a trucking company picks them up and delivers them to the dealers. As discussed earlier, Toyota strives to ensure that all components of the supply chain are streamlined and operate efficiently and effectively. Therefore, if vehicles are produced and shipped randomly without regard to railhead destination, then vehicles arrive in an uneven manner and eventually create a bottleneck. To prevent that from happening, Toyota includes the destination code as one of the parameters that is considered in the heijunka process. That inclusion ensures a smooth and even flow of vehicles through the distribution network.

Finally, the vehicles arrive at a dealer and are placed into inventory until sold. (Remember driving past dealerships that proudly park their vehicles in large lots in front and around the dealership? Those vehicles are the inventory.) Again, you may question, how does heijunka affect the dealerships? Just as at the railhead, a bottleneck can occur at a dealer if too many vehicles arrive in a short period of time. Dealership personnel must prep the vehicles once they arrive and get them ready for sale. It is best if this work is spread throughout the month. In addition, it is important to have a steady flow of vehicles to each dealer to avoid unnecessary buildup of inventory. Heijunka is again used to smooth the number of vehicles scheduled throughout the month by region. The region then allocates its vehicles to the dealers proportionally based on sales volume. Doing so will ensure a smooth flow of vehicles to each dealer throughout the month.

In summary, heijunka plays a vital role in Toyota's supply chain operations. It is used to create a smooth flow of parts from suppliers to the assembly plant as well as for maintaining a smooth flow of vehicles from each assembly plant to the dealers.

Why Is Production Sequence Important?

The sequence the vehicle is produced within the day is important because the assembly plant operations need to be well balanced to ensure that there are no bottlenecks within the production process or overburden on selected teams. Again, Toyota's focus is to guarantee smooth operations throughout the assembly process. In an assembly plant, there are hundreds of workstations along the line that install parts on the vehicle as the vehicle body passes through. The objective is to make sure that each work team's effort is similar and that the work can be completed within the takt time. Therefore, the production sequence is established based on smoothing options that create extra work for one or more work teams.

Once the sequence is set within each day, then the estimated line-off time (or completion time) can be assigned to each vehicle. A typical production day for a plant that runs two production shifts starts at 6 a.m. and completes at about 2 a.m. the next calendar day. So the first vehicle would have a planned line-off date/time of production D: 06:01, whereas the last vehicle planned line-off date/time would be D + 1: 02:00.

The planned line-off date/time is used by sales to calculate the estimated time of arrival (ETA). The ETA is used by dealers to keep customers posted on the scheduled arrival of their vehicle. The process to create the ETA will be explained in Chapter 8.

The line-off date/time is also sent to the parts ordering process to determine when parts will need to be shipped from the suppliers to arrive just-in-time to be installed on each vehicle. This process will be discussed in more detail in Chapter 6.

How Does Toyota's Scheduling Process Compare to Others?

Master production scheduling (MPS) is the process used in the manufacturing planning and control framework to initiate more production. A master production scheduling process plans production as forecasts are updated and also when orders are received. The master production schedule is often determined at the group level. [The final assembly schedule (FAS) also coordinates between the production plan and the rest of the manufacturing processes by specifying the *exact* build sequence.] A check is made to ascertain whether the aggregate of the detailed planned build equals the volume planned by the MPS. The master production schedule is the input to materials planning. Materials Requirements Planning (MRP) will be discussed and compared to Toyota's method of materials planning in Chapter 6. At this time it is enough to note that the material plan uses fixed lead times to decide when to schedule parts or assemblies.

Let us now compare these MRP processes to the scheduling processes at Toyota. MRP processes share many similarities with scheduling processes at Toyota; they have some differences too. As with scheduling at Toyota, there is an attempt to freeze the production plan using planning fences when developing the MPS. Typically, the planning horizon is split into zones that are called "ice," "slush," and "water." The ice part is frozen, the slush part is where some changes at the product family level are allowed, and the water part is open to changes. However, with MRP the attempt to manage the selling to match capacity is not undertaken with as much assiduousness as in Toyota.

It is well known that MRP tends to generate a significant amount of nervousness. That is so because small perturbations to the demand can lead to significant variations within the plant as well as for suppliers. This phenomenon is inadvertent and unavoidable because of the rules used to plan production. In MRP, production is considered to be taking place in discrete time (weeks, days, or hours); thus, the quantity to be produced is often "batched" so that the batch is the right size and started at the right time. Any such attempt at batching can lead to large changes in production requirements because of a small change in production plans. For example, say an economic batch size is 50. The demand in a period is 48. The next batch may not be started until the next period if the on-hand inventory is enough to cover current consumption requirements, even if the safety stock is low. For example, if safety stock is 10, current consumption demand is 30, and on-hand inventory is 43, then the planner might decide not to release a batch for production. Now, assume that either a customer places an order for five units or there is a change in forecast by the same five units. Then it is likely that a batch of 50 is released for production immediately. Toyota avoids such a scenario by using heijunka to create a level production plan. That stability prevents the nervousness associated with rules of batching in MRP within the plant and even when ordering from suppliers.

The materials plan is traditionally executed with a manufacturing execution system (MES). Often, the traditional scheduling process has to contend with managing orders through several complex steps to achieve the lead time promised by the material planners. For example, a stamping shop might have several processes. For material planning purposes, manufacturing a particular stamping is considered to be a single process. The average lead time plus some slack is used to plan production of this part in the shop. The shop therefore has leeway in scheduling the individual orders such that they meet the lead time; safety stock to cover scrap and rework is also added. The inclusion of slack in planning and the lack of step-by-step coordination inevitably lead to carrying inventory as work-in-process or finished goods. They also lead to temporary surges in capacity requirements that are seemingly unpredictable. In Toyota's process, the production plan is based on each shop working at its standard operations rate; thus, surges in workload are avoided. That approach makes scheduling easier to accomplish. Deviations are obvious and visible; they can be traced and addressed as and when they occur.

We say that the traditional (and common) methods use position-based planning because the position of inventories dictates the production planning and scheduling, not the rate of demand and supply. In summary, the processes mentioned previously deviate fundamentally from Toyota's because they use position-based planning instead of rate-based planning. They also differ significantly because of the lack of a "self" or "automatic" coordination/constraining mechanism such as heijunka, which forces collaboration across production and logistics planning, scheduling, and supplier planning processes.

Reflection Points

- *Variety* is planned and distributed across periods (using heijunka) to balance tasks.
- *Velocity* is maintained using a rate-based planning of flows balanced across the supply chain. By eliminating bottlenecks, the velocity is maximized.

- *Variability* is curtailed with heijunka to smooth out workload and loadings. That variability reduction enables suppliers to plan their capacity reliably and thus lower costs.
- *Visibility* is ensured by eliminating inventories, simplifying planning, ensuring buy-in, and so on.

The following are highlights of the learning practices:

- *Create awareness.* Heijunka makes deviations evident and forces planners to resolve issues as they arise. It enforces coordination at the supply chain level and makes problems evident to supply chain participants.
- *Establish capability.* Production control planners undergo intensive apprenticeship. Senior planners are asked to devote time to training.
- *Make action protocols.* Methods for taking actions to resolve heijunka are documented. The sequence in which different constraints are considered during planning are discussed and documented.
- *Generate system-level awareness.* Systemwide implications are captured by heijunka itself. It supersedes immediate concerns about local profit and loss. Heijunka makes deviations evident and forces planners to resolve issues as they arise. It enforces coordination at the supply chain level.

Endnote

1. Yasuhiro Monden, *Toyota Production System: An Integrated Approach to Just-In-Time*, 3d ed. Atlanta: Engineering & Management Press, December 1998.

Chapter 6

Parts Ordering

T oyota adopts different planning methods depending on which types of parts are involved. Some of the planning processes are unique to Toyota and so are worth contrasting with general practice.

There are many parts ordering processes for the different categories of parts. The four broad part categories are local parts, long lead time parts, in-house parts, and sequenced parts:

1. *Local parts* are parts supplied by suppliers located within the same global region as the assembly plants. For example, parts supplied by North American suppliers to assembly plants located in North America would be considered local.
2. Parts supplied by Japanese suppliers to North American and European assembly plants would be considered *long lead time parts*.
3. *In-house parts*, such as body panels, plastic bumpers, and engines, are produced at the same site as the assembly plant.
4. *Sequenced parts* are produced at suppliers located near to the assembly plant. Those parts are shipped to the assembly plant in the exact sequence of the vehicles being produced. A typical sequenced part for assembly is seats.

Each of these categories of parts has a unique parts ordering process that is described in this chapter. Note that the use of the term "parts" broadly includes individual parts as well as component assemblies. Also, parts orders are issued for parts and assemblies that are shipped from tier 1 suppliers to the original equipment manufacturer (OEM), which in this case is Toyota. The tier 1 suppliers are responsible for ordering their parts and materials from their suppliers.

Common Parts Ordering Processes

Some prerequisite processes are common to all of the parts ordering categories. These are necessary parts quantity calculations, parts and supplier master database maintenance, and parts forecasting. Each of these processes will be explained in the following paragraphs.

Necessary Parts Quantity

The necessary parts quantity calculation process translates the vehicle specification into the parts and components necessary to build the vehicle. The process uses a production schedule like the one discussed in Chapter 5 and a Toyota specification database that is similar to a bill of material (BOM).[1] The specification database is maintained by the engineering group and contains all of the specifications of each vehicle structure, including the necessary parts required to build each vehicle. The specifications are used by many functions within a manufacturing company including engineering, purchasing, manufacturing, and parts ordering. Toyota refers to its version of the BOM as the Specifications Management System (SMS). Because Toyota produces many of the same vehicles at plants around the world, it is imperative that the SMS database be the same source for vehicle structures.

Each plant also maintains a subset of the SMS database that provides the parts list for the vehicles produced at the plant. This database is the Plant Specifications Management System, or PSMS. Each parts ordering group uses the PSMS to identify the necessary parts and quantities required to build each vehicle. A key point here is that each unique vehicle build combination will have a different set of parts. For example, assume there are two vehicles with almost identical specifications:

- *Vehicle A:* Blue, four-door sedan, four-cylinder engine without spoiler
- *Vehicle B:* Blue, four-door sedan, four-cylinder engine with spoiler

The only difference between the two is that vehicle B has a spoiler; therefore, it would seem obvious that the only differences in the parts requirements are the spoiler and fasteners needed to attach it to the trunk. However, many spoilers contain a backlight. So, in addition to the spoiler parts, additional wiring harness parts are needed. This example emphasizes the need to consider each unique vehicle combination when performing the parts calculation.

The output of the necessary parts calculation process is a complete parts list along with the quantities needed for each vehicle. As will be explained later, Toyota retains the parts requirements by individual vehicles and does not aggregate the quantities by part number until the parts order is generated. In addition, each part is classified as local, long lead time, in-house, or sequenced.

Parts and Supplier Master

Another common process is to maintain a parts and supplier master database. The parts master contains information such as part name, supplier, lot size, and vendor share. Vendor share is used to allocate shares when a part is sourced to multiple suppliers. For example, one of three brands of tires might be installed on a vehicle. In our example, the share to each supplier could be Brand A, 40 percent; Brand B, 30 percent; Brand C, 30 percent. The supplier master contains information such as supplier name and location, lead time, and shipment frequency. The plant parts ordering groups maintain these data on an as-needed basis because they are closer to the actual operations. Of course, if significant changes with supplier volume or new suppliers occur, then purchasing would need to be consulted and assist with the supplier negotiations.

Forecasting

Each week, a 13-week rolling forecast is sent to all suppliers to provide them with guidance for future orders. The forecast gives suppliers an estimate of future orders so that they in turn can send forecasts to their suppliers. In some cases, long lead time component parts or raw materials may need to be ordered as a result of the forecast. For Toyota suppliers, the forecast is fairly consistent from week to week because, as discussed in Chapter 5, the strategy of Toyota is to *heijunka* (or "to smooth") the production schedule.

The forecast is created by summarizing the parts requirements by production week. As explained in Chapter 5, production is scheduled by production week. The process is straightforward: After all of the necessary part quantities are determined for each vehicle for the three-month rolling production, they are summarized by part number, by supplier, and by production week. Then the quantities are divided by the lot size to determine the number of lots to order for each part number for each supplier. Table 6-1 shows a sample parts forecast. Note that the lot size will vary by part number. In addition, the number of lots

Table 6-1. Sample Parts Forecast

| | | | Number of Lots Forecasted by Week | | | | |
Supplier Code	Part No.	Lot Size	W1	W2	W3	W4	W13
S-10001	PN-001	10	50	53	51	53	55
	PN-002	20	80	81	80	82	85
S-20001	PN-003	5	100	105	98	102	105
	PN-004	50	20	22	20	18	24

forecasted by week may vary, but that variance will be minimized because of heijunka.

The forecast and parts orders are communicated to the suppliers either by Electronic Data Interchange (EDI)[2] or via a supplier Web portal.

Local Parts Ordering

Local parts usually represent the largest number of part numbers. For each vehicle type there could be 300 to 400 suppliers that are located within a few days' travel time from the assembly plant. Although the suppliers receive a weekly forecast from Toyota, they must wait until they receive the final daily order prior to preparing the shipments. The final order is transmitted to the suppliers each day.

The formula for calculating the daily parts order is very precise in order to ensure that each part for each vehicle arrives so that it can be installed at the line side station in the assembly plant just-in-time. The following are key items that are used in the parts order calculation:

- The necessary parts quantities calculation for each vehicle
- The operating condition at the assembly plant:
  - The last vehicle lined off (the vehicle URN that was the last one off the line at the end of the previous day's production)
  - Current operations schedule based on latest overtime plan by day
  - The installation point on the assembly line where each part is installed and time offset calculated backward from the end of the line
  - Prior-day usage of parts based on kanban
- Key information for each supplier:
  - Part numbers for each supplier
  - The lot size for each part
  - The location of the supplier's plant and the lead time from the supplier's plant to the Toyota assembly plant

The objective of the daily parts ordering process is to send orders to each supplier for parts that will be needed for production based on the supplier's lead time.

The first step is to determine the adjusted vehicle production schedule based on the latest operating conditions. In Chapter 5 we demonstrated how vehicles are scheduled by production day and then sequenced within each day. That sequence will be the production plan, if everything at the plant runs on schedule. That assumption is a big one, because many things can happen to cause the plant to get off schedule. Therefore, each day prior to the determination of the daily parts order, the day-to-day production schedule is reset. The

Table 6-2. Plan versus Actual Production Adjustment

Item	Day 1	Day 2	Day 3	Day 4	Day 5
Plan	1,000	1,000	1,000	1,000	1,000
Actual	1,000	850			
Variance	0	(150)			
Revised plan			1,050	1,050	1,050

revised production schedule is created by starting with the last vehicle lined off and working backward to determine how many vehicles will be built each day based on the current operating plan. The daily operating plan is updated each day to reflect changes in daily overtime and/or working hours and days. For example, if at the end of the prior production day there was an equipment problem that caused the plant to lose three hours of production, then that lost production would most likely be made up by working overtime the next three days. Look at Table 6-2 to see the effect of this shift in the production schedule. The table reveals that on day two the actual vehicles produced were 850 versus the plan of 1,000. It means that the plant is 150 vehicles behind the plan. Therefore, the daily schedule will be revised showing 150 vehicles will be *made up over the next three days*. Observe the emphasis on not reacting too quickly, on smoothing the rate to ensure that the system is not stressed unduly, and the precision with which shortfalls are made up.

The importance of the adjustment is that if the parts were ordered based on the original plan, then the parts would be arriving at the plant ahead of the time needed. The result would be too much inventory at the plant. Too much inventory in the Toyota Production System is considered *muda*, or waste; thus, the schedule is adjusted to avoid ordering too many or too few parts.

Another factor used to determine when to order each part is the actual lead time for each supplier. To illustrate this point, refer to Table 6-3. This table shows a situation where a daily parts order is to be placed to two suppliers with different lead times. Part PN-001 is supplied from supplier S-10001, and the lead time is four days. This order will be issued on the sixteenth of the month for vehicles that will be produced on the twentieth. Part PN-003, on the other

Table 6-3. Order Lead Time

Supplier	Part No.	Lead Time	Order Day	Production Day
S-10001	PN-001	4 days	16th	20th
S-20001	PN-003	2 days	18th	20th

hand, is supplied from supplier S-20001 and the lead time is two days, so the order will be issued on the eighteenth for the same vehicles to be produced on the twentieth. The same process is repeated for all parts and all vehicles in the schedule until the part with the longest lead time has been ordered.

Keep in mind that all parts for a vehicle will not be ordered on the same day because each part may have a different lead time, depending on each supplier's location. Specifically, the aggregate order for parts is always linked to specific vehicle orders! This real-time connection between parts ordering and actual vehicle requirements keeps the supply line taut and coordinated throughout the manufacturing and supply systems.

Once the initial requirements are determined for each part, several adjustments need to be made before the order is finalized:

- Specifications may change in the vehicle content after parts have been ordered because dealers can change some specifications up to five days prior to production. That could mean that some parts that were ordered prior to the five-day freeze point were ordered incorrectly. Therefore, after the final vehicle specifications are known, parts ordered based on the tentative specifications must be compared to the parts requirements based on the final specifications, and an adjustment is added to or subtracted from the next order.
- Usage variations because of scrap, misuse, or inventory loss adjustments are calculated by comparing the actual usage based on the internal kanbans to the expected usage based on the necessary parts calculation of the final vehicle specifications. These adjustments are added to or subtracted from the next order.
- Operating conditions may also necessitate miscellaneous adjustments that can also be manually added or subtracted.

Although this process may seem very similar to the traditional MRP,[3] there is one significant difference: traditional MRP systems rely on the parts inventory count to determine what is on hand and on order. The inventory quantity is then subtracted from the total parts requirement to determine the quantity to be ordered. One risk in using inventory quantity in the parts calculation is that it does not automatically adjust for scrap and/or misusage. Moreover, the connection between orders and parts gets broken in most MRP systems. It may exist through information linkages, but not as tightly as Toyota intends—the company aims to keep the physical vehicle orders and parts orders tightly coupled. That is achieved by insisting on accurate specifications, keeping vehicle parts requirements separate, planning on adjustments on a frequent basis instead of weekly or monthly, and by grouping parts that need different types of controls and planning systems.

Once the quantities of each part and supplier have been determined, the actual order by lot and shipping time needs to be determined. One of Toyota's philosophies is to have "small lots, frequent deliveries," so most suppliers will have multiple shipments per day, or at least one shipment per day. The following is an example of a final parts ordering calculation:

1. The number of parts required (130) less carryover (0) equals parts to be ordered (130)
2. The parts to be ordered (130) divided by lot size (25) equals 6 lots and 20 carryover (Note: always round up to the next lot; the carryover will be subtracted from the next day's order.)
3. The number of lots (6) divided by the number of shipments per day (3) equals 2 lots per shipment

Long Lead Time Parts Ordering

Long lead time parts are handled differently than locally procured parts. The reason is quite obvious: long lead time parts must be ordered several weeks in advance of production. For example, most of the long lead time parts for Toyota's North American and European plants are shipped from Japan with a lead time of about six weeks. But this means that there will be some inaccuracies because the final vehicle specifications are not frozen until about five to ten days prior to production. The final freeze point varies by each plant and is based on local lead time conditions. The general rule of thumb is that 80 percent of the local parts lead time should be shorter than the final freeze point. For example, if the freeze point is five days, then 80 percent of local parts will have a lead time of five days or less.

Another factor that makes the planning tricky is that the work schedules are different in Japan than in North America or Europe, and in some cases they vary by country. For example, Canada celebrates Thanksgiving in October, whereas the United States celebrates it in November. Japan does not recognize Thanksgiving, but the country shuts down in May for Golden Week.[4]

To accommodate these differences each month, the working calendars of each plant are mapped to the working calendar of Japan. Working backward from the production schedule at the overseas assembly plant, each day's vehicle schedule would be mapped back to the day it must be shipped from Japan. That procedure gets a little more complicated because a production day of June 15 in the United States means that the parts must be ordered from Japan around May 1, assuming a six-week lead time. The actual shipment time is about four weeks, so these parts would be shipped in early May to arrive at the overseas plant on June 15. Now, if there is a holiday in Japan during early May, then the parts ordering schedule must be shifted to ensure that the shipment date is met. The process of mapping these schedules is sometimes referred to as a "rundown."

Table 6-4. Long Lead Time Parts Rundown Schedule

	May					June				
	18	19	20	21	22	15	16	17	18	19
Shipments	1,000	1,000	1,000	1,000	1,000					
Receipts						1,000	1,000	1,000	1,000	1,000
Production						1,000	1,000	1,000	1,000	1,000
Shipments	1,250	1,250	1,250	1,250	Holiday					
Receipts						1,250	1,250	1,250	1,250	
Production						1,000	1,000	1,000	1,000	1,000

Refer to Table 6-4 to grasp how the concept works. In the example, the daily production rate for the week of June 15 is 1,000 vehicles per day. Therefore, the parts required to build these vehicles will be shipped four weeks earlier, or the week of May 18. So when the daily work schedules are the same, the shipping and production will mirror each other.

But bear in mind that May 22 is a holiday in Japan. In Table 6-4, you can see that the parts required to build the 1,000 vehicles are spread evenly over the first four days of the week. The result is that 1,250 equivalent vehicles of parts will be shipped each of the four days preceding the holiday. Note: if the capacity in Japan cannot absorb this daily increase, then the pull ahead would be spread across more days. Keep in mind that the parts shipments are based on the *exact* sequence of the vehicle production, on the daily production schedule and vehicle sequence within the day. In other words, the 250 extra vehicle parts added to each day would not be the original vehicles scheduled for Friday. Thursday's shipments would consist of 1,000 of Friday's plus 250 from Thursday's. Wednesday's would consist of 750 of Thursday's plus 500 from Wednesday's. This pattern would continue until all of Friday's shipments were made up. Again, you can see from this example that it is extremely important to order parts based on the planned build sequence within each production day to maintain a tight link between parts delivered and associated vehicle specifications. This rundown schedule is created at the beginning of the order month; however, the actual parts orders are released on a daily basis.

As with the local adjustment process, the daily order for long lead time parts will include adjustments. Most of the adjustments will be the result of specification changes made by dealers after the initial parts order is released for the long lead time parts. Because of the long lead time, the adjustments could be considerable. Typically, Toyota caps the allowable change for long lead time parts to 10 percent. They do so because safety stock must be kept for the maximum weekly change allowance times the number of weeks of lead time. For example, if the normal weekly order for a part is 1,000 units and the allowable change is 10 percent, then the safety stock required to absorb these changes would be 600 units. The calculation is as follows:

1,000 × 10% = 100 per week, × 6 weeks = 600 units of safety stock

An example of how Toyota continues to learn and kaizen its operations is the modifications the company has made to its long lead time parts ordering process over time. When Toyota initially began production at overseas plants, the company had a very simple approach to ordering long lead time parts. The approach was to take the total quantity of parts required for a month and divide by the number of production days and place a daily order based on the average parts per day. What Toyota learned was that there were special circumstances when this approach did not work. One of these circumstances was when there was a running change implemented midmonth at a plant. A running change during a month would result in both a shortage of the old part and an overflow of the new part.

Table 6-5 illustrates this problem: the 100 pieces of the old part were needed during the first half of the month, and then the new part was required for the last half at the same 100-piece rate. The problem is that if parts were ordered based on the average of the usage of both parts over the month, the daily order would be 50 pieces of both parts over the month. At that rate, a shortage of the old part would be created as well as too many of the new parts during the first half of the month.

Table 6-5. Midmonth Parts Change

| Part Type | Daily Rate | | | |
	W1	W2	W3	W4
Actual Requirement				
Old part	100	100		
New part			100	100
Order Based on Average				
Old part	50	50	50	50
New part	50	50	50	50
Order-Based Sequence				
Old part	100	100		
New part			100	100

Once Toyota management analyzed this problem, they changed the method of ordering based on the daily production plan and sequence. This is another example of why the method of ordering based on the daily production planned sequence is so important.

In-house Parts Ordering

In-house parts are parts produced at the assembly plant—for example, stamping parts and plastic parts. There are two primary methods for ordering in-house parts: internal kanbans and sequenced orders.

The word *kanban* literally stands for the word *card*. In its simplest form, the planning department assigns a specific number of kanbans for each part that is ordered by a user department from a supplier department. Each kanban (or card) authorizes the production of a fixed number of parts that are to be placed in a container. Each full container and the accompanying card are transported to the user department. When the user department runs out of the part, before it starts using the parts from a full container, it removes the card from the container and places it on a kanban post. The kanban is then moved from the post to the supplier department, thereby authorizing the supplier department to make another full container. The supplier department cannot produce unless there is a kanban. Thus, the number of parts in circulation at any one time can never exceed the number authorized by the kanbans. Numerous articles have been written about the different types of kanbans and calculations of kanbans. Therefore, we do not dwell on these details here.

Sequence Parts Ordering

Sequence parts are parts such as seats and wheels ordered from a supplier at the time the vehicle enters final assembly. The supplier then builds and ships these parts in the exact sequence as the vehicles are being built. The actual order is generated by sending an electronic transmission to the supplier based on a radio frequency scan of the vehicle number as it starts down the final assembly line. The order is not sent earlier than that because prior to final assembly the vehicle can get out of sequence during paint operations. The time between when the signal is sent to the supplier and when it is needed on the assembly line varies. It could be as many as five hours and as few as two. The supplier does not keep stock of these parts because it is impossible to provide a service level of 100 percent with some types of parts (such as seats). Suppliers build the parts upon receipt of the orders and ship them in the precise sequence in a truck every 30 minutes or every hour. Clearly, significant resources are expended to develop supplier capabilities to accomplish this level of performance (as described in Chapter 7).

Reflection Points

- *Variety* of parts is managed by linking parts delivery to production sequence, particularly for sequence suppliers. Mix planning ensures that the aggregate mix across options is stable.
- *Velocity* of parts flow is directly linked to production sequence and takt time; thus, supplier velocity is tied to production velocity.
- *Variability* of orders is controlled by heijunka at the plant, which prevents large order fluctuations of the supplier orders.
- *Visibility* is maintained by tightly linking deliveries and lots to production sequence, which permits dealer order changes to be accommodated by direct adjustments to part orders.

The following are several examples that demonstrate how Toyota extends its learning across the extended enterprise:

- *Create awareness.* In the parts ordering process, the deviations are immediately noticeable because there is little or no inventory. The only action that is taken in most cases (except for long lead time parts) is to slow down or halt production. That slowdown or stoppage creates a sense of urgency to identify the root cause of the deviation and to implement both short-term and long-term countermeasures.
- *Make action protocols.* Adjustments to working production days are absorbed by the production schedule by maintaining the sequence of production to match shipments. There is constant effort to scientifically experiment with lead times and lot sizes.
- *Generate system-level awareness.* Changes in specifications for a vehicle are directly linked to parts changes and thus orders to suppliers. A common specification management system enables many functions to understand the impact of making changes to designs.
- *Adapt processes.* Tailor its parts ordering system according to the specific type of parts ordered. That accommodation makes it easier to link to other supply chain processes and thus make deviations across the supply chain evident to everyone. Toyota achieves that objective by keeping the physical product orders and parts orders tightly coupled.

Endnotes

1. BOM is a common industry term that refers to the bill of material. The bill of material defines the structure of the end product working back from the product to each level of components and eventually to the lowest level of parts.

2. EDI, or Electronic Data Interchange, is a standard method of exchanging data to and from OEMs and suppliers. There are many different types of transaction types, each with a unique transaction code and format.

3. MRP is an acronym for Materials Requirements Planning—a process in the manufacturing industry that is widely used to calculate parts orders.

4. Golden Week is a national holiday in Japan.

Chapter 7

Managing Suppliers

I magine you are a supplier to Toyota. What is your role in the Toyota supply chain? What is your expected productivity improvement over time? How would your experience as a part of Toyota's supply chain differ from your experience supplying other auto original equipment manufacturers? How would your processes have to operate to synchronize with Toyota's system? How would you have to adjust organizationally to collaborate with other suppliers to Toyota? How can the v4L framework enable an understanding of Toyota's supplier management system and its impact across the supply chain? These questions form the basis for this chapter.

Measured Performance Differences for Toyota and Suppliers

A study by John Henke from Planning Perspectives provides data regarding the supplier Working Relations Index (WRI) across auto OEMs. This analysis includes 1,112 buying situations of OEM-supplier relations. The index ranks OEMs based on 17 criteria, including: "supplier trust of the OEM, open and honest communication, timely information, degree of help to decrease costs, extent of late engineering changes, early involvement in the product development process, flexibility to recover from canceled or delayed engineering programs, etc." These criteria could thus be classified as focusing on the relationship, communication, help, and profit opportunity.[1] In 2005, the working index value for Toyota, Honda, and Nissan was between 298 and 415. The index for Chrysler, Ford, and General Motors (GM) was between 114 and 196. Eighty-five percent of the suppliers to the Big 3 OEMs characterize their relationship as "poor," with around half the suppliers claiming they would prefer not to do business with the OEM.

Table 7-1. Overall OEM—Supplier Working Relation Index for 2002–2006*

	Year					Percent Change	
OEM	2002	2003	2004	2005	2006	2005–2006	2002–2006
Toyota	314	334	399	415	407	−1.9	29.6
Honda	292	307	384	375	368	−1.8	26.0
Nissan	225	262	294	298	300	0.6	33.3
Industry mean	223	234	263	259	266	0.2	19.3
Chrysler	176	180	186	196	218	11.2	23.8
Ford	166	161	163	157	174	10.8	4.8
GM	164	157	150	114	131	14.9	−20.1

* A rating between 0 and 249 is considered to be "poor"; a rating between 250 and 359 is considered to be "adequate"; and a rating between 350 and 500 is considered to be "good to very good."

Source: From Planning Perspectives Web site at http://sev.prnewswire.com/auto/20060612/DEM00812062006-1.html.

Table 7-1 shows that Toyota's supplier performance is consistently superior compared to other OEMs, and it has been so over long periods of time. Thus, data suggest that the approaches used by Toyota to identify and engage with a supplier might well be superior to approaches chosen by other OEMs.

In addition, Table 7-2 shows that supplier performance may vary across departments for a given OEM. For example, at GM, which has an overall WRI

Table 7-2. Overall Ratings

	Purchasing Area			
OEM	Highest Scoring	WRI	Lowest Scoring	WRI
Toyota	Electrical and electronics	461	Body in White	381
General Motors	Power train	156	Body in White	74
Ford	Chassis	194	Electrical and electronics	154
Chrysler	Electrical and electronics	263	Exterior	167
Nissan	Chassis	316	Body in White	245
Honda	Exterior	401	Power train	328

ranking of 131, the power train area is ranked at 156, while the Body in White[2] group is at a very low 74. All other GM purchasing groups fall in between. In contrast, Toyota scores an overall 407. Toyota's electrical and electronics group scores a very high 461, while its Body in White group is at 381. The ratings suggest that the purchasing function and Toyota's management of relationships with suppliers may affect their satisfaction with the working relationship.

The supplier performance is closely correlated with the desires expressed by the OEMs. Suppliers for Toyota, Nissan, and Honda have been observed to be providing greater improvements in product quality year after year than have other OEMs. That increase reflects the priorities for quality versus cost focus by the OEMs. GM has a fivefold focus on cost over quality; Ford and Chrysler a fourfold focus on cost; Nissan a focus on cost 2.5 times that of quality; and Honda and Toyota have a weight of 1.7 on cost versus 1 on quality. Clearly OEMs' preferences get reflected in supplier performance.

An OESA/McKinsey study[3] suggests that interface costs are estimated at 5.2 percent of program cost. (The interface costs are expenses related to the issues in the WRI.) The study also estimates that 80 percent of the waste in the auto industry is a result of poor supplier management. Such waste occurs because of misinterpretation of product specifications, a poor understanding and/or manufacture of complex parts, and ineffective coordination of capacity and demand. The estimated cost related to such waste is estimated to be $10 billion. Clearly, then, supplier management represents an important supply chain capability. The bottom line is that the way a supplier is managed affects product specifications and innovation, delivery performance, cost, and quality.

Links to Toyota's Processes

A key feature of Toyota's selling strategy is to build in schemes that prevent unilateral actions to change volumes or commitments. The use of a consensus approach, fostered by visibility across the supply chain, minimizes actions that result in additional costs at different parts of the supply chain. As discussed in Chapters 3 through 6, Toyota strives to reduce variability to ensure stable operations by systematic mix planning, careful sales and operations planning, and sensitivity to the impact of product changes throughout the supply chain. Such deliberate planning provides suppliers with phased-in design changes and stable order volumes.

As Chapter 3 suggested, in order to maintain the guarantee of stability in Toyota's supply chain, the optimal mix trades off revenue versus the cost impact on operations. As the number of variants offered in each region is reduced, the choices for customers will be more limited. Toyota compensates for this limitation by increasing customer value so that customers are willing either to choose one of the offered choices or to wait for their preferred variant to be available. Thus, for Toyota's strategy to limit customer choice to be competitive, it must result in a significant improvement in product value to the customer. Given the large role played by suppliers in Toyota's supply chain, that value creation must begin at the suppliers.

Gary Dodd, former president of Tire & Wheel Assembly, a Toyota supplier, describes the level of collaboration between the supplier and Toyota. The focus on "bad news first" (so that problems identified can be fixed immediately) provides an environment in which suppliers have a greater incentive to offer visibility about their operations. In addition, the level of visibility provided to the supplier about Toyota's annual volume goals and discussions regarding its feasibility from the supplier's perspective increase the probability that product and production objectives will be achieved.

Most studies of TQM suggest that stable processes are an important component of improving quality and productivity. Given that suppliers are offered stable order commitments by Toyota, they are expected to use this opportunity to develop superior quality products and achieve productivity improvements. As described earlier, Toyota's suppliers consistently deliver quality improvements year after year. In addition, suppliers attain productivity improvements by implementing TPS practices. These quality and cost improvements are then reflected in improved customer value. Thus, the supplier responsibility is to capitalize on the order stability and deliver cost and quality improvements to a level that makes the supply chain competitive.

In addition to the quality and productivity focus, Toyota suppliers must be flexible so they can respond to daily order changes. They do not attempt to build ahead based on the forecast but instead wait until the final order is received. For example, a sequence supplier would have to be synchronized with the exact color or mix of products as they move through the production line. But that sequence may be expected to be adjusted in response to changes made by dealers, quality issues, manufacturing backlogs, and so on. Therefore, the sequence suppliers must wait until about four hours prior to delivery to receive the final order.

Choosing Suppliers

At Toyota, choosing a supplier is a long, drawn-out process that involves verifying whether the supplier will mesh with the supply network. In some cases, suppliers are selected because they have innovations that improve processes or decrease costs. Both new and existing suppliers are expected to share their innovations with other suppliers that supply similar products. Thus, being a supplier brings along with it an opportunity to receive ideas generated across the supply network. Toyota's goal is to minimize the number of suppliers and create long-term partnerships by nurturing existing suppliers to expand and grow with Toyota instead of growing the number of suppliers to induce competitive price bidding.

Individual suppliers receive a contract for a fraction of the total market over the life of a model. Empirical data collected by Japanese economist Asanuma[4] suggest that suppliers are promised all of the orders associated with a market segment (e.g., exports versus domestic) or a fixed fraction of a certain market (e.g., a fraction of the domestic market volume) or all of the orders for a particular car model. The goal of the supplier is to maintain delivery performance, high quality, productivity improvements, and so on, over the life of the model. Asanuma's study suggests little use for the supplier as a source of slack capacity.

Asanuma studied the Japanese auto industry, the rice cooker industry, and the electronics industry. These three industries differ in their product life cycles, ranging from four years to one year to a few months. Some key features in managing suppliers included independent but closely linked suppliers, long-term relationships, frequent collaboration, exchange of employees between companies over long periods, and cross-linked shareholding. The impact has been observed in terms of long-term cooperation in innovation, cost cutting, quick response to demand fluctuations, and high levels of trust. However, the extent of close relationships varies across suppliers and products and over time as is warranted by competitive forces for the end product. Thus, while suppliers often are organized as a *keiretsu* (a group of companies with investments in one another), their role varies across product type.

Studies of the Japanese OEMs suggest a significant difference between U.S. and Japanese auto OEMs. Published reports show that Japanese auto suppliers won renewal of their contracts 90 percent of the time versus 71 percent for suppliers to U.S. auto OEMs. A study in 1992 found that a typical Toyota plant had only 125 suppliers compared to 800 for the typical General Motors plant. At the corporate level, Toyota had 224 suppliers compared to 5,500 suppliers for General Motors. In addition, Japanese OEMs make about 27 percent of their components in house versus 54 percent for U.S. auto OEMs. While Japanese automakers accounted for 33 percent of world output in 2002, Japanese suppliers accounted for less than 19 of the world's top 100 auto suppliers. That ratio suggests that Japanese suppliers are smaller than their U.S. counterparts. All of these statistics imply that there are differences between the approaches used by Japanese and U.S. auto OEMs to manage suppliers.

Toyota Supplier Selection[5]

The United Kingdom provides a good example of how Toyota selects its suppliers. A supplier must meet extremely tough conditions to qualify. When Toyota set up its plant in Derbyshire, England, in 1991, it initially started with a list of 2,000 potential suppliers. It reduced that list to 400, which it then evaluated using criteria such as "assessment of management attitudes, production facilities, quality levels, and research-and-development capability." The final group was whittled down to 150. Some of the candidate companies had been discouraged by the amount of detail that had been requested. Others found that that requirement was to their advantage and held that the advice on improving quality and competitive factors provided by the Japanese technicians saved the cost of employing outside consultants.

Toyota asked its potential suppliers to provide evidence that they could cut costs immediately with improved designs. One supplier came up with a design that was not only cheaper but simpler and better than that of Toyota's own Japanese supplier. The component was a simple gear stick knob costing pennies, but the British found a way of making it in two plastic parts instead of four, as in Japan. Jim Robinson, Toyota UK's general manager for purchasing, said: "We get suppliers thinking immediately about cost. In the case of the gear knob, it involves only a small cost. But if that part costs two pounds [approximately US$2.90] today and we can make it for one pound [about US$1.45], that is a huge saving over 200,000 cars a year."[6] He added that some of Toyota's suppliers have doubled productivity with negligible defects.

Such success helps the whole economy. The change in the auto-parts industry was highlighted by the decision of Daimler-Benz, of Germany, to turn to Britain for component suppliers. More than 30 German executives met 100 British component firms. Dr Gerhard Liener, a Daimler board member in charge of the company's $35 billion materials purchases from 60,000 contractors in 100 countries, made no bones about why he was in Britain. The arrival of Japanese manufacturers, he said, had helped improve the technological and quality achievements of British supply firms.

Tiered Supplier Organization and Managing Relationships

For the auto OEMs, suppliers are organized into tiers, with tier 1 suppliers being assemblers of systems, who manage all relationships with tier 2 suppliers, and so on. The bottom of the pyramid consists of tier 4 suppliers who form, perhaps, about 40,000 entrepreneurs who own a lot of the intellectual capital that is required to produce excellent components. There are many of those suppliers that own patents, have customized machinery, and may be owned by an individual family. For example, a series of detailed interviews by Nishiguchi[7] provides examples of one tier 4 supplier who had 200 patents for a specific process and thus had considerable leverage in the supply chain. Similarly, another supplier offered the flexibility to adjust for demand surges by adjusting his working hours to flex with demand surges. An example examined by Roy Vasher was a situation in which a government regulation required a change in antirust coatings. More than 4,000 parts were impacted by this change, but there were only a small number of suppliers that supplied the coating materials. Thus, Toyota was able to focus attention on a few suppliers to develop the new coating materials to be provided to suppliers that coated the 4,000 parts. Working with these lower-tier suppliers was the key to making the necessary changes in a timely and efficient manner. Purchasing executive Jamey Lykins echoes the idea that Toyota chooses suppliers across multiple tiers so as to guarantee availability of innovative solutions across the supply chain. He describes cases in which Toyota engineers and supplier personnel dedicate a somewhat substantial period of time—say, three months—to solve a seemingly insurmountable problem but succeed through collaboration. Such organizational approaches tap into the knowledge base of the supplier network effectively.

The extent of the business relationship between Toyota and its tier 1 suppliers exceeded 10 trillion yen in 1995. In addition to these 28 companies, in 1995 there were 234 primary parts suppliers and another 77 manufacturers of production equipment and other products. Data collected for the same period showed that, as a result of such a tiered system, 300 purchasing managers at Toyota bought components for 3.6 million cars, thus generating 12,000 cars per purchasing manager.

Pressure on Suppliers to Perform

The pressure on a supplier is maintained by using a staggered system of model changes, which in turn entails a staggered system of negotiations. The usual price commitment by Toyota to a supplier is for a one-year period, and prices are reviewed every six months, but the contract award is kept in place over the model life. The impact is to keep the pressure on a supplier to perform even while offering a long-term contract. The absence of desired performance after winning the contract will jeopardize chances to win a contract for other vehicle models made by the same supplier. This approach balances the stability of orders over a longer time frame with pressure that is uniformly maintained for compliance.

Nishiguchi also suggests that an ALPS system of supplier organization (referring to the jagged outline of the Swiss Alps), with staggered contractual links across vehicle models, provides a secondary source for most components while permitting sole sourcing for a component for a car model. The availability of alternate suppliers, who can step in readily, places pressure on the existing supplier to conform.

Depth of Supplier Relationships

The relationship with suppliers, from drawing-supplied to drawing-approved ones, can vary based on what is being produced. Intermediate relationships exist as well, such as when the OEM provides rough drawings and the suppliers complete all details. A study by Asanuma[8] suggests that there could be up to six different levels of relationships between the OEM and the supplier:

1. The OEM provides drawings and detailed manufacturing instructions (e.g., when small parts are assembled by an assembly-service provider).
2. The OEM provides drawings but the supplier designs the manufacturing process (e.g., when a supplier is providing stamping).
3. The OEM provides rough drawings and entrusts the completion of the drawings and the entire manufacturing process to the supplier (e.g., when products are plastic parts used for dashboards).
4. The OEM provides specifications while the supplier generates the drawings, but the OEM has detailed knowledge about the manufacturing process (e.g., when the product is a seat).
5. The OEM provides specifications, the supplier generates the drawings but the OEM has limited knowledge about the manufacturing process (e.g., when products are brakes, bearings, and tires).
6. The OEM purchases the product out of a catalog (e.g., with commodity off-the-shelf items).

Suppliers may provide flexibility during design but are subject to tight monitoring during manufacturing. Studies by Clark and Fujimoto[9] suggest that black box suppliers, (i.e., suppliers that are offered considerable flexibility during product design) constitute a larger percentage of Toyota's supply base than for other OEM's. But even this proportion varies across products, as studies by Kamath and Liker indicate.[10] They show that the relationship between the OEM and the suppliers is as a parent or as an equal. Their example suggests that for some crucial products, detailed specifications are provided. For other components, the relationship is at arm's length, with considerable latitude provided to the supplier in product design. In Chapter 11 we suggest that this decision depends on what stage of development the supplier is at with regard to knowledge and practice of the Toyota Way.

When monitoring the manufacturing process is involved, data show a different pattern. Japanese OEMs exert considerable control over supplier manufacturing processes, requiring information if there is a change such as a substitution in raw material supply or a reset of a machine. The data suggest that this process control enables the OEMs to ensure stable component performance and quality, thus permitting just-in-time delivery and reducing receiving costs. The detailed monitoring of supplier performance requires OEM purchasing managers to spend considerable time at supplier facilities. One OEM even shares one desk and chair with three purchasing managers, the assumption is that no more than one out of the three managers will be in the OEM facility, with the rest being in supplier locations. The Japanese word *shukko* refers to this type of transplant who may well spend his or her entire career at the supplier facility managing the relationship on behalf of the OEM. The role of the shukko varies from being a temporary shukko to a more permanent one. This flexibility both enables adjustment of the workforce across the supply chain and permits better coordination across the supply chain.

Helper[11] characterizes the U.S. model of supplier management as involving adversarial relationships, easy switching among suppliers, a high level of sole sourcing, low information exchange, low commitment, price-based competition for supplier selection, and a search for new suppliers (if problems arise). In contrast, the Japanese model encourages close relationships, competition over quality, delivery, engineering capability rather than price, high levels of information exchange, high levels of commitment, many suppliers, long-term relationships, and working with existing suppliers to resolve problems.

In addition, suppliers to lean producers are often required to make daily deliveries and to be involved in product development. Thus, suppliers to lean producers often are ensured a reasonable return as long as they make a good-faith effort to perform as they should.[12] Anecdotal evidence suggests that once suppliers win business from Toyota, it is theirs to lose by not performing. The average percentage of suppliers that maintained their buyer relationship was 84 percent in the Japanese auto industry.

Other authors suggest that Japanese OEMs absorb a part of the business risk for their suppliers based on the intensity of the business relationship. Stabilizing the corporate performance of selected suppliers enables improvement in the OEM's components and product. Nishiguchi reports anecdotal evidence of a Japanese supplier to a U.S. OEM who claims that doing business with U.S. buyers is easy because if things go wrong the supplier only has to claim that the work was due to buyer specifications and manufacturing instructions. (Such excuses are not permitted by its Japanese OEMs.) One supplier provides an example of cable components ordered by a U.S. OEM that ended up being too short for the assembly to be successful. The OEM then announced that the car model was to be discontinued. However, as per the purchasing contract, the OEM paid the Japanese supplier to cover the few months of inventory already in process.

The flip side of this type of relationship is highly unstable orders. A Japanese supplier provides an example of a 50 percent increase in an electrical component by a U.S. OEM. Because past experience suggested that such increases were not real, the supplier collected data from the past and checked whether the order was real. The U.S. OEM purchasing department claimed that it was just passing along order increases from sales and was not responsible for the validity of costs associated with such order changes. The OEM then demanded immediate fulfillment and, if not, airfreight of the order. Such interactions with suppliers would be unthinkable within the Toyota supply chain.

Evans and Wolf[13] compare Toyota's processes to the open source movement and their product improvements (e.g., Linux). They suggest that Toyota's processes have a few characteristics that enable their success, namely:

- Pervasive collaboration tools that have common standards and are compatible with one another
- Visibility and visual control not fogged by analysis
- Trust to share intellectual property without fear of abuse
- Modular view of teams and processes and flexible planning to keep goals aligned with customer needs
- Encouragement of teams as a vehicle to solve problems

Given marked differences in supplier management by U.S. and Japanese OEMs and the adoption of lean principles for manufacturing, is it important to adopt all of the components of the Toyota supplier management system to be successful? Are there other approaches? Honda, for example, claims a much looser relationship with suppliers and is also successful. For example, authors who have studied Honda over several decades show that adjustments to the balance between cooperation and competition have proven to be a competitive weapon for Honda over a long period of time. The real answer might lie in understanding how the entire supply chain functions and whether the practices are consistent from that viewpoint.

Assisting Suppliers

A key feature of Toyota's supply chain is the automaker's role in supplier capability development. Sako[14] describes the use of *jishuken* at Toyota: "Jishuken is a closely knit gathering of middle-level production technologists from a stable group of companies who jointly develop better capabilities for applying the Toyota Production System through mutual criticism and concrete application."

Sako describes an example from the late 1990s involving 56 factories from 52 separate suppliers that accounted for 80 percent of the purchasing costs spent by Toyota in Japan. Each jishuken company chooses a specific theme but works within the broad policy direction set by Toyota's Operations Management Consulting Division. Toyota does not charge for its consultant's time but makes it a resource that can be used by the Toyota Group. The supplier typically hosts a study over two months. Toyota's senior engineers visit the supplier three times every two months while junior engineers from Toyota visit more frequently.

Members of the jishuken group meet every week. The study sessions consist of concrete performance targets such as productivity, cost reduction, inventory turns, and the like. Most of the kaizen ideas suggested are implemented during the two months. At the end of the year, jishuken groups gather in one location to present their achievements.

There are two types of assistance provided: individual and group. The individual assistance is provided to get some quick results. The focus is to deal with an immediate supplier problem such as a sharp drop in profits or difficulty in keeping up with a model launch. Toyota's experts then go to the supplier, observe, and suggest improvements. These improvements get quick results but do not ensure that the supplier has imbibed the underlying principles. The jishuken group develops supplier personnel and also assists Toyota. As a result of frequent jishukens, Toyota retains the manufacturing know-how for components it does not produce in-house. That approach enhances Toyota's capability to do target costing—a technique to manage and reduce costs over a product's life cycle.

In another example, during the recession in Japan, only three of its main suppliers saw profit increases, while 57 saw profit and revenue decreases. Toyota responded by creating a kaizen promotion section within its purchasing department. The group worked with suppliers to decrease pay and cut investments and thus enable recovery of loss. In addition, suppliers were able to enhance their long-term capability. All of this works on an informal, personal level. To prevent supplier information gathered by these working groups from being used to extract cost reductions, supplier productivity improvement results may not even be communicated to the purchasing group. Data seem to suggest that the supplier is permitted to keep the gains from improvement due to Toyota's assistance.

Data collected from suppliers suggest that plants that supply Toyota have a 14 percent higher output per worker, 25 percent lower inventories, and 50 percent fewer defects than operations that supply Toyota's rivals.[15] Between 1965 and 1992, Toyota and its suppliers increased their labor productivity by 700 percent. During the same period, U.S. automakers and their suppliers improved productivity by 250 percent and 50 percent, respectively.

In the United States, Toyota has created the Bluegrass Automotive Manufacturers Association (BAMA), modeled after the Japanese supplier association. The supplier association holds general meetings bimonthly where production plans, policies, market trends, and the like are shared with the supply network. In addition, committee meetings are held monthly to focus on quality, cost, safety, and social activities that benefit all members of the network.

Like its organization in Japan, the Toyota Supplier Support Center (TSSC) in the United States requires that suppliers who use its services share their results with others. Doing so allows best practice suppliers to be showcased and encourages supplier openness. Toyota believes that the ability to see a working solution increases the chance that suppliers can replicate that knowledge. Most projects take at least one and a half years or longer from start to completion. Summit Polymers is an example quoted by Dyer and Hatch.[16] Toyota consultants (two to four personnel) visited Summit every day for four months to provide ongoing support for the next five years. In the United States, TSSC suppliers have seen productivity (i.e., output per worker) increase by 123 percent and inventory reduced by 74 percent. Continental Metal Specialty (CMS), a supplier of metal stampings, found only four value-added steps out of 30. Toyota and CMS jointly reconfigured the production system and, through process changes, eliminated 19 steps. Setups were reduced from 2 hours to 12 minutes. Inventories were reduced to 10 percent of the original levels. The chairman of CMS claims that 75 to 80 percent of the learning from their customers has been contributed by Toyota. Suppliers also got to keep all their benefits. Ultimately, Toyota does reap benefits during annual price reviews through a target pricing exercise in which customer price is defined and used to work backward to a supplier cost target.

The jishuken concept is called the "plant development activity" (PDA) in the United States. Because PDAs are context-specific, they permit transfer of tacit knowledge. In the United States, Toyota purchases lower volumes than U.S. automakers. However, Toyota still provides suppliers with knowledge and technology to improve their productivity, and the company sends personnel to visit supplier plants an average of 13 days per visit (versus 6 days for the U.S. automakers). Such assistance showed that suppliers decreased defects for Toyota by 84 percent (versus 46 percent for the U.S. automakers), decreased inventories for Toyota by 35 percent (versus 6 percent for the U.S. automakers), and improved sales per direct employee by 36 percent (versus 1 percent for U.S. automakers). All of these results were achieved in plants that supplied U.S. automakers.

Steven Spear,[17] in a detailed study of process specifications at Toyota and its suppliers, describes the processes as follows: The process starts with a description of a pathway rule that specifies system design and decides who receives the product. The next specification is a connection rule that decides how requests will be made to this supplier. The activity rule specifies work content, timing, sequence, and outcome. Finally the improvement rule specifies who is responsible for resolution of problems, specifies a qualified teacher for assistance, and so on. That sequence of specifications of processes guarantees that the process as well as its improvement mechanisms is identified in advance. Such a process specification permits adaptability in the face of disturbances, external changes, and emerging opportunities. That sequence also conforms to the learning principles we identify throughout the book.

The CCC21 System

In 2000, Toyota announced a plan to cut costs by 30 percent across the board for parts it buys to guarantee that it retains its competitive edge. By 2005, the program had already saved $10 billion over five years, but it had done so while improving quality (Figure 7-1).

In addition, for about 180 key parts the team identified the world's most competitive suppliers and created benchmarks for the supply base to meet. In one case, the number of air-conditioning vents was decreased from 27 to 3, generating a 28 percent cost reduction. Why 30 percent? The number came from the commonly called "China price," that is, the expected price drop by moving orders to Chinese suppliers.

The following is a summary of the results achieved from that special initiative, CCC21.

Innovation at Toyota[18]

When it comes to being innovative and making fundamental changes in the organization, Toyota has shown that size does not matter and even a giant can reinvent itself.

In July 2000, Toyota launched the Construction of Cost Competitiveness in the 21st Century program, also known as CCC21. That initiative focused on cutting the purchasing costs of 170 major components. Katsuaki Watanabe, Toyota's president and CEO, spearheaded this effort because he was then a

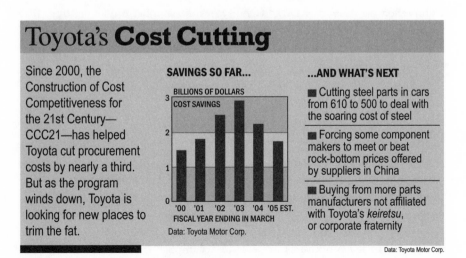

Figure 7-1. Toyota cost cutting results

purchasing specialist. This program brought together engineers from Toyota and the parts suppliers, eliminating unnecessary costs with methods such as standardizing parts across the entire Toyota range or reducing the number of components required to make a part. For example, reducing the parts in a horn from 28 to 22 led to a 40 percent savings in cost. In another example, Toyota helped to improve suppliers' economies of scale by approving 3 inside hand grips, down from 35. At the end of five years, the program led to a total savings of US$9 billion.

Never satisfied with its success, Toyota started the Value Innovation (VI) program in 2005 to follow up on the CCC21 program, which goes beyond lean manufacturing to lean product development practices. The VI program refocused Toyota on the production and design processes, continuing its quest for waste elimination and cost reduction. Toyota expects the VI program to show its main benefits by 2010, raising the operating profit margin from 9.3 percent to 10 percent.

What happens when that goal is achieved as well? Toyota already is thinking of plans to use the benefits of the VI program to invest in technologies, researching new vehicle structures that will reduce weight and lower fuel consumption.

Toyota Checklist for Supplier Audits

The Toyota purchasing organization expects suppliers to be available for comprehensive system audits. The audit process specifies the goals and the associated documents that will be used to check for confirmation of compliance. The Comprehensive Assessment Tool (CAT) rates the supplier on a scale from 0 to 5 on a set of specific performance measures, namely:

1. Mission
2. Reporting structure
3. Involvement of top management
4. Localization and self-reliance
5. Open mind to operating procedures such as kaizen
6. Organization with respect to Toyota interactions

For each of the measures, equal weight is allocated to subparts such as vision, long-term plan, annual plan, finances, and risk management. The evaluation score out of a maximum of 100 units is used to provide a supplier assessment score.

To provide data to support its adherence to processes, the supplier in turn is expected to list procedures in place to accomplish each of the stated tasks. Those specific procedures include tracking to improve quality, scrap handling, poka yoke management, warranty claims handling, returns processing, offline inspections, and final shipping.

Supplier Guest Engineers

One key coordination mechanism used at Toyota is the role of supplier guest engineers at Toyota's facility. The guest engineer is typically a specialist, employed by the supplier, who resides in the OEM's (Toyota's) organization. The role of this engineer is to provide tacit knowledge during product development and thus facilitate integration of the supplier's expertise with the OEM's needs.

The common approach is for suppliers to send its design engineers to Toyota to work for two to three years prior to product launch. After product manufacturing starts, the design engineers return to their company and production engineers are sent to the OEM. Production engineers ensure that components are assembled correctly in the vehicle. They also report problems, suggest design changes for easier manufacture, and propose approaches for cost reduction. Finally, the supplier development engineer's role is to see to it that kaizen processes are implemented.

Significantly, Toyota had 5 design engineers per supplier while General Motors had 0.2 guest engineers per supplier. The roles played by the guest engineers are shown in an empirical study by Daniel Twigg.[19] The study also found four types of roles by guest engineers at an OEM location, from preconcept to concept to product development through production phases.

The presence of supplier personnel within the Toyota facility enables faster changes in response to failures, quicker adjustment to information generated from customer complaints, chances to reduce engineering change order processing times, and opportunities to generate kaizen-type cost improvements, among other things. These shared resources allow effective coordination between the supplier and Toyota. What is the benefit to frequent interactions with a supplier? A study by Dyer[20] suggests that defects decrease with increased supplier interaction.

Supplier Location Decisions

Toyota's planning for assembly plant sites assumes that most suppliers will be located at a reasonable distance from the assembly plant and that their delivery schedules will permit efficient operation of the assembly plant to produce vehicles based on the final vehicle mix and sequence. The low lot sizes of assembly plant parts orders imply that suppliers need to be located close to the assembly plant.

Toyota suggests that a planning rule be used of 50-mile-per-hour travel time from supplier location to assembly plant. That assumption is one factor that is used to determine when supplier parts orders are released. Many suppliers choose to be located close to an assembly plant. In Japan, 85 percent of the volume comes from suppliers located within a 50-mile radius of a plant (i.e., within a one-hour drive). In North America and Europe, the goal is for 80 percent of the parts to be delivered within three to five days lead time.

Similarly, supplier location closer to the OEM results in lower inventories for the supplier and assembly plant. For Toyota in Japan, the average distance is short, in contrast to other OEMs. The resulting inventory as a percentage of sales is thus the lowest of the OEMs.

So, what can a supplier expect? Suppliers need to consider building factories near Toyota plants, especially as Toyota continues to expand and build new plants around the globe. The proximity of supplier location to the Toyota plant enables frequent deliveries to be made to the assembly plant, and in return, observed lower inventories at the supplier and the Toyota plant. In addition, the completed vehicle has fewer defects, because frequent interaction due to more deliveries enables quick feedback and more opportunities to fix defects.

Reflection Points

This chapter provides a rich context to review the use of the v4L approach in managing suppliers at Toyota. There are several good examples of how the learning principles are applied and linked to the v4L framework:

- *Variety* of components produced by suppliers is consistent with their flexibility. Because designs of components allow efficient manufacturability by suppliers, suppliers can reliably commit to capacity.
- *Velocity* of the parts flow is matched between the assembly line and suppliers. Sequence suppliers receive orders in the precise sequence of assembly. Other suppliers have orders picked up during delivery milk runs to Toyota. In short, the supplier velocity is matched to the assembly plant production rate.
- *Variability* of orders to suppliers is stabilized through communication of planned volumes in advance, through JIT pickups and by limiting the amount of day-to-day fluctuation in orders.
- *Visibility* of supplier operations and of Toyota plants is encouraged by the approach at Toyota to discuss problems first. The attitude that it is better to inform Toyota of problems early so as to enable efficient solutions with the company's assistance encourages increased visibility. In addition, frequent deliveries from suppliers ensure that Toyota is constantly informed about those suppliers' performance.

Learning by the supplier system is guaranteed by the various supplier organizations as well as by proactive steps such as the CCC21 program, which continually emphasize the need to reduce waste and increase efficiency. The following are some of the key steps taken by Toyota and the suppliers to achieve that goal:

- *Create awareness.* Constant pressure is placed on suppliers with a staggered system of model changes, supplier audits, and programs such as jishuken.
- *Establish capability.* Long-term relationships are carefully nurtured. Suppliers are involved at early stages of design and given ample scope to explore options and alternatives. Jishuken teams create capability both at the supplier as well as at Toyota for understanding how each other's systems function.
- *Make action protocols.* The work by the Toyota Supplier Support Center helps share best practices across the supply chain. The relationship-building process with the supplier is itself carefully planned and organized to maximize impact.
- *Generate system-level awareness.* A modular view of teams' processes and flexible planning are used to align the supply chain to the needs of the customer. Trust is fostered at the same time that value creation is emphasized.
- *Exercise control of processes.* Once the design is finalized, control is exercised on processes as if they were in-house systems.
- *Facilitate communication.* Communication is facilitated with a variety of methods, among them being that Toyota engineers are stationed for long periods at the supplier and the supplier's guest engineers are stationed at Toyota.
- *Provide stability.* Stability is provided to suppliers that require such support by absorbing business risk at times of difficulty.

Endnotes

1. "Strained Relationships with Suppliers Costing GM and Ford," Planning Perspectives, Inc., Birmingham, MI, 2006.
2. "*Body in White,*" or *BIW*, refers to the car body including doors, hoods, and deck lids but before other components are added to it.
3. OESA-McKinsey Study on Customer Supplier Interface, 2003.
4. Banri Asanuma, "Transactional Structure of Parts Supply in the Japanese Automobile and Electric Machinery Industries: A Comparative Analysis," Technical Report # 3, Socio-Economic Systems Research Project, Kyoto University, September 1986.
5. "British-Made Japanese Cars Mean Rising Sales for Parts Suppliers," *Agence France Presse,* August 2, 1991.
6. "Japan Tunes UK Part Makers," *The Times,* London, July 15, 1991.

7. T. Nishiguchi, "Japanese Subcontracting: Evolution Towards Flexibility," D.Phil. Thesis, University of Oxford, 1988.

8. B. Asanuma, "Manufacturer-Supplier Relationships in Japan and the Concept of Relation-Specific Skill," Working Paper # 2, Faculty of Economics, Kyoto University, February 1988.

9. K. B. Clark and T. Fujimoto, "The Product Development Imperative: Competing in the New Industrial Marathon." In Paula Baker Duffy, Ed., *The Relevance of a Decade: Essays to Mark the First Ten Years of the Harvard Business School Press*, Boston: Harvard Business School Press, 1994.

10. R. R. Kamath and J. K. Liker, "A Second Look at Japanese Product Development," *Harvard Business Review* 72, no. 6 (1994): 4–14.

11. S. Helper, "Strategy and Irreversibility in Supplier Relations: A Case Study of the US Automobile Industry," *Business History Review* 65 (Winter 1991).

12. J. P. Womack, D. T. Jones, and D. Roos, *The Machine that Changed the World: The Story of Lean Production*. New York: Scribner, 1990.

13. P. Evans and B. Wolf, "Collaboration Rules," *Harvard Business Review* 83, no. 7 (2005): 96–104.

14. M. Sako, "Supplier Development at Honda, Nissan, and Toyota: Comparative Case Studies of Organizational Capability Enhancement," *Industrial and Corporate Change* 13, no. 2 (2004): 281–308.

15. J. F. Dyer and N. W. Hatch, "Using Supplier Networks to Learn Faster," *Sloan Management Review* 45, no. 3 (2004): 57–63.

16. Dyer and Hatch, "Using Supplier Networks."

17. Steven J. Spear, "Just-in-Time in Practice at Toyota: Rules-in-Use for Building Self-Diagnostic, Adaptive Work-Systems," Harvard Business School Working Paper 02-043, December 2007.

18. "Toyota Aiming to Make US$2.7-bil.-Worth of Cost Cuts Annually," *Global Insight*, December 12, 2007.

19. D. Twigg, "Managing Product Development within a Design Chain," *International Journal of Operations and Production Management* 18, no. 5 (1988): 508–524.

20. J. Dyer, "Specialized Supplier Networks as a Source of Competitive Advantage: Evidence from the Auto Industry," *Strategic Management Journal* 17, no. 4 (1998): 271–291.

Chapter 8

Logistics

L ogistics is an extremely important component of the supply chain. It has two roles: (1) inbound logistics, which is responsible for transporting parts and materials from the tier 1 suppliers to the OEM plants; (2) outbound logistics, which is responsible for the distribution of vehicles from the assembly plants to the dealers. In this chapter we will examine both of these components.

Inbound Logistics

Inbound logistics encompasses two different operations: the first is the operation that transports parts from local suppliers to the local plants; the second is a separate operation, global inbound logistics, to transport parts from Japan to the North American and European plants. Because the inbound logistics operational models are very similar in both North America and Europe, we will explain only the North American operations. The local operation will be reviewed first, followed by an examination of the overseas operation.

Local Inbound Logistics

Toyota's success in operating a lean supply chain requires that the parts be transported from the suppliers in an efficient and timely matter; therefore, Toyota establishes a partnership with a limited number of third-party logistics providers (3PLs) to deliver logistics services.

Toyota's inbound logistics operation can best be described as a logistics network. The company organizes many of its suppliers into clusters based on geographic location. Parts are picked up from those suppliers by trucks on a "milk route" (i.e., a circuit in which a truck picks up multiple parts from various suppliers along the way), and then they are delivered to a regional cross-dock. (Suppliers that are located close to the plants, however, ship parts direct.)

At the cross-dock (a staging facility that is used to transfer parts), the parts are unloaded and staged for pickup and delivery to one of the Toyota plants. After the trucks arrive at the plant, the trailer is disconnected and parked in a numbered space in a staging lot. The trailers are not unloaded until the production progress triggers the need for the trailer to be unloaded. As discussed in Chapter 6, all incoming parts orders and deliveries are synchronized to the production rate. Doing so ensures that the parts unloaded and delivered to the lineside workstations are just what is needed and just-in-time.

Network Logistics

The network logistics model enables Toyota to operate a very efficient and effective inbound logistics operation. Figure 8-1 shows an example of a logistics network. The entities of the network are suppliers, cross-docks, and Toyota plants. The entities are connected by a continuous flow of trucks that move containers of parts inbound to the plants or move empty containers back to the suppliers. Plants include not only the assembly plants but also component plants that produce engines and transmissions. Toyota's strategy is "small lots, frequent deliveries." The ideal situation is for each supplier to ship parts every day to each plant. That course of events is where network design plays an important role.

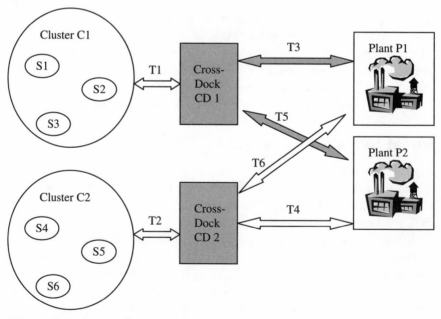

Figure 8-1. Network logistics

The first step in network design is to analyze the location of the suppliers and identify clusters of them that are located in close proximity to one another. Next, a determination is made as to which cross-dock is located nearest to the suppliers. The idea behind this design is that one truck picks up parts from multiple suppliers in what is called a "milk route." The truck then delivers the parts to the nearest cross-dock. The parts are unloaded and the corresponding empty containers are picked up and returned to the suppliers on the next run. The parts are then staged for pickup by trucks that are scheduled to deliver full truckloads of parts directly to each plant.

In the example in Figure 8-1, there are two clusters of suppliers, two cross-docks, and two plants. Parts from suppliers S1, S2, and S3 in cluster C1 are picked up by truck T1 and delivered to cross-dock CD1. Parts from suppliers S4, S5, and S6 in cluster C2 are picked up by truck T2 and delivered to cross-dock CD2. Then, truck T3 picks up parts from CD1 and delivers them to plant P1. Also, truck T5 picks up parts from CD1 and delivers them to plant P2. Truck T4 picks up parts from CD2 and delivers them to plant T2. Finally, truck T6 picks up parts from CD2 and delivers them to plant P1. As you can see from this example, there are two milk run routes picking up from suppliers and four main routes from two cross-docks to two plants.

The advantages of the network logistics structure is that it enables Toyota to pick up from most suppliers on a daily basis while at the same time minimizing transportation costs.[1] However, the network is extremely complex to operate and manage. Toyota's size enables it to maintain control over the logistics network by partnering with 3PL companies. The logistics partners provide a dedicated fleet of trucks and drivers to operate Toyota's logistics network. In addition, the entities in the network work closely with Toyota to design and plan routes. The shared transportation enables suppliers to receive small orders without increasing transportation costs.

Route Planning

Route planning is a key function that ensures efficient and effective operations. It is done once per month and is based on the next production month plan. Such planning is part of the production plan discussed in Chapter 5 and the parts ordering and forecast discussed in Chapter 6. In these chapters heijunka was discussed as a method for leveling parts orders by day. Without a level production and parts plan, developing a daily logistics route schedule and repeating it for the whole month would not be feasible.

The creation of a logistics route plan to transport parts from hundreds of suppliers to multiple manufacturing plants is like the making of an airline schedule. The planner needs to know the locations of the suppliers, cross-docks, and manufacturing plants. Then he needs to know the number of packages or containers of parts to be picked up from each supplier each day and to which cross-dock and plant those materials are to be delivered. In addition, he needs to know how the containers of parts can be arranged and stacked within a truck. It is important to optimize the cubic space of each truck so that one doesn't "ship air" and does avoid "blowouts"—in other words, one doesn't ship partial loads or create a condition in which all of the containers cannot be loaded on a truck because of weight or volume restrictions (a "blowout").

Another critical piece of information is the road routes and distances between all potential to/from destinations. A computer system is used to run simulations to create multiple route plans; they are then evaluated by logistics experts who select the optimal routes. The process is very complex, and numerous variables have to be considered (e.g., total miles, average miles per hour, number of trucks needed, number of drivers needed, and risks because of road conditions). The process used is an example of Toyota's emphasis of combining the talents of human beings and the power of machines—Toyota doesn't rely on the computer system alone.

Under normal conditions, the routes would not vary significantly from month to month. But in cases where there is a major change in production (either up or down) or if there are new suppliers, the change in routes could be drastic. That step would require more scrutiny to make sure that the plan is correct and that no error is in the simulation.

A Toyota logistics manager from the Princeton, Indiana, plant stated that for route planning, Toyota assumes a 50-mile-per-hour average speed of trucks and provides a desired route and travel time for deliveries. That time estimate is updated when snow or other weather conditions prevail. The planning thus shifts to this inclement weather route and associated lead time. Such detailed planning provides the plant with a good estimate of deliveries, and thus permits synchronization of parts flow with plant requirements.

Other situations that might arise include port-related unloading issues, border crossing delays because of tightened security checks, and strikes. In such cases, shipments are sometimes airlifted so that the flow is maintained. The capability to quickly react to impending crises enables alternate contingency plans to be generated and implemented to keep the parts flowing.

Pipeline Management

Toyota strives to operate an extremely lean supply chain, so it is critical for the plant production control personnel to understand the status of all parts in the pipeline. The "parts pipeline" is defined as all parts that have been ordered from a supplier and have not been unloaded at the receiving plant.

Toyota uses a variety of methods to track parts throughout the pipeline. The process starts with the parts order that is sent via Electronic Data Interchange (EDI), along with the kanban bar code label that the suppliers affix to the parts shipping container. Once the parts are shipped, the supplier sends an EDI Advanced Shipping Notice (ASN). The truck driver scans the kanban bar code label and identifies the truck onto which the parts are loaded. Once the truck arrives and is unloaded at the cross-dock, the parts status is changed to show arrival at the cross-dock. Again, as parts are loaded onto another truck bound for the plant, they are scanned and associated with the truck number. As the truck enters the gate at the plant, the parts status is updated to show that the parts are in the plant yard. The trailers remain in the yard until production progress dictates that they should be unloaded at the dock. As the parts are unloaded, each container is scanned to confirm the arrival at the plant. Pipeline data enable Toyota to have visibility into the parts pipeline. This pipeline database is especially important whenever there is a crisis situation such as parts shortage, short shipment, or transportation delay. It is thus clear that visibility plays a key role in the management of the inbound parts logistics process.

Some of the metrics used to monitor inbound logistics are percent of cubic capacity utilized, number of blowout loads, on-time pickup and delivery, and actual mileage versus plan.

Overseas Inbound Logistics

Overseas parts arriving from Japan are shipped via vessel to a port and then transported by railcar to the assembly plant. Once the railcar arrives at the assembly plant rail yard, the container is offloaded onto a truck and driven to the assembly dock. The trailers are parked in a large staging lot in a numbered space that can be used to locate the trailer.

One of the unique aspects of the parts flow from Japanese suppliers is the use of the vanning center. The vanning center is a consolidation point in Japan where parts are received from Japanese suppliers and packed for shipment to an overseas manufacturing plant. The vanning center operation is linked to the overseas parts shipping schedule described in Chapter 6. At the vanning center, parts are packed into plastic trays. These trays are then arranged into groups to fit into a module for shipment. The modules are then loaded into containers for shipment by a container ship to the overseas port. Figure 8-2 shows an example of the vanning packing process.

After the containers are loaded and shipped, it takes about four weeks for the containers to arrive at the overseas plant. After the containers arrive, they are staged in the lot outside the plant until needed. Normally, there are about three to five days of inventory in the lot. However, the containers are not unloaded

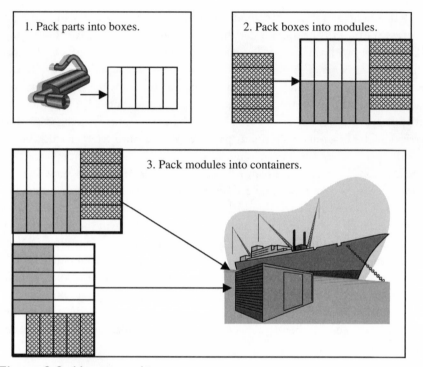

Figure 8-2. Vanning packing process

until the parts are needed for production. Similar to the method for local parts, overseas parts are unloaded based on the actual rate of production. Doing so keeps the parts inventory inside the plant to a minimum.

Because of the long lead time (six weeks) from when overseas parts are ordered until they are used for production, a risk arises that a parts shortage could require a part to be unloaded prior to its scheduled time in the production schedule. A parts shortage could occur for a variety of reasons such as an order error, excessive scrap, or a higher volume of vehicle order changes than expected. When a parts shortage occurs, a parts handling group at the plant must "tap" a container in the staging yard prior to its scheduled unload sequence. Tapping is a term that is used to describe the process for locating a container and unloading it out of sequence. There are several negative impacts on the plant when a container is tapped, two of which are excessive workload on the team members and a parts overflow. The reason why excessive workload results in a negative impact is fairly obvious, because it takes time to locate the container, move it to the dock, and unload the parts. However, it is not feasible to unload just the one part that is needed; the whole container must be unloaded. Doing so will create an overflow condition because there will not always be enough space to store these extra parts in the normal flow racks. That, in turn, creates an additional workload because these parts need to be handled multiple times and they could get misplaced.

The impact of variability at the plant is managed through appropriate use of buffer inventory for overseas logistics. That is facilitated by the visibility of the pipeline.

Long Lead Time Pipeline Management

Pipeline management is important for all parts, including local ones, but it is extremely important to monitor the pipeline for long lead time parts. Long lead time parts have a supply lead time of three to six weeks compared to less than two weeks for local parts. In addition, the vehicle order specifications are not frozen or finalized until about five to ten days prior to production. Therefore, if the dealers generate a high number of vehicle order specification changes, a parts shortage situation may be created because the long lead time parts ordered would be based on the forecast not the final order.

Toyota has developed a long lead time parts pipeline system to track changes to vehicle specifications on a daily basis and translate them into daily changes in parts. These changes are then compared to the parts pipeline inventory by day to highlight potential shortage and/or overflow conditions in advance. The results are presented in the form of graphs so that a visual representation is available of potential discrepancies that could result in a crisis situation. That information enables the parts manager to evaluate the situation, take an inventory of the parts in question, and, if necessary, place a special order for parts to be "air shipped" to avoid a production interruption. (Air shipments, however, are expensive and should be avoided unless a more expensive shutdown of production is imminent.)

To conclude this section on the inbound logistics operations at Toyota, it may be instructive to examine how the partnership between Toyota and its 3PL providers benefits not only to Toyota but also its partners.

Mutual Benefits from a Partnership

When Toyota partners with a supplier or a logistics provider, the benefits of the relationship are not for Toyota alone. The Transport Corporation of India (TCI) provides an example of how the partner can benefit. The company is a logistics provider in India that formed a joint venture with Toyota to deliver parts to Toyota, both imported (from the port) and sourced from more than 70 local suppliers. Initially, TCI learned how to better manage the delivery of auto parts from Toyota; since then, it has carried the best practices over to other manufacturers.

For example, using lessons learned from Toyota, in the two-wheeler segment (namely, bikes—a very popular mode of transport in India), TCI redesigned delivery trucks to increase the number of vehicles carried from 50 to 58. TCI went on to change them into flexible trucks, then to use trailers to carry 85 bikes, and then to improve the trailers so that they could carry 110 bikes. TCI also added Global Positioning System (GPS) units to the trucks, so that manufacturers could directly track pending deliveries and plan their operations accordingly. In a country with poor roads choked with traffic and red tape at state borders, deliveries are liable to get stuck unpredictably; thus, tracking information can be vital to a manufacturer's efficiency.

Starting out as a basic logistics company, TCI is now becoming a complex supply chain management provider. Other manufacturers have started listening to TCI. In some cases it has been asked to handle the entire inbound and outbound logistics. In other areas—for example, perishable products like chocolates—the company has made innovations such as linking the temperature of the truck with the GPS unit. In a one-year period from 2004 to 2005, the company's worth increased from approximately $160 million to nearly $200 million.[2]

Outbound Logistics

Outbound logistics is also known as product distribution, because the function of outbound logistics is to distribute the finished products from the OEM plants to the retailers. As discussed in Chapter 2, Toyota uses a different distribution flow in North America than in Europe. In addition, the relationship with the 3PL providers for outbound logistics differs from that for dedicated 3PL providers for inbound logistics. Although Toyota still considers outbound logistics providers to be its partners, those partners are not dedicated to Toyota because no one 3PL provider can control all transportation activities end to end from the plant to the dealer. Therefore, Toyota relies on common carriers, railroads and truck "car haulers," to transport its vehicles from the assembly plants to the dealers.

Railroads ship many types of goods and raw material in addition to vehicles. They also ship vehicles from multiple manufacturers on the same trains. Trucking companies, like the railroads, ship vehicles for multiple manufacturers—in many cases, they mix vehicles from different manufacturers on the same truck.

North American Vehicle Distribution

Figure 8-3 shows how vehicles move from the assembly plants through this distribution network in North America. After the vehicles are produced, they are shuttled into a marshaling yard. (Details of the marshaling yard operations will

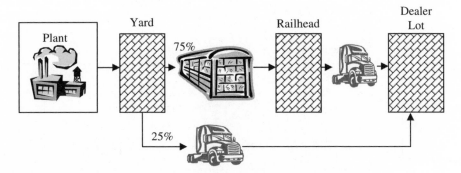

Figure 8-3. North American vehicle distribution flow

be explained next.) Once processing is completed in the marshaling yard, the vehicles are shuttled to the staging area for shipment. There are two options for shipment of vehicles to the dealers. The first option is rail shipment, in which vehicles are loaded onto railcars, shipped to a railhead, and then loaded onto a truck for delivery to the dealers. The second option is for direct truckaway: vehicles are loaded onto trucks and delivered directly to dealers. Option 1 is used for dealers that are located a long distance from the plant, usually greater than 500 miles. They represent about 75 percent of the volume. Option 2 is used for dealers near to the plant—within two to three days' travel time.

Toyota includes in its contracts with the trucking partners an on-time delivery objective of 48 hours from the time the vehicle is shuttled to the staging area to the time it is delivered to the dealership. A similar delivery standard does not exist for the railroads because so many variables, such as railcar switching time at rail yards, demand for empty railcars, congestion at final destination rail yards, etc., can impact rail shipment timing. Toyota also emphasizes quality by monitoring damage metrics for all of the trucking and rail partners. The company holds an annual meeting with all of its logistics providers to recognize the top performers in both on-time performance as well as quality performance. That recognition provides an incentive for the logistics providers to improve and also sets the benchmarks for future performance.

Marshaling Yard Operations

The marshaling yard operation is extremely important, as it ensures the efficient and timely delivery of vehicles to their final destination. Figure 8-4 shows how vehicles flow through the marshaling yard. After the vehicles are produced in the assembly plant, they are shuttled to one of two areas. Vehicles that require installation of accessories go to accessory staging; all other vehicles are shuttled

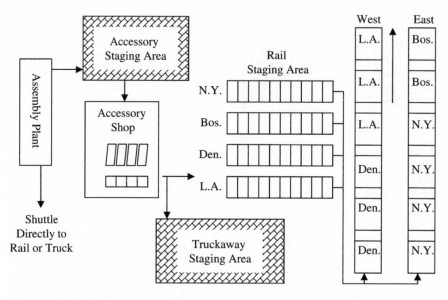

Figure 8-4. Marshaling yard flow

directly to the rail or truck staging areas. Once the accessories are installed, these vehicles are then shuttled to rail or truck staging areas. Accessory installation usually takes from one to three days.

After vehicles are parked in the truckaway staging area, the trucking partner has the responsibility of loading the vehicles onto the truck and getting them delivered to dealers within the delivery standard. Toyota provides the trucking partner with a weekly forecast of vehicles by dealer. That information enables the trucking company to plan its operation to ensure an adequate supply of trucks and drivers. Although some fluctuation of deliveries by dealer will occur, the volume of deliveries to a cluster of dealers will remain relatively even. This is another example of the benefit of Toyota's use of heijunka to smooth the production by destination to avoid spikes in deliveries.

Railcar loading is the responsibility of Toyota's logistics division. Note that not all railcars are the same. There are two types of railcars for automobiles: "bi-level" and "tri-level." Bi-levels are used to ship higher-height vehicles such as SUVs and pickups; tri-levels are used for smaller vehicles, including most cars. Some of the recent cars, especially the crossover models, are growing in height, which requires them to be shipped via bi-levels. That requirement results in increased transportation cost because rail shipment charges are based on a per-railcar cost. With a bi-level railcar, with a typical capacity of 10 vehicles (versus

15 for a tri-level), the cost could be as much as 50 percent higher. This is an example of a situation in which vehicle design can have a negative impact on the supply chain operations and costs.

Consider what happened at one of the Toyota plants: A major change for an existing model increased the height of the car by only a few inches, which resulted in the car being one inch too high to fit on a tri-level railcar. That extra height meant that the new model had to be shipped via bi-level instead of tri-level, resulting in an increased transportation cost.

The process for loading railcars is as follows:

- *Stage for rail shipment.* Vehicles are staged in lanes by destination and railcar type. See Figure 8-4, which illustrates a rail staging area. Note how vehicles are parked in lanes by destination. In this example, there is only one lane per destination. If both bi-level and tri-level railcars were to be used to ship to each destination, there would be two lanes for each destination.
- *Prestage empty railcars.* Empty railcars are shuttled by the rail company onto one or more rail spurs. These railcars are usually arranged in a string of six. See Figure 8-4 for an illustration of two strings of six railcars.
- *Assign destinations to railcars.* Once a new string of empty railcars is ready for loading, the dispatcher must decide which destinations are to be loaded. If possible, all six railcars should be loaded with vehicles for the same destination. The next best option is to combine destinations that will be on the same route; for example, vehicles shipped to New York and Boston would be picked up by an eastbound train. However, the dispatcher can load vehicles for destinations only if the staging lane is full. The dispatcher must take inventory of what is in the staging lanes to determine what can be loaded.
- *Load the vehicles.* Vehicles are driven onto the railcars and scanned as they are loaded so the tracking system knows which vehicles are loaded into each railcar.
- *Release the railcar for shipment.* Once the complete string of railcars is loaded, the dispatcher contacts the rail company to pull the full load out of the yard and replace it with an empty string.

This process appears to be a straightforward one; however, it does not always operate effectively. The following situation that occurred at one of Toyota's plants in 2003 provides some insight into how conflicting objectives can result in a negative impact on downstream operations.

At one of Toyota's North American assembly plants during 2003, there was a great deal of tension between the plant marshaling yard management and the rail company local management. The main concern of the yard management was that they were under strict orders from the plant manager to load railcars as quickly as possible; that sense of urgency ensured that vehicles were moved out with minimal delay so that delivery time to the dealers would be kept short. The yard managers suspected that the rail company personnel did not share the same sense of urgency, because each day when the plant manager passed by the rail yard on his way to work, he noticed that several railcars that were loaded the previous day were still parked along the fence. When the yard managers discussed the matter with the rail yard management, the reason given was that the rail yard personnel took several hours to shuttle railcars around and match them up with the proper outbound trains.

This conflict continued for several months; there did not seem to be any resolution. To make matters worse, the plant was planning a major increase in production within a year, so if this problem could not be resolved, the rail yard would need to be expanded at a cost of several millions of dollars.

Toyota management decided that the situation was critical, and so they dispatched an independent team from other Toyota locations. Team members could objectively study and evaluate the situation, recommend countermeasures, and attempt to find a compromise.

They arrived on site and met with the marshaling yard management to request a detailed explanation of the railcar loading process. After taking a walking tour of the yard, they were directed to a whiteboard that showed the number of vehicles ready for shipment by destination. That board was the dispatcher's "bible" and indicated visually the actual inventory in the staging lanes available to be shipped by destination. It was continuously updated during the day, and as soon as there were enough vehicles to load six railcars, the dispatcher called for an empty string of railcars and proceeded to load the vehicles. Because the rail yard's focus was to move the vehicles through the yard quickly, the sequence of the loading was based on FIFO, or first in, first out. Rail yard personnel were very proud of their operation because one of their key metrics was "days of yard inventory" and they were averaging less than one day.

Next, the team met with the rail yard management (the rail yard is owned by the rail company; these managers did not work for Toyota). The rail yard managers explained that the reason that some of the railcars were still sitting in the yard a day after they were loaded was because each string of six railcars had to be disassembled and rearranged into strings to connect to either the eastbound or westbound trains. Also, the vehicles were not always loaded in the proper sequence. The constant shuttling of railcars was a burden, and they indicated that they would need to add more engines and people to handle the increased volume.

The team asked, "Is there anything that Toyota could do to reduce your workload and increase the throughput?" The response was surprisingly quick. Rail yard managers suggested two changes to the process for loading railcars:

1. Load only vehicles with western destinations in the morning so that they can be shipped on the westbound train that departs at 1 p.m. Then, load only vehicles with eastern destinations in the afternoon so they can be shipped on the eastbound train at 9 p.m.

2. Load a string of six railcars based on the sequence in which the destinations will be delivered. For example, if there are railcars going west to Los Angeles and there are both Denver and L.A. railcars on the string, place the L.A. railcars at the front and Denver railcars at the rear. With that arrangement, when the train arrives at Denver on the way to L.A., the Denver railcars can simply be disconnected without affecting the L.A. railcars.

If the Toyota yard managers would agree to this change, then that decision would reduce the rail yard's need to disassemble and rearrange each string of railcars.

The team went back to the Toyota marshaling yard managers and explained that loading the railcars without regard to destination was causing extra work for the rail yard personnel. In fact, it was actually delaying the shipment to dealers because there were only two train departures per day: an eastbound train departing at 9 p.m. and a westbound train departing at 1 p.m. So, if vehicles for westbound destinations were loaded in the afternoon, they would not depart until the next day, and if vehicles for eastbound destinations were loaded in the morning, they would not depart until 9 p.m.

The response from the Toyota yard managers was lukewarm. Although they could understand the potential benefit, their concern was that such a change would result in an increase in yard inventory and would most likely require Toyota to expand the yard capacity to accommodate the future increase in volume. The team was concerned that an impasse seemed to have been reached, so they made a proposal: create a simulation based on the last month's loading data to show what would have happened if the railcars were loaded based on the process recommended by the rail yard manager. The simulation showed that the same number of railcars would be loaded each day and that there would not be a significant increase in yard inventory.

The next step was to do a pilot for two months to guarantee that there would not be any operational problems. The pilot was successful, and the new loading process was implemented. The increased throughput was great enough to avoid any expansion of either the marshaling yard or the rail yard. The benefit was not only a cost avoidance of millions of dollars but also a shortening of the vehicle delivery time because the railcars did not stagnate in the rail yard.

This example illustrates that it is imperative for logistics managers to consider the impact on downstream operations when they are establishing or modifying processes.

Tracking Progress

Tracking the shipment of vehicles from the plant all the way to the dealer is crucial. Toyota has created a tracking system that receives input from the rail companies on a real-time basis that reports the progress of each railcar. It also gets input from the trucking companies when vehicles are delivered to the dealers.

Toyota uses this information internally to monitor the distribution progress throughout the logistics network. It also provides an estimated time of arrival (ETA) to the dealers. The ETA calculation is based on the date and time of the final quality assurance (FQA). The FQA is the point in the marshaling yard process at which a vehicle is ready for shipment. The calculation is a follows:

$$ETA = FQA + \text{estimated delivery elapse time}$$

The estimated delivery elapse time is based on the recent actual history for each route.

If a vehicle has not been produced, the ETA is still calculated; the FQA date must also be estimated. Because many variables can impact the actual transportation time, Toyota provides the dealers with an estimated three- to five-day arrival window instead of an exact date. That arrival window is updated as the vehicles get closer to delivery. The ETA information is used by the dealer to provide its customers with expected delivery time.

Distribution Flow in Europe

Toyota's distribution flow in Europe is different than its flow in North America because the dealers in Europe do not have enough space to maintain a large inventory of vehicles. In fact, many dealers operate in an urban area and have room for only a few showroom vehicles. Figure 8-5 shows the normal flow in

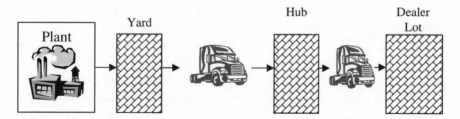

Figure 8-5. Europe vehicle distribution flow

Europe. As in the North American flow, the vehicles are released from the assembly plant and shuttled to the marshaling yard. In Europe, there is no additional processing in the marshaling yard. Instead, the vehicles are shuttled directly to the staging area for shipment via truck to one of the regional hubs. The hubs are where the installation of accessories and the application of the price label take place. Once the vehicle is sold by a dealer, the hub is notified to prepare the vehicle for shipment and install the accessories. Then the vehicle is shipped via truck to the dealer.

One of the other differences in Europe is that most transportation is via truck, not rail. Nevertheless, there is some limited use of rail for long-distance routes, and of course ferries or ships are used to cross waterways.

Another difference is the method for calculating the ETA. The ETA is based on the FQA date and time from the *hub*, not the marshaling yard at the factory. Also, the ETA is a promise date, not a delivery window. The promise date reflects the latest estimated arrival date.

Toyota's distribution processes in North America and Europe are just one example of how Toyota has the agility to adapt its processes to different environments around the world.

The paragraphs that follow give an example of how other OEMs value the importance of logistics as a key component of the supply chain.

Outbound Logistics at Ford and General Motors

As Ford and General Motors try to reduce the cost and increase the reliability of delivery in their outbound logistics, they both have tried using specialists to manage their operations. Ford created an alliance with UPS Logistics Group (a subsidiary of United Parcel Service) in 2000 and GM formed a joint venture with the logistics and freight giant Con-way (then called CNF).

UPS did not actually transport cars for Ford but provided their logistics expertise for management and tracking of deliveries. Ford's distribution network, based on a hub-and-spoke system with rail and ground transportation, utilized 14 different carriers that worked independently on their own lane optimization. UPS reengineered the network for simultaneous delivery planning across all the carriers, enabling optimum analysis of vehicle demand, assignment of sourcing, and scheduling of loads and delivery for all Ford dealers. According to a joint press release by Ford and UPS in 2001,[3] within one year they had shaved off four days of delivery time. They saved $1 billion in inventory and more than $125 million in annual inventory carrying costs for Ford.

General Motors went a step further to create the largest such venture in the automotive industry, outsourcing its entire inbound and outbound logistics operation worldwide to a joint venture formed with Con-way.[4] This new company, called Vector, was responsible for managing shipment of parts to plants, vehicles to dealers, and aftermarket parts and materials. The idea was to use a common information technology system to obtain seamless visibility of materials, parts, and vehicles moving through GM's supply chain worldwide. By July 2002, GM had reduced logistics costs by 10 percent and reduced time for delivery from 15 days (in 1999) to about nine days.[5]

Although this experiment was successful, GM ended the joint venture in 2006 by buying out Con-way's 85 percent share in the company. The reason cited was a response to changing fortunes to support GM's turnaround activities in North America.[6]

Reflection Points

Toyota's logistics operation is an excellent example of where Toyota's organizational learning practices are extended beyond the enterprise to include the 3PL partners. The continuous sharing of the Toyota Way principles and use of v4L with their partners ensures that parts and vehicles are transported in an effective and timely manner.

- *Velocity*. Parts inflow, production rate at the assembly plant, and rail departures are synchronized to ensure heijunka across the supply chain. This process enables a steady velocity to be maintained.
- *Variety* across vehicles affects vehicle height, which in turn affects loading efficiency in the railcar (bi-level or tri-level) and thus affects associated costs. Destination of delivery affects vehicle options and flow time and is in turn linked to parts inflow and finished goods outflow. Dealers have some limited flexibility to swap vehicle orders with other dealers' orders in the pipeline.
- *Variability* is managed by combining pickups across suppliers to create milk routes and the use of cross-docks. Tapping parts compensates for variability by using pipeline inventory.
- *Visibility* across the pipeline of parts inflow plays a key role in maintaining a lean system, particularly for long lead time parts. Scanners, ASNs, and the like enable visibility across the supply chain. Continuous monitoring of outbound flows from the plant all the way to the dealers provides visibility for dealers.

Toyota takes many steps to foster learning and continuous improvement in its logistics operations. These include the following:

- *Create awareness*. Toyota monitors the pipeline both to obtain early signals of problems that might arise and to take corrective action based on pipeline information. Progress of shipments is tracked with precise calculation.

- *Make action protocols.* Trade-offs that must be considered when designing the logistics systems (e.g., on-time pickup, capacity utilized, and total actual mileage) are clearly defined. Contingency plans are drawn with care to address exceptions that arise from time to time.
- *Generate system-level awareness.* The information system makes the supply pipeline visible. System-level exceptions are studied to isolate major issues, and those concerns are addressed on a priority basis.
- *Practice "go-and-see."* The highest-ranking managers go to the site with the logistics problem so they can see firsthand. These managers take a systems approach to solving problems, considering the impact both upstream and downstream.
- *Make deviations visible.* Toyota levels the workload with milk runs. That step makes deviations obvious and immediately visible.

Endnotes

1. Transportation costs are directly related to the cost of fuel. As the cost of fuel increases, the cost of transportation will be negatively impacted.
2. "We Are Doing a Lot More Than Just Basic Logistics," *Business Line*, April 18, 2005.
3. "Ford Motor Company and UPS Logistics Group Ahead of Schedule in Vehicle Delivery Improvements," Ford Motor Company press release, February 21, 2001.
4. "GM Joint Venture to Oversee Deliveries," *Automotive News*, December 18, 2000.
5. "GM System Reduces Parts Shortages," *Automotive News*, July 1, 2002.
6. "GM Buys Out Vector SCM, Brings Logistics Back In-house," *Logistics Management*, August 1, 2006.

Chapter 9

Dealer and Demand Fulfillment

Dealers use a number of different processes to fulfill retail customer demand. This chapter will explore the major ones; it will be subdivided into three areas: vehicle allocation, demand fulfillment options, and dealer operations.

Vehicle Allocation

At Toyota, vehicle allocation in North America is a two-step process. In the first step, the national sales company allocates vehicles to their regional areas. In the second step, the regional areas allocate these vehicles to dealers.

Regional Allocation

The regional allocation is performed monthly, about six weeks prior to the start of the production month. If the next production month is July, then the regional allocation would occur in mid-May. The purpose of the regional area allocation is to allocate the quantity of vehicles by model to each region. The quantity is calculated using a share or percentage of the total national market that each region will receive. The following are some of the factors that are used to determine each region's share:

- Sales versus previous month and model-to-date objectives
- Regional weather conditions that can impact future sales such as floods, snowstorms, drought, etc.
- Regional economic conditions and trends that impact future sales
- Competitive strategies that may affect market share in a region and necessitate more aggressive marketing strategies

Once the volume of each model is allocated to the regional area, the region must create a vehicle order for each unit. The regional vehicle order is an input to the sales and operations planning process, which was described in Chapter 4. After the monthly order is scheduled by manufacturing, regions receive a file containing the details of each vehicle along with the tentative scheduled date. These data are used to perform the dealer allocation.

Dealer Allocation

Toyota uses three methods in the United States to allocate vehicles to dealers. The methods vary for the three Toyota brands: Toyota, Scion, and Lexus.

Toyota Brand Allocation

Dealer allocation is based on the fair share of the regional volume for each model. That apportionment is intended to be a very objective calculation based on a turn-and-earn concept. Turn-and-earn is a results-oriented methodology that rewards the dealers for increasing their sales. The goal is to ensure that all dealers are treated fairly and to avoid the perception of favorable treatment. Therefore, the initial dealer allocation is based on each dealer's share of the regional market, as calculated based on actual sales. The allocation is performed twice each month and, unlike with the regional allocation, dealers are allocated or assigned unique vehicles with full specifications.

The vehicle specifications that the dealer is allocated are matched to two inputs that are provided by dealers. The dealers can maintain an allocation preference database that describes the type of vehicle specifications that they desire—or do not desire. We return to the example that dealers in Arizona may not want dark colors and dealers in northern cities may want cold weather kits. Dealers can also submit special orders from customers.

Once the dealers receive their allocation of vehicles, they have a few days to accept the vehicles. If there are reasons why dealers do not want some vehicles, they may turn down specific units. Those units will be placed in a supplemental pool and offered to other dealers. In the situation where there is a surplus of some models because of slow sales, the region may offer dealers a financial incentive to take these slow-selling vehicles.

After the dealers accept the vehicles, they appear in a pipeline inventory report. At this time, dealers can make changes to some of the factory specifications and also add accessories that will be installed at the marshaling yard and/or port. Now that the dealers know which vehicles are scheduled for production and approximately when they will be built, they can use information regarding these vehicles in combination with the dealer stock to fulfill demand.

Scion Brand Allocation

The method of allocating Scion is similar to the method of allocating the tradi-tional Toyota vehicles, with one major difference. For Scion, the vehicles allo-cated to each dealer are held at the port until the vehicle is sold. Once the vehicle is sold, additional accessories are installed based on customer request. Those accessories can be installed at the port or at the dealer. The flexibility to add accessories after the base vehicle is built enables Toyota to market to younger buyers. Younger buyers are usually first-time buyers and tend to want to person-alize their vehicle.

The model for distribution of the Scion is similar to the way Toyota distrib-utes vehicles in Europe. In Europe the vehicles are held at a hub until the dealer receives a customer contract. Then additional accessories are installed and the vehicle is shipped to the dealer.

Lexus Brand Allocation

The primary difference between the Lexus allocation model and the other allo-cation models described previously is that Lexus vehicles are allocated to dealers based on a quarterly sales plan. Unlike the Toyota models that are based on actual sales to "turn-and-earn," Lexus's vehicle allocation is based on the fore-casted sales of each dealer as a share of each region's total sales. The allocation share is revised each quarter to adjust for market changes. The allocation process is consistent with the idea that firms can take greater risk with products that have a higher margin.

Toyota's Order Fulfillment Process: U.S. Model

There are four options for dealers to fulfill customer demand, as outlined in Figure 9-1.

The first option is to fulfill the customer's order from dealer stock. The salesperson will attempt to influence the customer to select a vehicle already in stock. Such an approach is preferred by the dealer because the sale can be consummated immediately, before the customer leaves the dealership. The sales-person is always concerned that once a customer leaves without the keys to the car, she will change her mind and end up buying from another dealer or a competitor. The order-to-delivery lead time for vehicles purchased from stock is usually zero to two days.

The second option for fulfillment is a dealer trade. In that case, the sales-person can access a dealer locator system to determine if the vehicle is in another dealer's stock in a nearby city or state. Usually the distance is limited to less than

Option	Fulfillment Approach	Description	Order-to-Delivery Time
Option 1	Dealer Stock	The car is bought from the visited dealer.	Instantly available
Option 2	Dealer Trade	The car is located at another dealer within the Sales region and transported to the dealer. The additional cost occurred is > $250 for dealer trade in United States.	2–3 days
Option 3	Order Change	Orders are scheduled based on the forecast, and once the customer specifies an order, the dealer submits a change request to change a specific vehicle in the pipeline to match the customer requirements. In that event, another dealer submits an offsetting request, and a virtual trade is performed by simply changing the dealer/vehicle assignments.	Variable— 30 days on average
Option 4	Build-to-Order	The order is entered as new into the system. That happens only in 2% of the new vehicle purchases in the United States.	90–120 days

Figure 9-1. Toyota's options for demand fulfillment

500 miles, because if the vehicle is driven more than 500 miles before it is sold, the excessive mileage may violate the warranty. This issue can be avoided by hauling the vehicle on a trailer. In most cases, the dealers actually swap vehicles, meaning that two vehicles need to be transported instead of one. This method of fulfillment will add several hundred dollars to the dealer cost, because the dealer must pay a driver as well as cover the cost of fuel to transport the vehicle. That extra cost may or may not be passed along to the customer depending on how anxious the dealer is to sell the vehicle. It also adds miles to a new car before customer possession. The order-to-delivery lead time is usually two to three days.

The third option is to locate the vehicle in the dealer's pipeline. The pipeline consists of vehicles that have been allocated or assigned to the dealer but have not arrived at the dealer. The pipeline can be divided into three segments:

1. Vehicles produced and in transit from the plant
2. Vehicles that are either in the process of being built or for which the specifications have been frozen just prior to production
3. Vehicles scheduled for production with specifications that have not yet been frozen

If an exact match of the customer's specifications can be located in the first two groups, then the vehicle can be reserved for the customer and should be delivered in two to three weeks.

The next choice is to locate a vehicle that is scheduled for future production and request a change in specifications. That step requires the manufacturing plant to agree to change the vehicle specification. The process is as follows:

- The dealer submits an online request to change a vehicle that has still not been produced. The change request can be a simple one-for-one change; for example, "I have a red Camry and I want a blue Camry." The change request can also be one-to-many or many-to-one; for example, "I have a red Camry and I want either a blue or white Camry," or, "I have a blue Camry and a black Camry and I want a silver Camry."

- The next step is for the sales company's computer system to analyze and determine if any of the change requests can be satisfied by simply swapping the vehicle with a dealer who has submitted a change that is the exact reverse change request. For example, if a dealer in Boston wants to exchange a blue Camry LE for a black Camry XLE and a dealer in Chicago has a black Camry XLE and wants a blue Camry LE, then the computer can simply swap the dealer assignments. If this online swap is successful, then the virtual swap is made and both dealers will be notified.

- If the above swap is not available, then the changes are sent to the manufacturing computer system that checks to ensure that the change can be made without exceeding any of the manufacturing constraints. Each assembly plant establishes a fluctuation allowance for each vehicle option, including color. Each dealer change request is systematically evaluated to make sure that none of the allowances are exceeded. If the change is accepted, the vehicle specifications are changed and the result is sent back to the dealer via the sales company. Also, the dealer will be notified if the change cannot be accepted, so the dealer can modify it or leave it in a pending status to be reprocessed the next day. Vehicles changed at the factory are usually delivered in 30 to 40 days.

- The last resort (or fourth option) is to request a build-to-order vehicle from the regional office. That step would require the region to input the special order in the next month's order cycle. A special request order typically has a very long lead time (usually three or more months).

In addition to the order-to-delivery lead time for each of the fulfillment options as shown in Figure 9-2, it is also important to provide an accurate ETA (expected time of arrival) for the dealer to keep its customer updated. Not only should a date be provided, but the actual progress should be updated daily, similar to the way UPS tracks packages. Initially, the ETA is calculated using the estimated production build day and adding the standard transit time from the factory to the dealer. As can be seen from Figure 9-2, the longer lead time orders will result in a less accurate ETA. This calculation must take into account the standard deviation,

Monthly Order	Pipeline			Stock		Order Fulfillment		
	Schedule	Production	In-Transit	Trade	Stock	Lead Time	Percent	Option
					▓	0–2 days	60–70%	1
				▓	▓	1–3 days	20–25%	2
			▓			1–2 weeks	<5%	3
		▓				2–3 weeks	<5%	3
	▓					3–6 weeks	5–10%	3
▓						>3 months	<2%	4

Figure 9-2. Order-to-delivery time for U.S. market

because the transit time for each route will vary depending on many external factors. Toyota believes that it is better to underpromise and then overdeliver.

Choice versus Value Trade-off

What is a dealer's perspective on how customers respond to Toyota's strategy to limit the mix of vehicles produced in a market area? Steve Gates, an owner of a Toyota dealership in Kentucky, explained that most customers are repeat customers; they have owned Toyota cars previously or are familiar with other Japanese manufacturers and understand the concept that variety will be limited so that quality and value can be maintained. The remaining customers may require salesperson assistance to be guided to the increased features that accompany the limited variety, thus providing the "added value" for the cars offered. Steve Gates did not feel that limitations of variety were a deterrent. He did highlight the fact that dealers did have a voice in Toyota's product planning and their perceptions regarding customer needs were considered when allocations were made.

The concept that Toyota offers added value is interesting, but can it be measured? How should one measure the "added value" of a Toyota? While quality is measured and controlled by suppliers and assemblers using thousands (perhaps millions) of data points among all parts, how is a consumer to measure the difference in value between a Toyota vehicle and one produced, say, by an American or Korean competitor? One way of estimating value could be to compare used car values of vehicles in the same class: how much of its value does a car retain after three, five, or seven years of use? To measure the difference, we obtained suggested used car retail values from the *Kelley Blue Book (KBB)*, which reports the residual values for vehicles of different makes, models, and years. This value is calculated by analyzing thousands of actual transactions across the United States, producing prices for a varied set of mileage and vehicle conditions. These data are presented in Figure 9-3, which shows how Honda and Toyota cars not only command a premium at initial sale but also retain their values more than other vehicles sold at comparable prices. While Honda Accord and Toyota Camry retained 85 percent and 89 percent of their values, respectively,

	Year Purchased >>>	2001	2003	2005
Honda Accord	Model	DX	DX	DX
	MSRP	$15,400	$15,800	$16,295
	KBB Suggested Retail Value	$9,075	$12,350	$13,920
	Value Retained as of 2008	59%	78%	85%
Toyota Camry	Model	CE	LE	CE
	MSRP	$17,675	$19,045	$18,195
	KBB Suggested Retail Value	$9,915	$13,330	$16,105
	Value Retained as of 2008	56%	70%	89%
Chevrolet Malibu	Model	Base	Base	Base
	MSRP	$17,150	$18,075	$19,200
	KBB Suggested Retail Value	$6,290	$7,890	$10,825
	Value Retained as of 2008	37%	44%	56%
Ford Taurus	Model	LX	LX	SE
	MSRP	$18,550	$19,630	$21,200
	KBB Suggested Retail Value	$6,215	$7,525	$10,225
	Value Retained as of 2008	34%	38%	48%
Hyundai Sonata	Model	GLS	GLS	GLS
	MSRP	$16,999	$17,349	$18,999
	KBB Suggested Retail Value	$8,370	$10,055	$12,325
	Value Retained as of 2008	49%	58%	65%

Figure 9-3. Vehicle residual value chart

after three years, General Motors, Ford, and Hyundai cars that were similar retained only 56 percent, 48 percent, and 65 percent of their values, respectively. The *Kelley Blue Book* Suggested Retail Value for these vehicles was sampled in August 2008 and is updated every two months.[1]

Toyota's Order Fulfillment Process: Europe Model

One of the big differences between the order fulfillment model in Europe and in the United States is that most European dealers do not have space for dealer stock; therefore, stock is owned by Toyota or one of its distributors and is stored in a central hub. There is at least one hub in each major country. The other major difference is that the production and stock are not allocated to dealers until they are sold to customers.

Several government regulations in Europe also impact automobile operations, among which are the following:

- In Europe, various countries have different tax laws, which may skew how options are ordered. For example, if a country calculates value-added tax based on the invoice price from the factory, then a customer may order a vehicle with very few options and contract with a dealer or private shop to install accessories.

- Laws pertaining to the registration process could also affect the delivery time. Some countries require several days to process the vehicle registration, so even if the vehicle arrives at the dealer quickly, the customer may not be able to take delivery until registration is approved.

- In the past, the Block Exemption Agreement for automobiles affected the way OEMs set up their dealer network, which resulted in there being many small dealerships (for example, Germany has as many dealers as the entire United States). That arrangement also negatively affected customers, because they ended up paying a 35 percent premium to get repairs done at the local dealership. In addition, dealerships located in premium real estate locations meant that dealer inventory space was limited. However, the recent repeal of the Block Exemption Agreement means that the European dealer networks are expected to change considerably. Already several dealerships have been consolidated, and more aggregation is expected. Manufacturers have to choose an exclusive dealer or exclusive territory. The impact is expected to decrease customer costs and increase competition.

In summary, the order fulfillment process in Europe is more complex because there are over 25 countries involved, each with different laws and policies. Figure 9-4 illustrates the five options for fulfilling demand in Europe.

As in the U.S. market, in the European market too it is important to provide an accurate ETA. Not only should a date be provided, but the actual progress should be updated daily. For vehicles in the central hub, the ETA is calculated by adding the hub processing time to transit time from hub to dealer. If the vehicle is not yet produced, the ETA is calculated using the estimated production build day and adding the standard transit time from the factory to the dealer. As can be seen in Figure 9-5, the longer lead time orders will result in a less accurate ETA. That calculation must take into account the standard deviation, because each route transit time will vary depending on external factors. It is better to underpromise and then overdeliver. If too much buffer is built into the estimate, however, then the customer may not be willing to wait. Figure 9-5 shows the estimated order-to-delivery time for each option.

Metrics

Metrics are an important method to monitor order fulfillment. The following are some of the key metrics:

- *Sales*. The total sales by model and by mix
- *Daily selling rate*. The sales divided by the selling days in a month

Option	Demand Fulfillment Approach	Description	Order-to-Delivery Time
Option 1	Dealer Stock	The car is bought from the visited dealer. This option is limited in Europe due to limited space at dealerships to store stock.	Instantly available
Option 2	Dealer Swap	The car is located at another dealer in the country and transported to the dealer. Again this is limited in Europe for same reason as option 1.	3 days
Option 3	Central Hub	The vehicle is sourced from central stock location that is controlled by Toyota. Once a customer signs a contract to purchase a vehicle, the dealer issues a call-off request to the hub for a vehicle. In addition, some accessories can be installed at the hub. After installation, the vehicle is shipped to dealer via truck.	7 days
Option 4	Order Match	Vehicles are scheduled for production based on the mix forecasted for each country. Once the customer specifies his order, the pipeline of unsold vehicles is searched for the order that either matches or can be changed to match the customer order. The primary difference between the market in Europe and the market in the United States is that in Europe unsold stock in pipeline is not assigned to a dealer. The unsold stock is allocated to a country so any dealer within a country can match any unsold stock.	Variable—30 days on average
Option 5	Build-to-Order	A build-to-order is entered into the system as a new order. The dealer sends an order request to the central country office, and the order is entered into the next monthly production order.	90–120 days

Figure 9-4. Europe fulfillment model

- *Dealer stock.* The number of units in dealer stock that have not been delivered to a customer or put into demo service
- *Company stock.* The number of vehicles produced that are still at the factory or in transit to the dealer
- *Days supply.* The number of vehicles in stock divided by the daily selling rate
- *Aged stock.* The number of vehicles in stock over N days (usually 90 or 120 days)
- *Order-to-delivery lead time.* The number of days from the time the customer orders to the day of delivery

Monthly Order	Pipeline			Stock		Order Fulfillment		
	Schedule	Production	In-Transit	Hub	Dealer	Lead Time	Percent	Method
						0–2 days	<5%	1a
						5–7 days	50–60%	1b
						1–2 weeks	<5%	2a
						2–3 weeks	<5%	2b
						3–6 weeks	20–30%	2c
						>3 months	<5%	3

Figure 9-5. Order-to-delivery time for European market

Dealer Operations

Dealer operations are an important part of the automobile supply chain. Dealers receive vehicles from the OEM, hold them in inventory, negotiate the sale with a customer, assist in financing, take a used vehicle in trade, prepare the vehicle for delivery, and familiarize the customer with the vehicle features and operations during the handover process. In addition, the dealer provides after-sales warranty and service support.

Dealer operations include providing after-sales service and support to Toyota's customers. Toyota's service chain management is based on establishing strong links with its customers using a two-pronged strategy of supporting dealers and directly interacting with customers. The majority of customers are served by dealers for their after-sales service needs. Therefore, Toyota has created an efficient supply network to provide reliable supply of service parts to dealers. Toyota also trains and helps dealers in providing excellent service. In addition, Toyota is not averse to using advanced technologies, such as e-commerce and telematics, to directly interact with vehicle owners. We do not describe these systems in detail as they are somewhat tangential to the description of the main auto supply chain. Instead, we refer the reader to Lee, Peleg, and Whang's case study[2] for a detailed description on how the after-sales service systems at Toyota help build customer loyalty.

Dealer operations are considered so important that they merit a special section under the *Toyota Way* document titled "The Positioning of The Toyota Way in Sales and Marketing." The section related to dealers lays out the ideas that form the basis for continuous improvement and learning, both for and about dealer operations. For example, the mission statement for sales and marketing is "Customer First/Lifetime Customers as Well as Radar for All of Toyota." The historic concept at Toyota is that benefit should first go to the customer, then to the dealer; only after that does it go to Toyota. The sales operation is itself broken into five linked "targeted processes," namely:

1. Obtain necessary information quickly.
2. Drop into sales outlets with ease and without pressure from sales staff.
3. Understand the value of the purchased vehicles.
4. Obtain the vehicles with ease of mind.
5. Own the vehicle with confidence.

Each of these items is further broken down into subprocesses with objectives and clearly defined metrics. The following are some specific ideas discussed in this chapter and outlined in the *Toyota Way* document:

- The process of allocation, dealer feedback, and various methods to resolve issues related to the process are standardized and rigidly timed.

Those procedures allow problems to be noticed immediately and corrective action taken as soon as they have been identified. The system is practical and allows for changes in orders but within the specified time limit and cost. The sequence of corrective actions is also scripted: look at dealer stock, then dealer trade, then dealer pipeline, and finally the scheduled pipeline of vehicles.

- The amount of flexibility necessary to respond to requests is carefully controlled with a fluctuation allowance.
- One of the missions of sales and marketing is to "support the dealer in conducting constant kaizen." That objective involves planned sales activities and measures based on Plan, Do, Check, and Act (PDCA), creating a high-performing sales cycle and practice of field activities based on "Genchi Genbutsu," or "go to the source."

All that effort at sharing knowledge, learning, and process know-how pays off. In a 2007 Dealer Attitude Study for Japan by J.D. Power Asia Pacific,[3] Toyota was ranked the highest for the thirteenth consecutive year. The study measured dealer satisfaction with vehicle manufacturers or importers and determined dealer attitudes toward the automotive sales business. It was based on eight factors: product attractiveness (31 percent), responsiveness to dealers (21 percent), sales support (13 percent), service relations (12 percent), warranty (6 percent), sales representatives (6 percent), vehicle ordering systems (6 percent), and parts (5 percent).

For Toyota, profitability of its supply chain partners—including dealers—is important for its success in the long term. Therefore, it is still trying to improve its dealer operations and continuously increase the value delivered to customers. For example, Toyota Motor Europe (TME) is trying to determine how best to make the Toyota Production System work for car retailing as well. To that end, it has created the Toyota Retailing System (TRS), which takes a bottom-up approach to developing the best practices for Toyota dealers. It works somewhat like Wikipedia, the Web-based encyclopedia that is maintained and improved by its own readers. Both Toyota's production and retailing systems adhere to a straightforward problem-solving methodology called PDCA, where problems are solved by teams, not individuals. This approach offers the benefit of better structure and measurability in problem solving than other methods have. The solution created by the team is used to create a kaizen module that can be shared with all other retailers in Europe through a common database.

This bottom-up construction is a big advantage of TRS, says Dave Cussell, the general manager of market development at TME. In his view, dealers are more open to listen to positive experiences from colleagues than to top-down case histories presented by carmakers.

Reflection Points

The following is a summary of the link between ideas in this chapter and the v4L framework:

- *Variety* differs in Europe, where customers expect more customization than in the United States. Dealers work to convince customers that the limited variety is compensated by higher attribute levels.
- *Velocity* of the dealer sales is matched to shipments to dealers to maintain a lean supply chain.
- *Variability* of sales is minimized by mix planning, which restricts variety sold in each region.
- *Visibility* of the product flows is ensured by providing each dealer with a specific delivery date for a car. This date is updated as the product flows through the supply chain. It permits the final customer to have a good idea regarding the expected delivery date.

The following are highlights of the learning practices:

- *Create awareness.* The dealers are made aware that the Toyota Way extends to their processes.
- *Establish capability.* Dealers are trained and supported in conducting constant kaizen.
- *Make action protocols.* The process of allocation, dealer feedback, and various methods to resolve issues related to the process are standardized and rigidly timed.
- *Generate system-level awareness.* Toyota uses both a top-down as well as bottom-up approach to provide the system level perspective for monitoring, planning, and continuously improving dealer operations.

Endnotes

1. See Kbb.com, Frequently Asked Questions (www.kbb.com/kbb/CompanyInfo/FAQ.aspx?section=UsedCar#uc_8).
2. Hau Lee, Barchi Peleg, and Seungjin Whang, "Toyota: Service Chain Management," Case GS-41, Stanford Graduate School of Business, Stanford University, Stanford, CA, 2005.
3. J.D. Power 2007 Dealer Attitude Survey for Japan, J.D. Power Asia Pacific.

Chapter 10

Crisis Management

Why would Toyota need to be concerned about crisis management when it has implemented processes throughout the supply chain that are synchronized and integrated to function like a fine Swiss clock? The reality is that Toyota is not immune to disruption of its operations because of natural disasters, strikes, fires, bankruptcies, and the like. Because of that vulnerability, Toyota has a process to respond to crisis situations.

But before we began with the discussion on how Toyota responds to crisis situations, let's learn how a Japanese official reacted to a crisis situation. The following is a true personal story.

An example of contingency planning involves one of the authors' visits with his family to the historic town of Koyasan in Japan. The rail ticket had been sold for two days, but because of a misunderstanding the return trip was scheduled after the first night, rather than after two nights as the family had planned. The Japan Rail official immediately realized the problem and wanted to create a solution that would hold whether the family traveled back the next day or the day after. He waited patiently for other lodging details to be finalized, and then he reprogrammed the ticketing system machines to recognize the return ticket for either day. He requested that the family merely inform the ticketing staff when they arrived and the programs would be activated so that the travel would be as if there was no issue with the tickets. In other words, plan B was as efficient as plan A. Such contingency planning is a hallmark of Toyota—plan B is as smooth as plan A.

Crisis Management Process

Unlike most of the Toyota operational process, crisis management is much less structured because the exact type and timing of a crisis event is unpredictable. In addition, there are two types of supply chain crises. The most obvious type

133

of crisis is one that occurs as a result of an unplanned event such as a fire or natural disaster. However, Toyota also will declare a crisis situation to mobilize internal staff and suppliers to create a sense of urgency in order to develop a new technology that gains a competitive and/or strategic advantage. Such a situation is analogous to President Kennedy announcing in 1960 that the United States would send a man to the moon within 10 years. The development of the Toyota Prius was the result of one of these strategic crises.

The crisis management process consists of the following steps:

1. *Identify the crisis.* Identification of a crisis may seem to be a simple thing, because so many crisis events are also big media events (e.g., the terrorist attacks of September 11, 2001; earthquakes; and hurricanes). However, many crises are much less obvious, such as suppliers that are in financial trouble. Therefore, the responsibility to identify supply chain issues is not that of the purchasing group alone. It is also important to detect a potential crisis before the actual event occurs. The following are some of the ways that a crisis or potential crisis can be identified:

   o The parts ordering group at a plant notices a pattern of short shipments
   o The quality control group at a plant detects a sudden change in parts defects
   o The purchasing buyer discovers during a periodic review of the supplier's financial records that there has been a serious deterioration in the supplier's finances that could lead to filing for bankruptcy
   o The purchasing buyer becomes aware of a potential strike at a supplier
   o News media report a natural disaster or terrorist attack

   In the event that a supplier detects a problem first, then it is important that the supplier contacts purchasing or the plant to alert them of a problem. This step is crucial, because it is human nature to attempt to resolve the problem by one's self. It is especially difficult for a supplier to admit that it has a problem. Therefore, Toyota's purchasing management continually communicates to suppliers that Toyota wants to be alerted to all potential problems. Gene Tabor, general manager of purchasing at Toyota Engineering and Manufacturing North America, stated, "Call even if it is 5 p.m. Friday afternoon. Don't try to solve the problem yourself over the weekend. We are here to help."[1] Gene claimed that "every supplier will have a problem; the question is how it is handled when it happens." There are no extra staff resources to help suppliers; everyone from purchasing to the assembly line team members may be used to solve a supply chain problem. If a supplier has a financial issue and is required to wind down production, a team from Toyota will go to the supplier location and assist with production changes while at the same time ensuring that all OEMs receive a fair share of product. In addition, many times the subsuppliers to the supplier in trouble may be requested to continue to work closely with an alternate supplier so that shipments to Toyota can be continued.

2. *Communicate!* Both internal and external communications must be timely and effective. Initially, it is critical that all affected plants be alerted as well as sales organizations. Ongoing daily phone conferences need to be conducted to obtain the latest status and to share information. In addition, status reports must be e-mailed to all interested parties on a daily basis. External communication has to be managed to avoid misinformation being leaked to the media. Community leaders in the affected area must also be kept informed on a regular basis.

3. *Make an assessment.* Preliminary assessment determines the potential impact of the crisis. Questions that must be asked to probe the scope of the crisis include: "Which supplier or suppliers are impacted?" "What parts will be affected?" "What models and plants are affected?" Another aspect would be to assess the timing of the crisis. Has the crisis event already occurred (e.g., a fire or earthquake), or is it something that might happen in the future (e.g., a strike)? If the crisis can be anticipated, Toyota can get ahead of the curve by establishing the crisis team in advance to implement mitigating actions before the event occurs. For example, in the situation of a pending strike at a supplier, Toyota can build up inventory and/or establish an alternative supplier.

4. *Assign "crisis owner."* An owner is assigned to manage each crisis across the enterprise and the supply chain. The crisis owner is determined based on the scope and type of the crisis. The following are some of the criteria used to determine the owner:

   ○ *Scope.* If the scope is limited to one plant, then the owner would most likely be a production control manager at the plant. On the other hand, if the crisis is worldwide, TMC headquarters in Japan might own and manage the crisis. Most crises fall in the middle. They impact multiple plants in one region and are the responsibility of the regional manufacturing headquarters.

   ○ *Type.* Once the entity responsible for the crisis has been determined, then it must be decided which function owns the crisis within the entity. The following are some examples: (1) Supplier financial and/or supplier employee relations issues would likely be assigned to purchasing, (2) parts shortages and/or supplier operation problems would be assigned to production control, and (3) parts quality issues would be assigned to quality. Even though who the owner is might vary, depending on the scope and type of crisis, all functions and entities will support the owner when and where necessary.

5. *Assemble crisis team.* There are two steps to assembling a crisis team. The first step is to identify the representatives from all of the parties affected. The representatives are the people who will be the focal points for each of the interested organizations. Toyota does not have extra staff to address crisis situations; therefore, the personnel assigned to work on the crisis must reprioritize their work and make necessary time to support the effort to mitigate the crisis. The second step is to gather together the on-the-ground team that is dispatched to the scene of the crisis. This team is the eyes and ears for the extended team and also provides direct support to resolve the problem. One of the principles of the Toyota Way is "Genchi Genbutsu," which means "go and see." This on-site team is able to provide the facts so that the crisis impact can be assessed and countermeasures can be developed. The team also provides technical assistance as needed.

6. *Mitigate:*

   o *Short-term mitigation.* The immediate requirement is to implement countermeasures to minimize the impact. As stated above, the on-site team works to resolve the problem by providing technical support. The production control group works with the plant to ensure that parts continue to be delivered to the plants on time and in the quantity needed to avoid a disruption in production. The first step is to grasp the inventory of the affected parts at each plant as well of the parts in the pipeline. Then decisions are made to air-ship parts or obtain extra parts from another supplier. In the event there are not adequate parts to maintain production, then scheduled overtime will be reduced at each plant and, if necessary, production is stopped for the models that are slowest in demand. On another front, the purchasing group investigates the feasibility of establishing a new source for the parts. If the supplier has a relationship with a Japanese parent company, then it may be practical to obtain parts from the parent company in Japan on a temporary basis. With such parallel activities, Toyota proceeds with a sense of urgency on multiple fronts, even though in many cases the crisis is avoided or mitigated quickly.

   o *Long-term mitigation.* Even as the crisis team is involved in the day-to-day activities to mitigate the crisis, Toyota managers are using their problem-solving skills to investigate potential long-term countermeasures. The objective is to learn from the experience and to attempt to either avoid that type of crisis from recurring in the future or, if it is impractical to avoid, consider ways in which the impact could be reduced. For example, based on a particular experience, Toyota might decide to source parts to multiple suppliers or ensure that there is a backup source for critical parts.

7. *Practice good corporate citizenship.* Toyota practices its corporate citizenship principles even during times of crisis. Two examples are Toyota's corporate donation to aid victims of a natural disaster and the company's sense of fairness to its competitors when multiple automotive manufacturers are affected by the same supplier. Although the company may be deeply involved with assisting a supplier with recovery from a crisis, Toyota will make the best effort to see to it that each manufacturer receives its fair share of the supplier's production.

8. *Reflect.* Toyota learns from a negative experience through reflection. After each crisis, a reflection report is prepared and shared throughout the organization. The report will include an analysis of the problem along with the short-term and long-term countermeasures. It also includes a reflection on what went right and what went wrong.

Crises Stories

Toyota has reacted to several crisis situations—no two of them the same—in a number of ways. Even though Toyota is not immune to crises, the company's ability to systematically manage them enables it not only to mitigate the impact of each crisis but also to strengthen the organization by learning from the experience.

Recovering from Disaster: The Aisin Seiki Story[2]

How do suppliers benefit from being part of the Toyota network? The story of Toyota's recovery from the fire at the Aisin Seiki plant provides an excellent example of how the supply chain reacted to a crisis. The story began at 4:18 a.m. on Saturday, February 1, 1997, when a fire erupted in the Aisin Seiki Kariya plant number 1. By 8:52 a.m., the lines devoted to P-valves and two other brake parts were completely destroyed. (The P-valve is a fairly standard product that was sourced solely to Aisin Seiki because of the supplier's long partnership with Toyota and its quality standards, dedicated machinery, and the like. The P-valve is a small rectangular object that controls pressure on rear wheels, thus preventing skidding of the car.) The plant was responsible for delivering 32,500 P-valves to Toyota and other companies such as Mitsubishi, Isuzu, and Suzuki. Because of just-in-time delivery of parts to Toyota, only two to three days of inventory existed in the system. The fire on February 1 caused Toyota to start idling plants within two days.

Almost immediately, Aisin Seiki sprang into action. At 5:30 a.m. it decided to create an emergency response team that, later in the day, contacted all suppliers to ask for assistance in producing P-valves for Toyota. About 62 firms responded to this call for help. Among them were 22 of Aisin's suppliers, Toyota itself, 36 of Toyota's regular suppliers, and 4 nonregular suppliers, including a sewing machine manufacturer that had never made car parts. Because there were 100 different types of P-valves, Aisin had to decide which valves would be made at each of the available supplier locations.

The next day, drawings were faxed to potential manufacturing sites; they did not contain detailed manufacturing specifications. Given the large volume of calls and communication congestion, there was limited direct contact with Aisin personnel as well. Toyota decided not to pressure these suppliers into providing the part as a priority. In the absence of the specialized machinery at Aisin that was destroyed in the fire, the P-valve production had to depend on a large number of improvised steps that used a significantly larger amount of labor. Historically, Aisin had 70 inspection steps per piece with specialized gauges. Therefore, to ensure that quality parts were being shipped to Toyota, all P-valves were shipped to Aisin for quality checks before they went to Toyota.

Each of the suppliers used different supply chain processes to produce the P-valve, but because all the suppliers were trained on the Toyota production system principle, those different approaches still fit within the Toyota way of manufacturing and delivery. The flexibility to create individual supply chains yet fit within the overall system is often held up as a shining example of the value of standardizing processes across the supply chain.

One supplier, Denso, decided to outsource its existing production to free up capacity to produce P-valves on more than 40 machines. It decided that because of evolving design understanding, process learning, and the like, the system would be too complex to manage if it were outsourced. Another supplier, Taiho, met with its suppliers and chose 11 suppliers to assist by providing machining centers at its plants. Toyota pulled employees from its experimental prototype division and set up a temporary production facility. Supplier Kayaba outsourced the P-valves to three of its suppliers and produced no valves itself. Each of these firms, in turn, created its own emergency response teams to coordinate production and delivery.

One supplier started delivering prototypes three days after the fire. Denso delivered its prototype on February 5, followed by two other large suppliers the same day. Kayaba delivered prototypes on February 6 from one supplier and February 7 and 8 from the other two suppliers. Volume production began within a day or the same day of prototype approval.

Denso took the lead in identifying and eliminating bottlenecks across all suppliers. Productivity improvement approaches were implemented to decrease processing times at machines.

During this period there was constant flow of personnel across all of these locations to disseminate information and resolve production bottlenecks.

Among them were Toyota personnel scattered across the production locations and individual supplier personnel. All of these steps were taken without any contracts regarding reimbursement of suppliers for costs. Meanwhile, Aisin Seiki started increasing its own production and boosted its production level to 100 percent by mid-March.

Aisin Seiki decided to compensate all of the suppliers for the costs incurred to manage this production, while Toyota compensated its supply base with 1 percent of its sales from January to March 1997. These funds in turn were passed along to individual component suppliers and others so that it disseminated throughout the system.

What does this show? Being part of the Toyota system and applying Toyota principles, and knowing that everyone else can be counted on to follow these processes as well, makes the system far more resilient to disruptions. The level of trust in the supply chain means that Toyota can comfortably expect a supplier to take the lead and solve problems without the need for centralized coordination. Low inventory in the system means that bottlenecks anywhere are every supplier's problem. The sharing of resources and the flexibility of response permit innovative individual suppliers to be both efficient and responsive.

West Coast Port Strike

During 2002, there was an extended shutdown of the U.S. West Coast ports. It had a devastating impact on the North American auto industry, including Toyota, as highlighted in an article from *Auto Parts Report*,[3] which stated: "Operations at many of the nation's vehicle assembly and auto parts plants are slowly returning to normal after a federal judge ordered an injunction under the 1947 Taft-Hartley Act to end lockout of about 10,500 union workers at U.S. West Coast ports. The lockout started Sept. 29th."

The U.S. economy was losing up to $1 billion a day, and the automotive industry was particularly hard hit because imported parts and vehicles could not be delivered. The Motor & Equipment Manufacturers Association (MEMA) estimated the value of automotive products and vehicles shipped into West Coast ports to be at least $42 billion in 2002.

This port work stoppage is a good example of how Toyota responds to crisis events when there is some advanced warning. In this case, negotiations were ongoing between management and the union for several months before the lockout actually occurred. Toyota was able to organize its crisis management team in advance to develop contingency plans. The following were some of the actions taken to mitigate the impact of the potential shutdown of the ports:

- Build up inventory of parts at the North American plants by gradually increasing parts orders for several weeks prior to the projected shutdown.

Doing so would enable Toyota to continue to operate its plants until alternate shipping arrangements could be implemented.

- Contract with air cargo companies to lease several cargo planes to transport parts during the shutdown.
- Investigate alternative ports of entry where ships at sea could be diverted. For example, ports in Mexico and Canada remained open during this time.

That advanced planning paid off, because Toyota was able to move quickly to implement its initiatives to minimize the impact on North American plant operations. The availability of fast air transportation shortened the inventory pipeline and enabled plants to receive parts shipments during the time when the ports were closed. Those capabilities allowed plant velocity to be maintained at the highest level possible. Likewise, adjusting inventory in advance based on visibility of planned production provided effective temporary buffers. This example shows how Toyota compromised the "lean manufacturing" paradigm to manage during the crisis.

9/11 Terrorist Attacks

The terrorist attacks on September 11, 2001 (9/11) are an example of a major crisis that certainly was not predicted. Toyota as well as other automotive companies did not have any opportunity to do any advance planning for that event.

One of the immediate impacts to the supply chain was the heightened security measures implemented at all ports as well as the border crossings between the United States, Canada, and Mexico. Those increased security measures created an uncertainty for the delivery times for parts shipments coming into the United States, and there was not any indication of how long this slowdown would last. Another impact that would become apparent in a short time was the slowdown in vehicle sales because of the ensuing recession.

Toyota had to assemble a crisis team with members from all North American plants, North American sales companies, and TMC in Japan. Because of the nature of the crisis, Toyota had to take immediate action to temporarily stop production at its North American plants until an assessment could be made of the impact of the crisis. The following are some of the actions that were taken:

- Production schedules and rates were adjusted to react to the slower delivery of parts.
- Sales prioritized the production volume of each model based on the projected selling rate and dealer inventory.

- Logistics evaluated the impact on parts shipments of additional security checks at border crossings and ports. That effort required an adjustment of parts lead time schedules for some of its suppliers.

The adjusted system involved velocity changes to synchronize with deliveries, variety adjustment to prioritize parts use, and visibility across the system to enable rapid adjustments based on available parts.

Freescale Worldwide Capacity Issue

Freescale is a leading manufacturer of semiconductor chips that it supplies to the auto industry. During 2005, Freescale was unable to produce wafers at a high enough volume to provide an adequate supply of chips to the auto industry because of manufacturing problems at one of its plants in France. At that time, auto industry sales were at a peak and all auto companies were producing and selling vehicles at very high levels. Therefore, when the news hit that Freescale was not able to meet demand for an extended period of time, a worldwide auto crisis ensued. To make matters worse, the shortage situation was not one that could be resolved quickly; the problem would take several months to fix.

Toyota responded by assembling a crisis team that included sales and manufacturing groups in North America, Europe, and Japan. The following were some of the multiple parallel actions that were initiated:

- Establish daily communications with the crisis team.
- Dispatch a team to assist the plant in France that was the source of the problem.
- Assess the on-hand and pipeline inventory of all related parts.
- Pull ahead pipeline inventory when necessary to maintain plant operations by air shipping parts to shorten lead time.
- Allocate common parts to vehicles in highest demand and slow production of parts for slower-selling vehicles.
- Work closely with other auto manufacturers and Freescale to ensure that Freescale's production was allocated fairly to all auto companies.

Parts allocation based on variety with the highest demand enabled prioritization of production. Daily communications and visibility made possible optimal use of all available inventories. Use of air shipments permitted shortening of the pipeline, which provided greater physical inventory. Collaboration with the supplier brought about reduction of variability in yields and improved parts availability. Synchronization of production velocity with parts availability allowed plant production to continue and use the same principles as during normal operations.

Dealing with the Asian Financial Crisis[4,5,6,7]

Attracted by market opportunities in the Association of Southeast Asian Nations (ASEAN) region, Toyota had steadily increased production in Thailand in the 1990s. When the industry had hit a peak in 1996, Toyota had invested US$200 million in a new facility to increase production capacity from 120,000 units to 220,000 units a year.

As the financial crisis hit the region beginning in July 1997, auto sales in Thailand started to slump, ultimately falling 60 percent from 1997 to 1998. However, Toyota saw the long-term potential for the region, and instead of scaling back production like other manufacturers, it instituted several other changes to help sustain its operations in the region:

- *Shift to exports.* As local sales slumped, Toyota undertook a major restructuring of its operations to shift its Thailand production to exports. For example, Toyota Motor Thailand (TMT) increased exports of Hilux trucks to Australia from 600 in 1997 to 20,000 in 1998. To incorporate this shift, Hino, a Toyota-affiliated manufacturer in Japan, had to decrease its output of Hilux trucks by the same number and had to be compensated by an additional capital investment by Toyota. Vehicle specifications also had to be harmonized across several countries. In addition to vehicle exports, Toyota also began exporting diesel engines from Thailand to Japan.
- *Sustain suppliers and parts manufacturers.* To help parts suppliers through the decreased output levels, Toyota accepted price increases of 6 to 20 percent, which was contrary to its policy of continuous price reduction; the company also provided preshipment payments to help suppliers deal with the severe credit crunch. To absorb these costs, and also to provide financing to car buyers, the Japanese parent also supplied additional capital to the tune of 4 billion Thai baht to Toyota Motor Thailand.
- *Sustain the workforce.* Toyota did not lay off any of the workers, taking this time instead to retrain part of the workforce and send large teams to Japan to upgrade their skills. The number of employees was reduced to some extent through an early-retirement scheme, and jobs done by outside subcontractors were transferred in-house.

This long-term vision proved to be successful for Toyota, and today it dominates the Thai auto market, with a 2007 market share of 44.7 percent and leadership in both the car and commercial vehicle segments.

Prius Story

The development of the Prius provides an example of a remarkable "going to the moon" type event at Toyota. At the time that plans for the Prius were finalized, large cars were in vogue and gas was under $1 per gallon. Gas mileage was not a consideration for many people, and for those interested in the environment, riding a bicycle was thought to be a better thing to do than driving a car. It was in this environment that Toyota developed the Prius, a car designed to better the average mileage of an automobile by 50 percent. (The highest-mileage car at the time, the basic Corolla, had an average mileage of 30.8 miles per gallon.)

As Liker reports,[8] the team consisted of a general manager and his group of 10 middle managers who reported directly to a high-level committee of board members. The choice of a hybrid engine was significant because it had not (at the time) been proven on a mass production basis. As the project unfolded, the deadline shrank to less than one year to develop the hybrid engine and vehicle. At the time of this design goal, there was no plan regarding how this goal would be attained. The team was provided a time frame of two years to develop such a car. Long before this design decision, Toyota had been working to best leverage the use of information technology in enhancing car performance. A quote from a senior Toyota executive is appropriate: "Each time, a new business model changed the ground rules for the industry. Each time the new model seemed invincible. And each time, it gave way to changing circumstances and a new business model. . . . Our old business model is breaking down for four main reasons. One, we need to decentralize our manufacturing and R&D [research and development] activities. . . . Two, the product and process paradigms that Henry Ford established are themselves breaking down. . . . Three, information technology is transforming the inner workings of the automobile. It is also transforming the way we develop and make and sell our products. And four, the changing product paradigm and the growing role of information technology (IT) will open our industry to a vast array of competitors."[9]

Given such a long-ranging plan for the use of IT, it is not surprising that IT was used significantly to coordinate the development of a battery that would operate with an internal combustion engine. The challenge during the development of the Prius was the highly compressed time frame for the development of the car. All of the principal engineers worked eagerly to complete model development in 15 months. Some engineers were moved to a company dormitory to be away from distractions and devote them to the project. As the project evolved, over 1,000 engineers who were involved in the project left their families and moved into a dorm for about 18 months. Team members focused their entire energies on creating a product that conformed to the principles of the Toyota Way (described in further detail in Chapter 11) by enabling car technologies that were consistent with the booming demands of emerging markets. In the process, they created value for consumers and the society by generating environmental benefits.

Clearly, the development of the Prius was an internal crisis trigger that served to motivate the product development team to create a car with new technology in 15 months. But such pressures only serve to highlight the benefit of well-crafted processes and their success under testing circumstances.

Reflection Points

Crisis management at Toyota highlights how the v4L framework applies to many different situations. Learning and leadership are equally necessary to facilitate such execution. The following are links to the v4L framework:

- *Variety.* Careful balancing of the variety of products produced and the associated parts and capacity requirements, with available parts suppliers and in the pipeline, play an important role in maximizing the benefits and minimizing the corresponding impact on the system.
- *Velocity.* Synchronization of velocity across the supply chain is crucial to ensure that bottlenecks are avoided.
- *Variability.* Variability across the system is managed by insisting that new processes continue to follow accepted working processes so that quality and performance will not be compromised.
- *Visibility.* The role of managers in the system is both to create internal visibility to enable effective coordination and to provide an on-site presence to manage the problem. Also, a separate outside communications manager provides visibility to the outside world.

The learning methods of Toyota are certainly applicable to crisis management:

- *Create awareness.* Potential crises are identified by looking for patterns such as a bunch of shipments that are delayed or deterioration in supplier's financials.
- *Establish capability.* Toyota communicates both internally and externally to all interested parties so that they become aware of both the crisis management process as well as the steps taken to mitigate the impact of the crisis.
- *Make action protocols.* The process of crisis management is scripted and communicated to supply chain participants.
- *Generate system-level awareness.* Toyota selects the appropriate crisis owner and then discusses both short-term and long-term mitigation.
- *Produce the ability to teach.* Toyota's senior managers are able to articulate the crisis management steps clearly and provide examples to illustrate.

Endnotes

1. Interview with Gene Tabor, general manager of Toyota Purchasing, August 21, 2008.
2. T. Nishiguchi and A. Beaudet, "Self Organization and Clustered Control in the Toyota Group: Lessons from the Aisin Fire," MIT International Motor Vehicle Program, 1997.
3. "West Coast Port Shutdown Slowed Auto/Autoparts Production," *Autoparts Report*, October 18, 2002.
4. "Toyota Chief Sees Auto Crisis Reaching Bottom," *The Nation* (Thailand), October 8, 1998.
5. "Toyota Prepares Ground for Next-Century Blast," *The Nation* (Thailand), February 22, 1999.
6. "Japanese Direct Foreign Investment and the Asian Financial Crisis," *Geoforum*. 32, no. 1 (February 2001).
7. "Automakers Expect Rebound," *Bangkok Post*, January 18, 2008.
8. Jeffrey K. Liker, *The Toyota Way*. New York: McGraw-Hill, 2004.
9. H. Okuda, "When Ground Rules Change," speech at the Yale School of Management, 1998.

Chapter 11

The Toyota Way of Managing Supply Chains

he Toyota Way is made up of four major elements: long-term philosophy, right process, development of people, and continuous solving of root problems. Taken together, they are the secret recipe for continuous improvement, for creating value, and for developing people that will continue the mission of creating value into the future. In the paragraphs that follow, we will describe how these ideas are applied to supply chain management and how they manifest themselves in all chapters in this book. You might already be familiar with the components of the Toyota Production System. Writers such as Monden,[1] Liker,[2] and Suzaki,[3] as well as Toyota's own internal training documents, have explained in detail how the principles form a whole and consistent approach for running a manufacturing system. Moreover, they emphasize that the Toyota Way is not a collection of rules but a method for thinking about how systems work and evolve.

Our goal is not to restate these findings but to take them as given and explain how the Toyota Way applies to supply chain design and management. The focus is not limited to the production system; it also extends to the supply chain. One word of caution: when the authors initially inquired how Toyota manages its supply chain, we were greeted with bemused expressions. As we spoke with several people within and outside Toyota, the reason for that reaction became clear—Toyota considers itself part of the value chain. Therefore, asking company representatives how they manage the company's supply chain is like asking people how they manage the circulation to their feet.

As many people have said in the past, grand ideas by themselves do not make a Toyota. Even a casual observer will agree that Toyota did not arrive at the world markets all of a sudden but, as is common to many things that Toyota does, they arrived continuously over time. You only have to visit Toyota's Web site that describes its mission and also includes numerous statements over time[4] to obtain a sense of the continuous developments. Considering the fact that 30 million Corollas have been sold in more than 140 countries, it is still easy to identify the Corolla on the road in any part of the globe; however, it's hard to visualize all the design changes, supply chain reconfigurations, and channel changes that have accompanied the global expansion of the production of that sophisticated car since its introduction in Japan in 1966. On its Web site, Toyota attributes the success to "the evolving elements of the 'Corolla DNA,' which has been passed down from generation to generation within the Toyota Motor Corporation." The Corolla has indeed arrived over time.

As Toyota has globalized, the organization has felt it necessary to document the philosophy and goals that have enabled it to develop into the leader in manufacturing and supply chain management. The *Toyota Way* document (2001) was produced to keep the "Toyota DNA" strong as Toyota expanded globally. Similar documents were produced at Toyota Sales to record the history of the sales organization as well as to state the current understanding of the Toyota Way. Introducing the Toyota Way, Fujio Cho, president of Toyota Motor Corporation, said that Toyota is "preparing to operate as a truly global company guided by a common corporate culture." The booklet identifies the "company's fundamental DNA." Cho urges every Toyota team member to "take professional and personal responsibility for advancing the understanding and acceptance of the Toyota Way."

After we wrote several chapters and conducted interviews with managers who were familiar with the Toyota system and Toyota's supply chain, we saw that over and above simply using the ingredients of the Toyota Way the supply chain seemed to be capable of evolving and developing as challenges arose. Toyota manages to keep the supply chain focused on the tasks ahead, and they do so over a long period of time. We recapitulate the ideas used by Toyota in this regard from previous chapters. We also describe *Yokoten*—a method used to propagate best practices across the supply chain. We also compare the methods embedded in the Toyota Way to other planning, control, and process improvement methods that have been proposed and adopted by manufacturing and service organizations worldwide.

The ability to quickly identify problem patterns and solutions reminds us of a study by Herbert Simon and Jonathan Schaeffer[5] of ordinary chess players and grand masters. In their study, a feasible set of positions of 25 pieces on a chessboard were shown to ordinary chess players and grand masters for 5 to 10 seconds. Grand masters could replace more than 90 percent of the pieces correctly, while ordinary chess players replaced fewer than 30 percent. However, if the 25 pieces were placed randomly on the board, both groups could replace about 30 percent. In other words, when problems evolve following a pattern of moves, seasoned managers can identify issues rapidly and thus evolve solutions quickly. The Toyota Way, by emphasizing the use of specific problem-solving approaches, is designed to enable such pattern recognition and problem solving. One of the authors of this book, Roy Vasher, described a visit by a senior Toyota executive to a facility in Kentucky he had never visited before. Despite a long plane ride that preceded his trip, the man walked through the plant soon after his arrival and identified problems based on his prior experience. The ability to recognize patterns of evolution enabled him to get to the root causes of the problem rapidly.

The Essential Ingredients of the Toyota Way

The ingredients of the Toyota Way are unique and effective. To sequence their description, this chapter's layout follows Liker's approach. Examples specific to how Toyota applies these principles to managing its supply chain are drawn from previous chapters in this book. The trade-offs that are implicit in making these decisions are also illustrated.

Long-Term Philosophy

> We believe that our fundamental mission is to contribute to the economy and society through creating value, mainly by manufacturing high-quality products and providing related services.
> —Toyota Way document

The long-term philosophy of the Toyota Way is to create *value* for customers, suppliers, and the society.[6] That view is consistent with the idea of maximizing supply chain surplus. For example, we often hear that a firm should buy from a low-cost supplier and not from one whose price is low. A supplier who drops the price to gain business may not necessarily increase supply chain value. But, a low-cost supplier is always likely to increase supply chain value if demand is sufficiently inelastic. Chapter 7 revealed that instead of simply opting for a low-cost supplier, Toyota views *value* creation as a joint effort toward increasing supplier capabilities and reducing costs. Interviews with current Toyota managers David Burbidge, Gene Tabor, and Jamey Lykins reinforce the notion that Toyota's collaborative approach aims to solve problems and reduce costs and, thereby, prices. In Chapter 5, we saw that great emphasis is placed on heijunka. That chapter examined how Toyota keeps demand stable by using the 80/20 rule; these efforts help in the identification of problems and create value for all participants in the supply chain.

Likewise, we have heard and read about the pros and cons of price promotions. The famous case of Campbell's promoting chicken soup during the winter has made the rounds of every college and boardroom. By promoting demand just when it is high, the supply chain experiences a double dose of spike in demand: one due to natural factors and the other due to forward buys that are made to take advantage of the drop in price. Keeping prices steady certainly improves planning and efficiency. Data show that Toyota's promotion cost for cars is under $700 versus over $2,000 for other domestic manufacturers. Stable prices also permit a focus on increasing value as a way to sell the product. That idea is at the core of Toyota's philosophy, which goes beyond the average present-day corporation's goal of maximizing "short-term" profit (or the net present value at a steeply discounted rate). Instead of forswearing price promotions, Toyota attempts to increase *value* at the same price, thus forestalling competitive moves to grab market share. The trade-off is obvious once it is articulated. A low-cost strategy does not necessarily provide competitive edge into the future. However, accompanied by value-creating activities that are made possible by a stable system, the strategy continuously pushes the technology frontier out and keeps competition at bay.

Long-term philosophy goes beyond making profit. Value creation might provide the right focus. Supply chain planners need to consider how customer values might change over the next 10 to 15 years. The focus of Toyota on the development of hybrid vehicles and on green manufacturing is an example of long-term philosophy described in this book and elsewhere that at first glance seems to contradict the goal of profit maximization. The *Toyota Way* document states: "current trends are assessed in light of a long-range vision of as much as ten years."

Managers might wonder how to formulate such a problem in the profit maximization framework and how to make choices regarding the timeline of planning and what method to use for accumulating and comparing cash flows. What are the discount factors? How to evaluate the risk-return trade-offs? In an interview, Katsuaki Watanabe, Toyota's president, provides a rare insight into making the trade-offs.[7] Watanabe mentions the three keys to long-term health: improve product quality, keep reducing costs, and develop human resources. He explicitly mentions that "we have to create a stronger foundation at every stage of the supply chain."

Readers might pause and reflect that these principles are probably easy to focus upon in isolation but not in combination. Watanabe goes on to say that the focus of current investments in new products, new technology, and human resources is improving quality. Thus, an explicit prioritization is made. We have seen that in previous chapters too: customers first, dealers second, and the plant third. (As early as 1937, Kiichiro Toyoda, the founder of auto making at Toyota, set the price to dealers based on market price rather than cost. The *Toyota Way* document quotes: "The price for the dealer is to be 2,400 yen regardless of cost.") What does that prioritization do? Basically, Toyota makes the trade-offs obvious. If a firm's focus is on only one idea of self-interest, such as growth, that firm can neglect its supply chain obligations. Every Toyota manager realizes that the obligations do not go away; instead, they are ranked as subordinate goals. By specifying that Toyota's products will be among the top three products considered by every customer while making a purchasing decision, the planner is constrained to make choices that fit the long-term goal of creating value. The *Toyota Way* document includes this statement: "Prioritization: Priorities are established and resources concentrated for the greatest possible outcomes." It also urges decision making to focus on continuous improvement and optimization as a whole company overcoming barriers among functions and organizations.

As a final example of this thinking, we quote: "Toyota now stands at the threshold of unprecedented transition in the race for survival in the 21st century. We must be careful not to become complacent through our past achievements, but unite and take on the challenges of the new world."[8]

Right Process

The Toyota Way emphasizes having a good knowledge of the process before attempting to improve it. It insists on standardizing work. To many people, standardizing work in order to improve it often seems to be a contradiction, until one takes the teachings of W. Edwards Deming and Joseph M. Juran[9] into account. What is the purpose of standardization if the intent is to change the way work is done?

The statistical process control theory proposed by Juran states that every process has natural variations. It is impossible to try to control natural (i.e., truly random) variation, whereas it is important to look for variation that is systematic. Thus, a standard process is one that is in control, stable, and, if it has to be satisfactory, also capable of meeting the customer's requirements. Moreover, in order to determine whether improvements should be aimed at reducing the natural variation or the systematic causes, it is necessary to isolate the two sources of variation: random and systematic. The techniques and solutions required for dealing with each source of variation, random and systematic, are different. In the section on learning, we shall see that one of the pitfalls of fast learning is associating incorrect causes to effects because it leads to superstitious learning—that is, falsely associating success to irrelevant causes, such as touching one's nose before entering an office will lead to a good day at work.

Indeed, even the journey of feedback regarding this book from Toyota was transformed into a process by Nancy Banks, our liaison at Toyota. The first step that was necessary was for us to get a signed contract from the publisher so that Toyota could be sure we were serious about the book and had a detailed plan.

Next, we shared drafts of the overall details with potential managers before we met them. A visit to the plant was included in our trip so as to ground the academic authors of the book into plant realities. All interviews were exchanged with appropriate managers to ensure that their perspectives were reflected accurately. Finally, after style edits, the final copy was sent to Toyota for review. This process was designed to guarantee flow only if necessary, and managers contacted had specific roles that were directly related to chapter descriptions. In other words, the designed process had a goal of being efficient while maximizing our value creation writing this book.

The Toyota Way goes one step further. It proposes to design, plan, and execute processes so that variations and scope for improvement become evident. To this end, the definition of the right process is enlarged to include steps that we interpret using our v4L framework.

Managing Velocity Using Continuous Process Flow

By making the flow in the supply chain at the global level even and uniform to the most practical extent, the designers of the supply chain are able to detect systematic variations quickly. This detection is based on managing random variations using well-designed systems and processes that adjust to the random variations with small and permissible perturbations. Chapters 4 and 5 revealed how adjustments are made continuously as more accurate information becomes available. Possible adjustments are prioritized, with volume adjustments being the most difficult to make. Volume adjustments require overall consensus, whereas parts that are supplied from nearby sources can be adjusted within preset limits. So, if the mechanisms that have been prescribed to address variations fail to match demand and supply, then it is a signal that a systematic shift has occurred. The dealer interview describes how data regarding product volumes and appropriate sales stimulation are continuously shared between Toyota and dealers. The inbound logistics process describes how milk runs ensure pickup in small volumes from suppliers on a continuous basis. All of these processes ensure a flow view of the entire supply chain.

Managing Visibility Using a Pull System

The pull system is used to link successive production units together. Clearly, in a supply chain the role of a pull system is to match demand and supply by linking the flow of information to the flow of material. The extraordinary simplicity of having suppliers that are located in close proximity to the plant minimizes the need for coordinating activities at the operational level (but not at the planning level). The pull system is also Toyota's way of executing so that variations become visible. Let us take for example the famous seat supply case,[10] in which a supplier delivers seats to the assembly line. As cars leave the paint area, a signal is sent to the seat supplier that indicates the seat required. Seats are made in the order in which the signal is received and delivered by truck to the assembly line just-in-time for the seats to be put in place at the final assembly lines. In the normal course of things, a few seats might be damaged and a few might not fit the car. However, the case describes a situation in which not only do several cars wait in the "clinic area" following assembly for replacement seats but also no one seems to be aware of the seat problem. Has the pull system failed? One view is that the problems accumulate because of the pull system. Another, and our view, is that the pull system worked. It has revealed systematic problems that need to be addressed. One or more seats waiting is to be expected because of random variations. Several cars waiting for replacement seats is a sign that something has gone wrong.

But how does the supply chain benefit by forcing the seat supplier or a tire and wheel assembly supplier to produce with a pull system? It forces the supplier to standardize the process, to level production, and to make its own suppliers deliver in a smooth fashion. Thus, if a critical part holds up production, the Toyota engineers as well as the seat supplier become alerted to the problem early. The benefit of managing random variations using the capabilities built into the systems is that it allows for an early warning of truly systematic problems. Moreover, it brings to bear the expertise of the supply chain community to solve problems.

Managing Visibility Using Visual Controls

Visual controls have several purposes. The first is to make problems visible, thus enabling the team member to recognize variation and forcing a decision to be made within a given time. If the decision cannot be made by the team member, the case is deemed to be a special one and should be escalated. In a supply chain, as we have seen, it includes setting limits on the mix variations allowed and using visits to suppliers and dealers to understand their processes. Toyota Motor Corp. Chairman Fujio Cho recently extended the definition of going to see the problem to, "Have you seen it yourself?"[11] We have also described the practice of sending engineers to visit suppliers and dealerships. That customary action reveals the second purpose of visual controls, especially in a supply chain: to learn about different systems firsthand. One might wonder how much firsthand learning is necessary to manage supply chains. We shall address this issue in the section on The Theory of Learning. A third purpose of visual controls is to provide transparency to any observer regardless of function or ownership. The Toyota Way document states: "We share a common understanding of actual conditions by using visual controls."

Managing Visibility by Leveling the Workload

Heijunka—the leveling of the workload—serves many purposes. First, it is a prerequisite to having continuous flow and pull production. Second, at the supply chain level, it reduces artificial demand fluctuations, or the bullwhip effect. Third, it provides visibility into systematic changes such as shift in product mix or slowing of demand, and allows the planner to use rate-based planning techniques. It allows the match of production and sales rates (using the concept of takt time). Thus, heijunka along with mix planning are keys to maintaining a stable supply chain. As Chapter 3 revealed, a mix strategy does not mean that the same product mix needs to be produced and supplied to every dealer in the world. The supply chain allows each dealer and each region to focus on the 80 percent that sells the best. At the national and even the regional level, the variations accumulate and are accommodated through careful planning to fit the overall sales goals. Thus, what is produced is a much larger set than what is sold at the dealer. That is another wonderful example of allowing local (or random) variations and adapting to them at the central level, where the control is better and planning more precise. Moreover, heijunka when applied to sales trends provides a quicker signal of bigger and more difficult issues to manage, such as the recent drop in sales of Tundras and the upswing in demand of the Prius. Every supply chain manager, if asked which is more difficult to manage, mix or volume fluctuations, can use Toyota's principles to articulate the trade-off precisely.

In an interview, Katsuaki Watanabe gives yet another use of heijunka, namely, in managing risk. It is difficult to respond to global shifts in demand. How does one supply more cars to the hot market in China or trucks in the United States and at the same time practice heijunka? The Toyota solution is to use production capacity in Japan to smooth out production. How does that work? Suppose we make the following assumptions: There will always be ups and downs in individual global markets, but collectively, these fluctuations will tend to cancel each other out. However, in order to meet an upswing in China, it might not be possible to supply from the relatively slow U.S. market (for trucks) due to logistical problems as well as the tremendous effort required to retool the plant. Instead, a very flexible factory in Japan can be utilized to supply the upswings. Watanabe calls this concept "global-link production." The advantage is that all plants are used fully, demand is met, and flexibility is tested.

Managing Variability by Stopping the Line to Fix Problems

The virtues of stopping to fix problems are well known. In a supply chain, that method might not work the best. In the seat example above, it is not possible to stop the line to fix the problem each time a defective seat is noticed. Doing so will take too long and be too costly. Does that mean one gives up the principle? What exactly is the logic behind stopping to fix the problem? There are two concerns: (1) The link between cause and effect becomes attenuated the longer the corrective action is postponed. (Try an exercise in recall: go back and read the first hundred pages in this book; then try to recall what exactly you were reading prior to revisiting those 100 pages.) (2) Unless production or supply is halted, the problem is never given the priority it requires for a permanent solution to be found. The latter issue is more subtle. It is possible to record problems so that the information is not completely lost, which addresses the first concern. But how would one design a supply chain that focuses attention on the special causes that need to be addressed? How should causes of root problems be uncovered and eliminated permanently?

Watanabe provides an example of how to do so in a supply chain. Soon after he took over as president of the company, several quality problems arose. Engineers were instructed to find the root cause. The investigators found that the problems were due to either design defects or insufficient lead time. They decided to experiment thoroughly and test a large number of prototypes. In response, Watanabe states, "I will not allow the same problems to recur." He halted several projects just as workers do when they stop production.

When we visited the Toyota plant in Kentucky, we were told of another instance where this seemingly bullheaded persistence of eliminating defects prevailed. The problem was with the canopy of the Solara convertible; the first canopies delivered to Toyota had many quality defects. The supplier of the canopies had moved close to the plant and set up a facility to supply exclusively to Toyota. The root cause required several changes to the management style and practices of the supplier. A senior manager at the plant was told to work with the supplier exclusively until all root causes were eliminated. The manager worked for several months at the supplier plant before returning to Toyota.

Managers usually seem perplexed when we discuss the idea of finding permanent cures. In response, we tell them to find the most important cause for problems and address it. That effort requires a combination of the prioritization method (i.e., customer first, suppliers and dealers second, and factory last) as well as tools to uncover the systematic issues that need addressing. Moreover, it requires halting production once a threshold limit is exceeded, thus signaling a special case. The three have to be used in combination. The *Toyota Way* document provides guidance as "Focus on Concrete Proof/Exhaustive Due Diligence: Actions are undertaken only after thorough study and testing to determine what must be done."

Managing Variety Using Standardized Tasks

Most firms have realized the importance of standardizing tasks; however, the degree of standardization often stops at the tasks that directly relate to producing a product or, to a lesser extent, service. For example, how to machine a part is often documented at length simply because an industrial engineer and a stopwatch can achieve the desired end. But how does a worker load a truck? How are invoices filled? How are cars driven to the parking lot? In what sequence are lights switched on or off at a factory or office? How is food ordered for a meeting? People who work on projects are often frustrated by competing demands. How does one standardize their tasks? Help them prioritize?

The unfortunate problem is that 85 to 90 percent of the tasks in most supply chains are not performed according to a standard procedure. Many of these tasks involve repetitive activity such as loading and unloading trucks, moving material in and out of warehouses, scheduling a route for picking up parts, and scheduling deliveries to dealers. In various chapters we have described these activities. In order to standardize pickups, a determination would need to be made as to how many deliveries are necessary from each supplier. Then, the trucks would be routed so that those that have similar frequency are picked up together. Doing so would allow the operator to find the route and routine that works the best. The operator can then be tasked with improvement of the process.

Wherever task standardization is difficult, it is possible to standardize recording and reporting so that similar activities can be compared across multiple locations or with the same reference framework. Toyota uses reports on one side of a standard A3 sheet in the same format to record problems and solutions. For example, if a heavy load needs to be moved across one plant to another, it should be possible to quickly access how it was done previously or at a similar location.

Standardization also facilitates the transfer of successful practices across the supply chains. The *Toyota Way* document puts it like this: "Successful practices are adopted as standard and then transferred, spread, and entrenched in the organization to leverage their effect." Moreover, standardization facilitates coordination; for example, if there is a fire in the supplier's factory (see the description of the Aisin Seiki episode in Chapter 10), a rapid response to the crisis is possible. Solutions can be brought to bear quickly because there is familiarity with operations and operating systems.

Task standardization also enables senior managers to recognize issues well before they go out of control by matching evolving patterns, similar to the innate capacity of chess grand masters.

Managing Variety Using Reliable Tested Technology That Serves People and Processes

The planning and control systems we have described are simple but effective because they serve people and processes. Many of the planning systems used at

Toyota combine simplicity and visual controls into powerful tools. For example, new production lines are created virtually through use of ergonomic design in the workplace. The program can identify such issues as excessive bending, requirement of excessive force, and tools that cannot reach recesses. Spreadsheets that use color codes are utilized to plan the mix of cars to ship to different regions in Europe. Parts are associated with each car to be assembled in the precise sequence. Toyota is also not averse to using the most advanced technology if it serves people and processes. With the most recent technology, the car that leaves the paint line signals the seat producer.

This emphasis on serving people and processes does not preclude experimentation. Often design projects begin with several parallel paths until careful experimentation leads to pruning and convergence on the technology.[12]

Applying the Above Process Design Principles

When inventories accumulate in a supply chain at different stages, they make demand less visible and the reaction to changes slower than if there were less inventory. (This topic is covered in detail in Chapter 13.) Inventory might indicate a slow-moving product, defective items, problems with transportation, picking and packing bottlenecks, and the like. To keep products flowing requires a synchronized supply chain, with each stage and each player not only knowing what to do but also when and where to deliver. Handoffs must be made perfectly.

Now, imagine that the supply chain designer attempted to level out the flows to a large extent. Miraculously, many decisions that are difficult would become easier. For example, if the volume of shipments to a region were relatively stable, or the inbound transportation needs were relatively stable, then these activities could be conducted on a fixed schedule. Thus, visual controls can be used. It is possible to standardize tasks, such as where to stop, what to load first, where to unload, where to drop off documents, and whom to contact for a problem or suggestion. Real problems surface quickly, because deviations become visible. For example, if deliveries had to leave a warehouse within two hours and were color coded by the time of the day, then identifying and fixing problems would be easy. But in order to do that, the work flow would have to be stable and standard; otherwise, the manager would be firefighting to handle temporary surges with no permanent solution to the real problem, which is the demand surge (other than adding flexible capacity). Similarly, when a substantial degree of work is standardized, it is possible to use reliable and tested technology that serves your people and processes. Changes are easily evaluated. They can be studied in a controlled environment to see if the impact is substantial and then adopted into practice after being vetted by a team. The team itself is aware of many of the issues, even before studying the problem.

Consider, for example, the use of recyclable containers. Even though the concept is simple, it is hard to evaluate the costs in a nonstandard environment. But if every shipping quantity and frequency were known, if the loading and unloading methods were specified, and if the routing patterns of the trucks were well established, then one could figure out the optimal size of the containers, the required number of containers, the change in loading and unloading patterns, and the additional cost to ship back the containers. It is no wonder that Toyota implemented this idea smoothly and with visible improvements within a short span of time. Thus, reliable and tested technology does not mean it has to be "boring," "traditional," or "inferior"; rather, it clearly balances requirements in the system.

In an increasingly complex world Toyota has continuously adapted its processes to deal with complexity in a small but cumulative manner. One of the major innovations that supports these process innovations is the concept of a virtual supply chain. How does this process compare with the production planning techniques found in the literature? Consider first Materials Requirements Planning, or MRP. One of the drawbacks of MRP is that it does not include scheduling details that allow the planner to visualize how the system will work at a given point in time. Any manufacturing planning system that uses a "time bucket" that is greater than the rate at which operations take place requires an additional system to synchronize the flow of parts into each vehicle as it gets produced. Rate-based planning is also often inadequate for scheduling complex tasks because it fails to observe the discrete handoffs in scheduling. Thus, both MRP and rate-based planning methods miss out on certain details. However, Toyota's system that assigns parts to each car exactly in the required sequence combines the virtues of both systems. That illustration of visual controls is also an illustration of an innovation that combines the best of ideas available in supply chain management.

Developing Your People and Partners

At a very broad level, Toyota believes that continuous improvement and respect for people are at the core of its philosophy. Careful reading of the *Toyota Way* guidelines reveals what is meant by *respect*: respect for customers, respect for society, respect for suppliers and dealers, and respect for employees. The *Toyota Way* document puts it this way: "Our Company owes its existence to the support and satisfaction of customers, stockholders, employees, business partners and host societies who derive benefit from the added value Toyota provides. Our continued success depends on providing ever-greater satisfaction of customers by placing their interest ahead of all others."

Toyota commits to creating value for everyone. The commitment is genuine, based on numerous anecdotes and historical evidence. These commitments are as follows:

- *Time is to be used effectively.* "A person's life is an accumulation of time—just one hour is equivalent to a person's life. Employees provide their precious hours of life to the company, so we have to use it effectively; otherwise, we are wasting their life." (Eiji Toyoda, former chairman of the Toyota Motor Company)
- *The nature of relationships is long term.* For example, one of the authors asked why a particular joint venture in India gave only a 10 percent share to its local partner. The answer was that the partner was "terrific." The senior manager added that the local partner was expected to gradually earn enough to buy a larger share of the venture.
- *There is a commitment to make partnerships work.* (See, for example, the discussions in Chapter 7.) Among the many courses of action pursued by Toyota is dispatching senior managers for months to improve operations. The key issue is not just respect but also a commitment to create value for everyone.

Whether a relationship is transactional (one-time interaction) or relational (multiple interactions over time) depends to a great extent on respect. But that is not the only determinant; another is *improvement*, which counterbalances respect. Look at it this way: transactional relationships are like meetings between strangers in New York City who honk at each other from their cars. They exist and create friction. That very friction might make such relationships work well by making people cautious of venturing too close to another car. But when relationships happen over a long time, honking at the other person whom you know well (e.g., a coworker or fellow student) and whom you will meet every day is frowned upon. Relational partnerships cannot tolerate rudeness or disrespect; however, respect must be counterbalanced by demand for improvement and contribution to the joint venture. If it is not, the incentive to stay abreast of the system as well as the changes in the environment will go away.

This focus has yet another implication. Continuous improvement can be viewed as improving a person or an organization. The *Toyota Way* states: "We believe each individual has the creative power for the independent achievement of his or her personal goals. We respect the values, abilities, and way of thinking and motivation of all team members." The Father of the Toyota Production System, Taiichi Ohno[13] is quoted in the *Toyota Way* document as saying that "work is a contest of wit and wisdom with subordinates."

Employees at Toyota are asked to think as if they were two levels higher in the organization. Toyota prefers to give broad targets or vague instructions instead of rules. That approach is used, in our viewpoint, to inculcate the habit of assessing and setting one's own goals. That practice is fundamental to learning about how the system works. For example, asking a supplier to reduce the number of deliveries of water to an office might not lead to the most creative solution; a better approach would be to ask how to provide drinking water the best way.

Toyota uses five kinds of subjective criteria to evaluate managers. One of them emphasizes how results were obtained; others look at the trust and respect the manager has earned. Takeuchi, Osono, and Shimizu[14] suggest that the desired characteristics include willingness to listen and learn from others, enthusiasm for making continuous improvements, comfort with working in teams, ability to quickly solve a problem, interest in coaching other employees, and modesty. Clearly, these are not only fuzzy criteria but somewhat contradictory because quick solutions to problems do not seem consistent with modesty and a willingness to listen and learn. They provide great scope for developing people.

The system aims to develop exceptional people and teams, who will follow the philosophy and understand the system, by challenging them and helping them improve, both within Toyota and also in the extended network of partners and suppliers. Toyota uses many methods for helping its suppliers understand and adopt the company's way (see Chapter 7). In two fascinating articles, Ward and others and Tae-Hoon[15] describe the different levels of relationships that Toyota has with different suppliers. Those relationships range from suppliers that are given almost complete design freedom to suppliers who are given the entire design by Toyota. No matter which relationship is utilized, once the design is finalized, the production processes always seem to follow the more rigidly crafted Toyota Way principles.

How does one interpret that approach? We can use the framework developed above: different suppliers might have attained different levels of understanding of Toyota's system. That provides a different way of viewing strategic sourcing. Strategic sourcing (or supplier scorecards) is a term used to signify two aspects of sourcing:

1. Enormous effort is invested prior to selection of a supplier, but unless the same level of effort (or more) is maintained, the supplier tends to slacken.
2. It is impossible to maintain the same level of communication and relationship with all suppliers—some might be more important than others, from a strategic consideration viewpoint.

A third consideration based on the Toyota Way might be the degree of familiarity that a supplier has with both the buyer's and the seller's organization and organizational processes. Thus, the knowledge and stage of development of the supplier is another consideration, strategic or not.

Womack[16] in his weekly e-mails shares some aspect or other about lean production. His recent e-mail provided the following anecdote: "Many years ago, when I first visited Toyota in Japan, I had dinner with the purchasing director and asked how he could be sure that Toyota was getting good performance from its suppliers when only two suppliers were employed for a given category of need and when Toyota relied on target pricing rather than supplier bids. 'How,' I asked, 'do you know you aren't getting ripped off?' After an incredulous look, he answered, 'Because I know everything—every aspect of every value-creating process—running from raw materials at suppliers through Toyota's operations. That's my job.'"

Continuously Solving the Root Causes

How does continuous improvement take place in a supply chain? In our view, continuous improvement is learning and implementing the lessons learned; thus, much of what has been written about continuous improvement can be subsumed into the broader context of organizational learning. As we shall demonstrate, many of the methods used by Toyota in its effort to make continuous improvement happen are grounded strongly in theory.

The *Toyota Way* document states: "Learning is a continuous, company-wide process as superiors motivate and train subordinates; predecessors do the same for successors; and the team members at all levels share knowledge with one another. Every team member should be motivated to learn for his or her own development."

The Theory of Learning

Huber[17] writes about four learning-related constructs: knowledge acquisition, information distribution, information interpretation, and organizational memory. The reader can clearly identify how Toyota institutionalizes learning along each of these constructs from the following:

Spear[18] describes the gradual induction of a manager into the Toyota Way of experimentation and continuous improvement. The manager is gradually led into learning the workings of the system through direct observation (knowledge acquisition). Spear also recounts that the trainer concluded the training by having the manager present his findings to the plant manager, the shop manager, and group leaders. "Two-thirds of the audience actively took notes," noted Spear (information distribution). Thus, sometimes direct observation is substituted with structured formal presentations. Then the trainer taught the manager how to structure experiments with a carefully reasoned hypothesis; for example, if this change were made, it would change cycle time by six seconds. The objective of this exercise was as much to improve the system as to learn the workings of the system. Is the cause-effect relationship clear? Are there important variables we have forgotten to take into account? The next lesson was to make small incremental changes. Once again, the purpose of this cautious but exploratory approach is to minimize the risk of overlooking some aspect and learning about the system before moving to the next step (information interpretation). Finally, during the entire training the student was guided but never given direct answers. Toyota deploys coaches over a long period of time who are not only the repository of the lessons learned but also the chief conduits for passing them on to the next generation of managers (organizational memory).

In addition, theory emphasizes the role of communication and the implications of the learning rate as described below.

The Role of Communication

For a giant organization such as Toyota, communication is critical in order to learn. The structure of Toyota is very complex. Its informal information system mirrors that complexity. Takeuchi, Osono, and Shimizu[19] write that information flows freely up and down and across the hierarchy. Employees are urged to "listen intently in an open environment." Senior salespeople share information with dealers and learn from dealers by talking to them. Toyota's word for lateral communication is *yokoten*. Yokoten means "open out sideways." Toyota has a global strategy to ensure yokoten. They have a matrix organization structure to ensure that processes are standardized by the functional area. The management for each affiliate is responsible for day-to-day operations, but the functional management is responsible for yokoten of processes. Figure 11-1 illustrates the structure. This is the "Guiding Hand" concept used by Toyota to spread the best supply chain practices not only to the parts of the supply chain internal to Toyota but also to dealers, suppliers, and contractors. The spread of practices is coordinated top-down. Herbert Simon[20] writes that "an important component of organizational learning is internal learning—that is, transmission of information from one organizational member to another. Individual learning is very much a social, not a solitary, phenomenon." Takeuchi, Osono, and Shimizu[21] list ways that communications are reinforced and employees and supply chain partners are kept informed. They include giving freedom to people to voice contrary opinions, having frequent face-to-face interactions, and making tacit knowledge explicit.

Learning Rate Implications

A classic problem studied by researchers from many fields is how firms allocate resources to the exploration of new possibilities versus the exploitation of known

Global Region >>>>>	Japan						North America						Europe					
Affiliate >>>>> / Function	WHQ	S&M	R&D	Plant 1	Plant 2	Plant 3	S&M	R&D	MHQ	Plant 1	Plant 2	Plant 3	S&M	R&D	MHQ	Plant 1	Plant 2	Plant 3
Plant Engineering	●			○	○	○			◐	○	○	○			◐	○	○	○
Production Control	●			○	○	○			◐	○	○	○			◐	○	○	○
Logistics	●			○	○	○			◐	○	○	○			◐	○	○	○
Quality	●			○	○	○			◐	○	○	○			◐	○	○	○
Information Systems	●			○	○	○			◐	○	○	○			◐	○	○	○
Accounting/Finance	●			○	○	○			◐	○	○	○			◐	○	○	○
Purchasing	●			○	○	○			◐						◐			
Marketing/Sales	●						◐						◐					
Distribution	●			○	○	○	◐			○	○	○	◐			○	○	○
Product Planning	●						◐						◐					
Design	●							◐						◐				
R&D	●							◐						◐				
Etc.	●																	

● Global Functional Leader

◐ Regional Functional Leader/Collaborator

○ Implementer

GHQ   Global Headquarters
MHQ   Manufacturing Headquarters
M&S   Marketing & Sales
R&D   Research & Design

Figure 11-1 Yokoten to ensure processes standardized according to function

certainties. The returns of exploration are more long term, uncertain, and therefore risky. As March[22] puts it: what is good in the long term is not always good in the short term. What is good for one part of an organization is not always good for another part of the organization (or the whole organization), and what is good for an organization is not always good for the society. "As organizations learn from experience, this distribution of consequences across time and space affects the lessons learned," says March. If distances are smaller, feedback is quicker. Thus, experiments that are more local and about the near term provide feedback quickly and tend to reinforce the "local" aspect of learning. Because of these differences, organizations that learn through feedback gained from experimentation and sharing knowledge of outcomes (or adaptive processes) tend to improve exploitation rather than exploration. As organizations specialize and become more and more competent at exploitation, they tend to stay with what they do best. Thus, organizations might gain competence in inferior activities at the expense of not switching to a superior activity. This effect is passed on to other firms with whom the firm interacts. There is also the effect of excessive specialization. Specifically, in the models proposed by researchers, agents are "trapped by immediate positive feedback from competence within a rather narrow domain."[23] For these reasons, March posits that organizations might want to control learning, and he suggests some ways of doing so.

For example, slow learning might preserve sufficient diversity among employees, thereby preserving exploration until convergence of ideas occur. Slow learning also avoids false association of causes to events (in the theory of learning, that is called "superstitious learning for obvious reasons"). In many places, we see the emphasis on slow learning in Toyota's supply chain. March also suggests that a modest amount of turnover preserves the heterogeneity until new employees are socialized into the organization and provided with the impetus for exploration. Too little turnover leads to greater homogeneity and less deviation from the "norm," whereas substantial turnover dissipates learning. Toyota provides "turnover" by rotating its employees through a variety of tasks.

Even though a modest amount of turnover is good, rapid socialization reduces the impact of new thinkers on the organization. Therefore, employees should be brought up to speed slowly. At Toyota, even suppliers and dealers are brought up to speed and attain full partnership slowly. Simon writes that "tasks of management are quite different in organizations that can recruit employees who are pre-fashioned, so to speak, than they are in organizations that wish to create and maintain, along some dimensions, idiosyncratic subcultures." If the idiosyncratic aspect we wish to create is "systems thinking," then Toyota's management has a formidable task. If it is protecting the bastion, then bureaucratic training might be necessary. If anyone can step in and do the job, then a mass production approach with limited on-the-job training might suffice.

Nevertheless, Toyota faces the risk of excessive exploitation by its supply chain partners and thus has to inculcate similar thinking into each of its partners. That fact might explain the "vague" instructions given to its partners. For example, Toyota might ask a supplier to "explore the range of improvement possible." Let us say the possible improvement is a 20 to 30 percent reduction in weight. The supplier might come back and present what it has learned about the design and what can be achieved. The target is then gradually narrowed down. As a general manager has said: "This process allows the (user) to understand trade-offs and set targets to produce the best possible design."[24] In universities, we train our Ph.D. students in a similar fashion. We give them vague targets, such as, "See what this assumption does" or "Can you relax this?" or even, "You may have forgotten something." Many times, the student comes back and suggests, "You said, 'Try doing this,' but I found something else"—we are looking for such opportunities to learn.

Herbert Simon[25] elaborates that in some cases research ideas get constrained by the market and customers; in other cases the needs of the customers are well known and the flow of ideas is in the opposite direction. In the former case, research can be facilitated by setting goals that have an element of exploration in them and by getting feedback on the results, both anticipated and otherwise. Simon acknowledges that for such transfer of ideas to occur, disparate groups need to respect one another's skills, understand the others' problems, and actually have experienced, in sufficient numbers, the other groups' activities and processes. For example, in a recent client engagement, one of the authors had the opportunity to work with a team member who had worked for several years with the client in many of the client's businesses. The person could be reliably counted upon to draw upon his experience and write down a business process in 85 percent of its detail. We realized that the remaining 15 percent could be had only by observing the processes at work! People were using rules written and unwritten to make decisions. Only by asking them for daily feedback based on our replication of their work were we able to uncover another 14 percent of the rules. The last 1 percent still eludes us.

The Practice of Learning

Learning requires optimism and the spirit to take up challenges. The *Toyota Way* document states that: "We accept the challenges with a creative spirit and the courage to realize our own dreams without losing drive or energy. We approach our work vigorously, with optimism and a sincere belief in the value of our contribution." It challenges its supply chain partners in a similar way and expects to be challenged by them.

Toyota provides a system where thinking pervades the organization. Moreover, Toyota has spread these ideas throughout its supply chain in its leadership role. Its approach to learning conforms to the theory of learning that has been referenced in this book and can be described as follows:

- *Create awareness.* Unless problems are seen, they will not be solved. The effort at raising awareness involves systems to report ideas, problems, deviations, and potential issues to one's direct contact with no delay.
- *Establish capability.* Unless a person is capable of solving a problem that might arise within the system boundaries set for him or her, that person will be unable to contribute to solving the problem or for recognizing the need for specialized help.
- *Make action protocols.* Actions have to be taken within a set of constraints and conform to certain standards. Doing so will help in the identification of the relationship between action and results. It will help codify the knowledge for future use. It will help to engender communication using the same language, format, and similar content.
- *Generate system-level awareness.* As more and more experience is obtained at solving problems, greater awareness needs to be instilled about other areas that might be affected or that might impact one's own performance.
- *Produce the ability to teach.* As more and more system-level awareness and experience accumulates, the capability to teach others about these methods needs to be created.

The practicality of Toyota's approach to learning is not only in establishing rules but also in translating thoughts to action. Managers at Toyota are taught that problems by themselves are frustrating unless people are shown a way to solve them. The problem must be well defined, the goals measurable, and the problem solvable in a given time with given resources. Likewise, learning should be accomplished systematically. That part of the Toyota Way emphasizes the practicality of making learning possible. Only by experimenting and scientifically understanding the dynamics involved can one master the supply chain.

In addition to learning through experimentation, Toyota learns vicariously, using secondhand sources and anything else it can lay its hands on. The *Toyota Way* document states, "We search for outstanding ideas inside the company and in the larger business community, regardless of their authorship, and investigate them thoroughly. Benchmarking is used to measure Toyota's accomplishments against those of other leading companies." And: "We continue to search for breakthroughs, refusing to be restrained by precedent or taboo."

Toyota realizes that mastering thinking for the long term is important. How does one accomplish goal setting in the long run? It is easy to have small successes if learning and problem solving as described previously are accomplished; however, it is very difficult to measure success and failure in the long run. Even if an overall direction is available, the goals might seem far away and irrelevant unless these ideas are applied over the long run. That keeps the focus on creating value and moves attention away from action to planning. Once a "long-term" problem has been identified, all the steps mentioned previously should be used to ensure that employees remain targeted and motivated. Therefore, it is important to break up the goal into targets.[26] Make it specific. Make people capable. Take action systematically. Think systemwide after each step. Pass on the learning. Make sure that each target is achievable with the available resources within the allowed time. For example, productivity improvement is a long-run goal. Simply exhorting employees to be more productive not only does not lead to results but it also results in frustration. Asking managers to reduce costs or improve productivity is too general a directive. The Toyota method emphasizes that targets be as specific as possible. If the manager or worker cannot control cost, then the endeavor will not be motivating. Therefore, the target has to be meaningful and focused. With regard to productivity, Toyota has many long-term goals. For example, Toyota sets a measure of hours of labor per car. A potential target would be: make labor per car 5 percent better.

Internal competition is used to set standards and compare achievable improvements. The target is made more specific by classifying labor into different categories: (1) labor actually making the product, (2) labor team leaders (supervisory), (3) maintenance, (4) accountants and purchasing, and so on. Different targets are set for different classifications.

Coordination and Lean

Going back 20 years, the national bestseller *The Machine that Changed the World: The Story of Lean Production* by Womack, Jones, and Roos devotes three chapters to supply chain coordination, dealing with customers, and managing the lean enterprise. The main ideas in these chapters have been translated into action in the Toyota supply chain setting. It is worth recapitulating the key difference between lean and mass production approaches to dealing with these three issues. "Don't be fooled into thinking that Western suppliers have been moving toward lean supply. They have not.... Indeed, without a fundamental shift away from a power-based bargaining relationship, it is almost impossible to move toward lean supply." In an almost fatalistic statement, the authors conclude the chapter on supply chain coordination with, "How can the Western post-mass-production supply system move toward true lean supply? We suspect that the key means will be the creation of lean-supply systems in the West by the Japanese producers."

In the chapter on customer relationships, they write that coordination is essential even in distribution. Thus, lean manufacturing by taking away the luxury of excess enforces careful planning to coordinate every activity. The present-day efforts toward customer relationship management seem to reflect these concerns.

In the last of three prophetic chapters, Womack, Jones, and Roos write about the emergence of the global enterprise. They note that Toyota trailed Honda and Ford. Today, Toyota's global presence rivals that of these firms. It seems to us that the principles of the lean production system underlie a great amount of the success of Toyota and other firms that have adopted them. Nevertheless, people are at the core of achieving these successes. As support to these ideas, we summarize below an e-mail from the chairman of the Lean Enterprise Institute (LEI) to all subscribers:

> *Many firms have introduced lean tools, starting with value stream mapping, then attending conferences and performing experiments on lean. We do not mean that the rules are meaningless or that if they are practiced to less than perfection, the results will be a disaster. As an example, look at the Lean Enterprise Institute (www.lean.org) that has advocated lean thinking for over a decade. Their "Five steps of lean implementation" are as follows: "specify value, map the value stream, and make the remaining steps flow, let the customer pull, and then pursue perfection relentlessly." Many organizations have adopted some (or most) of these steps. For example, according to a survey by Industry Week/Manufacturing Performance Institute 2007 Census of Manufacturers, 17.8 percent say continuous improvement programs led to a major increase in productivity and 67.2 percent report some increase.[27]*

As John Kerr wrote in his summary of Lean: "Despite the difficulty of implementing a lean system, companies have begun to consider it as a process-improvement tool, not just for manufacturing, but also for everything from transportation management to accounting. The beauty of the lean philosophy is that it focuses everyone on what matters, which is what the customer needs. This means that everything else is seen as non-essential and therefore as a cost that can be taken out, whether it is buffer stock or a business process that requires multiple manual sign-offs."[28] Despite the tremendous gains to be had, he cautions that several experts consider the PDCA cycle to be the hardest to follow because it is people intensive. He also suggests that lean production can be adopted by any manager.

Conclusion

Liker in his book on the Toyota Way summarizes at the very end the choice that managers have to make when deciding whether to treat the process management ideas of the Toyota Way as a toolkit or to adopt the Toyota Way to transform the organization into a learning enterprise. He frames the question on whether the focus is toward short-term success or long-term building of a top-notch learning organization.

Somewhere in this debate it seems the humble beginnings of the Toyota Way have been forgotten. Taiichi Ohno started with changes on the shop floor and they spread outward to the rest of the organization and outside it. For example, in the initial stages, Liker writes that Toyota did not have the bargaining power to convince suppliers to do things its way. All Toyota could offer was the opportunity to "grow together and mutually benefit in the long term." Even when Toyota became powerful it did not forget these beginnings. It views new supply chain partners cautiously. Matching value and commitment is essential before the supplier, dealer, designer, or contractor is taken into the family. Despite this caution, it has managed to grow. Despite the focus on the details, the Toyota supply chain functions as a single entity with a common purpose. Despite the long haul, it continues to produce superb supply chain players.

The sustained learning, growth, and adaptation of Toyota never cease to amaze bystanders. The Toyota Way is a small description of Toyota's endeavors to create a world-class organization. Our description of it is an even smaller small subset. We have tried to set out what we have learned by following its ways, albeit incompletely.

Endnotes

1. Yasuhiro Monden, *Toyota Production System: An Integrated Approach to Just-In-Time*, 3rd ed. Atlanta: Engineering & Management Press, 1998.
2. Jeffrey K. Liker, *The Toyota Way*. New York: McGraw-Hill, 2004.
3. Kiyoshi Suzaki, *The New Manufacturing Challenge: Techniques for Continuous Improvement*. New York: The Free Press, 1987.
4. www.toyota.co.jp/en/vision/message/index.html.
5. Herbert Simon and Jonathan Schaeffer, "The Game of Chess," in R. J. Aumann and S. Hart, eds., *Handbook of Game Theory*, vol. 1. New York: Elsevier Science, 1992.
6. See, for example, the statement of the corporate philosophy on Toyota's Web site: www.toyota.co.jp/en/vision/philosophy/index.html.
7. "Lessons from Toyota's Long Drive: An Interview with Katsuaki Watanabe," *Harvard Business Review* 85, no. 4 (July–August 2007): 1–10.
8. Words of Hiroshi Okuda, as reported in the *Toyota Way* document, speaking in December 1995 after being appointed president in the summer of 1995.
9. Dr. Deming and Dr. Juran were the foremost leaders in the quality movement during the last century. Both of them contributed significantly to Japan's emergence as a world-class manufacturing nation.

10. Kazuhiro Mishina, *Toyota Motor Manufacturing, U.S.A., Inc.* Boston: Harvard Business School Publishing, 1992.

11. Hirotaka Takeuchi, Emi Osono, and Norihiko Shimizu, "The Contradictions that Drive Toyota's Success," *Harvard Business Review* 86, no. 6, (June 2008): 96–104.

12. Allen Ward, Jeffrey K. Liker, John J. Cristiano, and Durward K. Sobek II, "The Second Toyota Paradox: How Delaying Decisions Can Make Better Cars Faster," *Sloan Management Review*, Spring 1995, 43–61. See also Park Rae-Hoon, "Hierarchical Structures and Competitive Strategies in Car Development: Inter-organizational Relationships with Toyota's First-, Second- and Third-Tier Suppliers," *Asian Business & Management* 6 (2007): 179–198, for the choice between postponement and speculation strategies.

13. Taiichi Ohno was an employee of Toyota. He wrote several bestselling books about the Toyota Production System.

14. Hirotaka Takeuchi, Emi Osono, and Norihiko Shimizu, "The Contradictions that Drive Toyota's Success."

15. Allen Ward, Jeffrey K. Liker, John J. Cristiano, and Durward K. Sobek II, "The Second Toyota Paradox: How Delaying Decisions Can Make Better Cars Faster," *Sloan Management Review*, Spring 1995: 43–61; and Park Tae-Hoon, "Hierarchical Structures and Competitive Strategies in Car Development: Inter-Organizational Relationships with Toyota's First-, Second- and Third-Tier Suppliers," *Asian Business & Management* 6 (2007): 179–198.

16. James P. Womack is the chairman and founder of the Lean Enterprise Institute. He is a coauthor of the bestseller *The Machine That Changed the World*," along with Daniel T. Jones and Daniel Roos. Boston: MIT Press, 1991.

17. George P. Huber, "Organizational Learning: The Contributing Processes and the Literatures," *Organization Science* 2 (1991): 88–115.

18. Steven J. Spear, "Learning to Lead at Toyota," *Harvard Business Review* 82, no. 5 (May 2004): 78–86, 151.

19. Hirotaka Takeuchi, Emi Osono, and Norihiko Shimizu, "The Contradictions that Drive Toyota's Success."

20. Herbert A. Simon, "Bounded Rationality and Organizational Learning," *Organization Science* 2, no. 1 (1991): 125–134.

21. Hirotaka Takeuchi, Emi Osono, and Norihiko Shimizu, "The Contradictions that Drive Toyota's Success."

22. J. G. March, "Exploration and Exploitation in Organizational Learning," *Management Science* 2, no. 1 (1991): 71–87.

23. D. A. Levinthal and J. G. March (1993), "The Myopia of Learning," *Strategic Management Journal* 14 (1993): 95–112.

24. Ward et al., "The Second Toyota Paradox."
25. Herbert A. Simon, "Bounded Rationality and Organizational Learning."
26. Christina Fang and Daniel Levinthal, "The Near-Term Liability of Exploitation: Exploration and Exploitation in Multi-Stage Problems," working paper, Stern School of Business, New York University, NY, 2007.
27. Jonathan Katz, "By the Numbers: Of All Firms Responding to the IW/MPI Census of U.S. Manufacturers," *IndustryWeek*, December 1, 2007, www.industryweek.com/ReadArticle.aspx?ArticleID=15327&SectionID=10.
28. John Kerr, "What Does 'Lean' Really Mean?" *Logistics Management*, May 1, 2006, www.logisticsmgmt.com/article/CA6334579.html.

Chapter 12

How to Apply Toyota Way Principles to Nonautomotive Supply Chains

The underlying principles associated with managing variety, velocity, and variability across the supply chain—the focus of Toyota's supply chain leadership and management process—are found in many different industrial contexts. We provide several examples from service industries such as health care, insurance, banking, credit processing, and retailing. Products and services covered include apparel, wine, brake linings, emerging market product development, concrete delivery, and more. In each of these cases, a supply chain leadership strategy delivered superior performance. If you are fired up and eager to develop your individual industry application using the Toyota supply chain principles, this chapter offers several different application prototypes.

Banking Example

Goland, Hall, and Clifford[1] provide a description of how the application of Toyota principles to banking can yield significant results. They describe the back-office check processing operations for a bank that faced capacity shortfalls and demands for added capacity to process checks. A couple of managers decided to follow the "Journey of Chuck the Check" by mapping the steps involved in processing checks at the bank. What they discovered was astounding. More than 45 percent of the time, the check processing machines sat idle. Though checks could be sent for processing two times a day, most banks accumulated checks and sent them in at the end of the day. Even when processing, the machines were subject to breakdowns, and checks had to be processed more than once.

Clearly, the process was not streamlined, and the capacity issues observed reflected deeper underlying problems. The managers then went back to the banks and worked to streamline the procedure of separating checks in batches before they were sent for processing. Checks that needed additional time at the bank before they were sent were kept until the evening, while others were shipped out earlier in the day. This smoothing of flows permitted the arrival of checks to the sorting facility to be better synchronized with capacity demands. Next, the bottleneck: check sorting equipment and its operation were examined and provided with additional resources to ensure its availability during peak demand periods.

The impact was faster check processing and lower capacity utilization, thus providing additional capacity to provide check processing capacity for other banks. What was a source of problems due to capacity-related congestion was not only improved with regard to service, but it was also converted to a revenue opportunity. Continuous improvement in this context would include examining the process to identify sources of waste and scope for increasing value to customers. Such process changes can lead to learning more about customer needs and supplier technologies leading to further cycles of PDCA.

Hospital Example

Mango and Shapiro[2] provide an application of Toyota supply chain principles to a cardiothoracic facility. Demand at the facility directly related to arrivals of patients for service. Capacity referred to the number of operating rooms or beds available for a step in the process. Time to complete a step varied based on patient- and doctor-related variables. The facility had frequently become a bottleneck, with patients kept waiting for surgery.

The typical process for a patient at the cardiothoracic facility involved: going to the operating room, then sometimes to the surgical anesthesia intensive care unit or the cardiothoracic intensive care unit, followed by a step-down unit, then to a general unit, and discharge. The system discharged about five patients per day, and demand exceeded capacity about 30 percent of the time.

A closer examination of the system showed that the time for surgery varied between 283 and 368 minutes, but when separated by surgeon, the time became quite predictable. Thus, rather than build in variability as buffer time, the system scheduled the right amount of time based on a surgeon's characteristics. Such a planning approach increased utilization and kept appointments on track.

The next variability observed was large demand surgeries on Fridays. A closer examination showed that many people who developed chest pains over the weekend went to see their primary care physician on Mondays or Tuesdays and arrived at labs for testing a couple of days later. Thus, Fridays became a bottleneck for operating rooms. The hospital decided to examine patients and prioritize surgeries based on the type of blockage. That step spread out the demand for operating rooms over the whole week. Finally, when a surgery was completed, the hospital created SWAT teams to clean and sterilize the operating room to return it to use.

The net effect was a streamlined facility with smoothed flow, reduced variability for surgery times, and quick turnaround of bottleneck operating room resources. Indeed, all of the elements of a Toyota supply chain thought process are illustrated in this example.

Continuous improvement might address further reduction in waste of patient and surgeon times, scheduling follow-ups and obtaining feedback, and the like. That step would in time create opportunities to kaizen supplier operations, service provider operations, and technology introduction.

IBM Credit

Hammer and Champy[3] provide a classic example of how changing the process can improve performance. The example concerns the credit division of IBM. This department was used by IBM salespeople to offer credit terms to businesses that agreed to purchase IBM software or hardware.

The original system consisted of a series of steps. First, orders were taken over the phone by customer service representatives. Those orders were passed along to a business department that focused on loan covenants based on business contexts. That step was followed by a credit check. The next department determined pricing. Finally, an administrator generated a letter providing all details and pulled together all related paperwork. That material was then express-shipped to the salesperson. The average lead time for the entire process, from start to completion, was eight days, but the observed time took as long as two weeks.

A couple of senior managers at IBM Credit decided to personally walk a credit request across all departments and discovered that the actual processing time was 90 minutes, while the lead time (as mentioned earlier) was as long as two weeks. The source of all of the delays was the batch and queue mode of operation, as each transaction waited at a step until its cohort batch of orders was processed, and then waited in line to start the next step.

A closer examination of the process showed that about 20 percent of the task types accounted for 80 percent of the volume. A careful standardization of the process for the 20 percent converted the steps into a menu-driven system that could be completely managed by one person. These generalists thus took a credit request from start to finish for 20 percent of the standard credit requests. Of course, standard rates for such requests may have potentially increased the risk of bad debts. The remaining 80 percent of requests that accounted for

20 percent of the volume were still handled by specialists. The net result of such a triage mode of operation was to increase the volume of credit requests handled by a factor of 100 (100 × old volume) while decreasing head count slightly. Clearly, redefining processes, changing work allocation, and standardizing tasks significantly increased delivered performance.

Kaizen would probably start with continuous appraisal of client needs, creation of a database to understand failures and long delays, further training in procedures, and the creation of teams to identify and solve problems.

Ford Accounts Payable

Another example from the book by Hammer and Champy describes changes in the accounts payable process at Ford Motor Co. Ford's accounts payable department had 500 employees handling transactions. Their task involved reconciling three documents: the purchase order, the receiving document, and the invoice.

In an attempt to streamline this department, Ford examined the accounts payable operation of a partner company, Mazda. Mazda operated its accounts payable department with five people. This stark contrast, despite company size differences, suggested a need to redefine the process to reduce overhead.

The first step was to change the way product was received. All open purchase orders were included in a computer system. All receipts were against these open purchase orders only. Thus, reconciliation of the receiving document and the purchase order was completed on receipt. Given this reconciliation, payment was scheduled as per the predetermined terms. This one change in the process reduced tasks for the accounts payable department significantly. In one section (engine components) the size of the staff decreased by over 80 percent.

The next change was to replace purchase orders with supplier-certified blanket purchase orders and vendor-managed inventory arrangements. Under this scheme, as parts are used in assembly, they are replenished and vendor payments are scheduled. The net effect is to eliminate reconciliation of the purchase order and receiving document with the invoice. Because this reconciliation is done upon usage of components, the role of accounts payable changed to enable supplier monitoring and certification.

All of these changes synchronized steps across the supply chain and thus reduced the need for the overhead at accounts payable. That synchronicity decreased capacity, increased efficiency, and thus improved overall performance.

Could the system be improved even further? Could suppliers be coaxed to take payments when cars are sold with their components? Under such an agreement, how would supplier designs change and what information would need to be shared with suppliers? How would marketing campaigns have to be managed to take into account supplier and OEM interests? Notice that all of these issues deal with continuous improvement in a synchronized supply chain.

The 7-Eleven Japan Story

With sales of over $21 billion in Japan and inventory turns of over 55 along with greater than 30 percent gross margins, management of 7-Eleven Japan's supply chain,[4] covering over 9,000 stores, provides a great case study of execution throughout the day. The 7-Eleven Japan stores are located in residential areas, within walking distance from homes. Given the average small size of the stores, to have appropriate stockkeeping units (SKUs) in stock over the course of the day requires repeated store variety changes.

The process starts with information systems that detect customer choice at each individual store. Analysis of individual stores and aggregation across stores permits shuffling inventory across stores to manage store-level variety and thus increase SKU velocity. Store shelves are reconfigured more than three times a day to reflect demand preferences by time of day. While morning items might focus on breakfast-ready SKUs, the same store caters to dinners by the evening. Trucks are scheduled to make deliveries in 30-minute windows, and products are unloaded and put away at stores without being checked against scheduled deliveries. Delivery flexibility is ensured by adjusting transportation mode (the company uses motorcycles, boats, trucks, and helicopters). In one example of this flexibility, the company was reported to have used 7 helicopters and 125 motorcycles to deliver 64,000 rice balls to the city of Kobe after a devastating earthquake hit the area.

Managing inventory across stores enables the inventory impact of variability to be kept in check. Reshuffling SKUs through the course of the day enables variety to be synchronized with demand and demand velocity to be maximized. In short, 7-Eleven Japan provides a retailing example of Toyota's supply chain management.

It does not require great effort to imagine the scope for kaizen. For example, a metric that measures truck utilization, mileage, and on-time delivery on a delivery-by-delivery basis will uncover enough to start the PDCA cycle.

Rane Brake Linings

Rane Brake Linings (RBL)[5] has enacted changes that enable it to compete globally as a manufacturer of brake linings. The company is a division of the Rane Group and won the Deming prize in 2003. It is a major supplier of brake linings to the Indian railways as well as to automotive companies. One of the capabilities that RBL has developed that permits it to be a global competitor is the ability to diagnose problems across the supply chain and solve system-level issues rapidly. One example of this capability involves the brake system provided to a two-wheeler company that experienced stickiness in the brakes. RBL was the brake provider that assembled the brake linings to stamped parts provided by a supplier. The resulting brake was assembled by the OEM into its product. Upon hearing of the issue faced by the OEM's customers, RBL installed its own engineers at every step in the supply chain. They then developed four different designs over a 10-day period that carefully identified adjustments to the supplier stampings, adjusted the brake lining manufacture and assembly, and then worked with the OEM to see that the parts were assembled appropriately at the OEM's assembly operation. The net result was an improved brake system while manufacturing productivity was maintained. The ability to coordinate upstream and downstream, develop multiple designs rapidly, and deploy the resulting designs suggests that there is a unique capability to synchronize across the supply chain. That ability to meld engineering design talent and manufacturing may well be a competitive capability that enables RBL to compete globally.

Another capability that RBL has is its approach to maintaining product costs through careful global sourcing. For example, one company was importing chemical inputs from Canada that were priced in dollars. There also was an opportunity to compensate for the rising dollar (at that time) by including sources from Russia. The adjustment in product designs and approval would generate a cost reduction. But at the same time there was another effort to improve productivity through a change in design of the existing product. The phasing in of the new design and then the change in sourcing resulted in both product design improvement as well as a cost reduction.

While Total Quality Management (TQM) approaches have not been shown to be profitable in many companies in mature markets, their success in emerging and growing markets is a new story. RBL's success after TQM implementation and the associated productivity gains has enabled it to remain a strong competitor in the Indian market and engage effectively in global markets.

Progressive Insurance

The typical insurance company operates its offices just during regular hours (ordinarily, 9 a.m. to 5 p.m.). Thus, when a client has an insurance claim, the client's call is usually recorded and followed by an attempt to contact the client. Following contact with the insurance company, the client is responsible, for example, for taking the damaged automobile to a repair facility, renting a car while repair is being completed, submitting receipts, and paying the deductible and thus completing the processing of the claim. The associated delays present a challenge to clients since they are responsible for doing many of the steps necessary to get back to a normal state.

Progressive's CEO Peter Lakrides had a different idea: "Process claims whenever the client has a need and fulfill the need on site whenever possible."[6] Implementing this idea meant that customer service agents were distributed spatially in Ford Explorers around towns so that they could get to the site of an accident quickly. The company invested in an information system that permitted all data to be accessed wirelessly by the agent on site. Clients were offered the option for a check cut on the spot of the accident to settle claims. If a client preferred, Progressive took charge of the car, completed all repairs, and delivered the car to the customer. The customer was given a ride home with arrangements for a rental car to be provided. In short, Progressive became available when the customer wanted assistance.

The net impact was a significant market share increase for Progressive as it targeted drivers who valued such superlative service. Because accidents were observed on site, both fraud claims and repair costs decreased. In short, improved service decreased overall costs, thus permitting increased profits. A supply chain view that takes the customer's perspective has played a crucial role in Progressive's success.

Progressive can continue to improve with analysis of clients' needs. Continuous improvement on these dimensions will require the most creative problem-solving teams imaginable.

Shouldice Hospital

Shouldice Hospital in Canada is often hailed as a great example of a service factory. The genesis of this hospital was the observation by Dr. Shouldice during the period of World War II that hernia surgery, which was a nonemergency procedure, was taking up three weeks of hospitalization during a time when hospital capacity was scarce. However, in a single operating room, Dr. Shouldice completed surgery for about two hernias per day. The facility expanded to several more buildings, and all surgery now takes place in an 89-bed facility in Thornhill.

Shouldice Hospital has been dedicated to the repair of hernias for over 55 years. The hospital focuses on the standard hernia surgery, staying away from complicated cases that frequently involve older patients. The facility focuses on maximizing the success rate by performing standardized steps, thus increasing the learning curve benefits and associated success. The founder likens Shouldice to McDonald's, with its emphasis on standardized processes to produce its specialties (e.g., fries at McDonald's).

The hospital has spartan rooms with no entertainment. Surgeons meet the patient on arrival and focus on surgery success. The large number of common spaces and self-serve focus for patients encourages the view of the facility as a nonhospital environment. The hospital focuses on management of processes used in the operating system, care path and procedures as well as a dedicated organizational and physical design. As a result of its high volume, the system can operate at low cost while delivering high quality. For example, hernia surgeries at Shouldice average US$954, versus US$2,000 to US$4,000 elsewhere.

Analysis of Shouldice Hospital's success suggests that the menu of services at the hospital limits what the facility does, but the volume of such activity enables increased success as well as speed. In addition, careful attention to detail and an emphasis on processes and efficiency put the focus on simplifying procedures and kaizen. That results in a constant emphasis on improving the process by using data. The overall impact is high performance on the dimensions of cost and quality.

Although Shouldice is a well-studied example of a facility that performs a specialized medical service (i.e., hernia operations), such focused operations are found in other specialties. The Texas Heart Institute does bypass surgeries for $27,000 (which is $16,000 cheaper than the national average); it has a five-year survival rate of over 92 percent, which is better than the rate at most other facilities. Likewise, Salick Health Care, Mid-America Dental, Hearing and Vision Care in Missouri, and the Mayo Clinic (which has a broader focus than the others mentioned but is very process oriented) all provide examples of supply chain–like operations, like those used at Toyota, in the health-care industry.

Shouldice has kaizen built into its systems. Interestingly, the impetus for change in procedures, processes, and equipment might also come from Shouldice's "mass production" system rather than 100 percent top-down from the equipment designers or pharmaceutical firms.

ALDI

ALDI, a German-based retailer, is a "limited assortment discount international retailer."[7] The company was founded after 1945 and has global sales of over €33 billion ($43 billion). It has more than 5,000 stores across Europe and Australia and 600 stores in the United States. Unlike supermarkets that have between 15,000 and 40,000 SKUs, ALDI stocks 700 items. These items are the most-needed, most-often-used products in the home. The store offers no bagging service, no check cashing, and no special displays. Prices are 20 percent lower than at Wal-Mart. The company generates sales of €30 million ($39 million) per SKU versus Wal-Mart's sales of 1.5 million per SKU. This figure is impressive, given that Wal-Mart is six times larger than ALDI.

The company keeps a sharp focus on price, and whenever a supplier lowers its price, ALDI's retail price is lowered so as to maintain the lowest price in the market. Executives in the company admit that adding 50 new items could increase sales revenue by €1 billion ($1.3 billion), but the company limits its assortment to 700 items. If any new items are added, existing ones are dropped to compensate. In many cases, the company produces its own brand, thus increasing buying power.

In Europe, the retailer has 51 percent of the fruit juice market, 42 percent of the canned vegetable market, and 50 percent of the packaged and preserved meats market. ALDI's sharp focus on a small selection of SKUs (700) that constitute around 80 percent of shoppers' baskets, private label manufacturing that enables supply chain efficiency, significant volumes that enable scale economies, lower price points, and low service levels all create a unique and competitive retail environment.

Continuous improvement in this context would involve tracking changing customer tastes, more cost reduction, reduction of waste (e.g., in perishable goods), and so on. The main metrics could be price compared to other stores while the most desired goods would be kept on the shelves.

Fujitsu Computer Services

Womack and Jones[8] describe the example of Fujitsu Computer Services and the management of its supply chain role for British Midland Airlines (BMI). When Fujitsu Services started its contract with BMI, it was paid based on the number of calls handled, and the focus was on the speed of processing calls.

But Fujitsu decided to analyze the calls and identify the reasons they were made. It discovered, for example, that printer malfunctions accounted for a large percentage (more than 26 percent) of calls. The problems arose with such things as printing baggage tags and boarding cards. Those issues translated into passenger delays, the need for backup printers, the necessity for quickly dispatching customer service agents to fix the printers, and so on. The average time to fix these errant printers was about 10 hours.

An analysis of the root cause of the problem, as well as the true impact on flight-related costs, suggested that BMI would have been better off spending more money on better printers. The new printers the company eventually bought decreased calls by over 80 percent and cut down the time to fix printer problems to less than three hours. A supply chain view enabled costs to be decreased systemwide.

As a result, Fujitsu offered a new contract to BMI. The computer services company would be paid based on the projected volume of calls but was free to focus on system improvements that lowered overall costs. The result has been a system in which Fujitsu monitors problems and anticipates issues before they arise. In addition, by identifying customer issues, Fujitsu is able to develop new custom products that can solve the customers' problems and kaizen its supply chain operations.

Tesco

Tesco is a British retailer that has significantly improved its in-stock availability while decreasing inventories. While observed fill rates in grocery stores is 92 percent, Tesco's systems ensure a fill rate of over 96 percent. Womack and Jones[9] suggest specific steps taken by Tesco to improve its in-stock position.

The retailer coordinates with large-volume suppliers for direct pickup from its warehouses, cross-dock through its own warehouses, and delivery to stores. The quantities provided to stores follow a replenishment mode of operation also known as a "pull system." Replenishing sold products guarantees that the mix of product shipped synchronizes with demand mix. Such a dynamic adjustment of inbound shipments to synchronize with demand enables assortment matching and thus ensures a uniform service level across SKUs. Shipping in quantities that match demand also allows inventory levels to be lowered. But what is needed is an effective logistics system that can maintain efficiency by aggregating volumes across stores to effectively use transport capacity.

The same approach has enabled Tesco to use a common back-end supply system to support multiple front-end retail formats. Tesco has local convenience stores (Tesco Express), midsized stores (Tesco Metro), large stores (Tesco Superstore), hypermarkets (Tesco Extra), and Web-based stores (Tesco.com). Each of these retail formats is optimized to satisfy its customer base. But because they all share common back-end operations, it is possible to offer buying-efficiency-related pricing across these formats. In addition, collecting data from customers with loyalty cards that can be used across formats enables a unique window into the total shopping basket of customers.

Tesco's multiformat supply chains suggest that it has a system similar to Toyota's common supply chain processes used to deliver different car experiences to the customer and adjusted for different selling geographies across the world. The opportunities for kaizen are likewise numerous due to the common back-end system.

Zara

Zara represents a new generation of supply chains in the apparel industry. The following anecdote regarding Zara says it all: "When Madonna went on tour in Spain in early 2001, she started in Madrid and ended in Barcelona 10 days later. The fashion that teenagers picked up from Madonna's outfits were developed, manufactured and available in stores in Barcelona by the time the tour ended. This was a remarkable accomplishment, 10 days from design, development, and manufacturing to store availability."[10]

Zara is a multi-billion-dollar company with stores all over the world. The Spanish company owns large sections of the apparel supply chain and manages the entire chain to speed innovation and product availability. One secret is the constant flow of customer requests and information from stores to the design studios. Zara relies on a constant flow of product from plants to stores and does not replenish product.

The apparel firm sources the fabric from all over the world (e.g., Italy, China, Japan, and India). It owns its own cutting machines that cut the fabric in batches within each roll to minimize scrap. Independent sewing shops in Europe do all of the stitching. The apparel comes back to Zara where it is ironed, packaged, and grouped by store. The company contracts with independent trucking companies to distribute the products to stores that are solely owned by Zara.

Customers expect fresh assortments every time they visit the store, and they do not expect products to be in stock for a long time. By controlling most steps in the supply chain, Zara is able to respond quickly to market trends. The degree of vertical control at Zara also decreases the cost of errors in the forecast. But Zara may also have identified that having a fast supply chain enables it to charge a price premium for the market segment it targets. Reports indicate that it also leaves sufficient value for customers so that they return to the Zara stores far more often than they do to competitors. In addition, Zara's store managers keep track of customer requests for changes to existing designs and pass along that information to buyers at Zara headquarters. That feedback from customers is incorporated, when appropriate, into new design changes that flow back to the store.

In fact, Zara used the services of Toyota to design several of its operations. Zara's kaizen during the season, fast cycle manufacturing, and control of the supply chain have resulted in the synchronization of the supply of SKUs with demand. That enables lower inventories and higher service levels and provides greater value for customers.

Reflection Points

The examples in this chapter show ideas related to the v4L framework applied to different industries.

- *Variety* is carefully chosen at Shouldice and ALDI in order to be able to offer a distinct operational advantage and cost competitiveness.
- *Velocity* of the flow of product at Progressive Insurance, IBM Credit, and Ford Accounts Payable comes from a careful process design that ensures rapid execution.

- *Variability* is managed at Rane Brake Linings, Tesco, Fujitsu, and the hospital and bank by smoothing flows, eliminating bottlenecks, and identifying reasons for and adjusting plans to observed variability.
- *Visibility* of data across the supply chain enables 7-Eleven Japan and Zara to offer rapid response and product changes that synchronize with demand.
- *Learning* is achieved by adopting systems to foster continuous improvement, and thus these firms can continue to deliver superior performance for years to come.

Endnotes

1. A. R. Goland, J. Hall, and D. A. Clifford, "First National Toyota," *The McKinsey Quarterly*, no. 4 (1998).
2. P. D. Mango and L. A. Shapiro, "Hospitals Get Serious about Operations," *The McKinsey Quarterly*, no. 2 (2001).
3. M. Hammer and J. Champy, *Reengineering the Corporation: A Manifesto for a Business Revolution*. New York: HarperCollins, 2003.
4. A. Ishikawa and Tai Nejo, "The Success of 7-Eleven Japan," *World Scientific* (2002).
5. A. Iyer and S. Seshadri, "Transforming an Indian Manufacturing Company: The Rane Brake Linings Case." In Hau Lee and Chung-Yee Lee, eds., *Building Supply Chain Excellence in Emerging Economies*. New York: Springer, 2006.
6. D. Bovet and J. Murtha, *Value Nets: Breaking the Supply Chain to Unlock Hidden Profits*. Hoboken, NJ: Wiley, 2000.
7. John L. Mariotti, *The Complexity Crisis: Why Too Many Products, Markets, and Customers Are Crippling Your Company and What You Can Do About It*. Avon, Mass.: Adams Media, 2008.
8. J. T. Womack and D. Jones, "Lean Consumption," *Harvard Business Review* (March 2005).
9. Ibid.
10. "The Future of Fast Fashion," *The Economist* (June 18, 2005): 57–58.

Chapter 13

The Beer Game and the Toyota Supply Chain

The beer game was introduced as an exercise in industrial dynamics in 1960. And what has beer to do with automobiles? The beer game is used as a fun way to illustrate some of the pitfalls of operating a supply chain. Certainly, beer gets the attention of students. Even though the product used in the game is beer, the processes are similar to most supply chains, including those involving automobiles. This chapter will compare and contrast how the original beer game is played versus how Toyota's managers would play the game, which will illustrate how Toyota's processes can streamline the supply chain.

The Beer Game Rules

In the beer game, four players play the roles of managing a serial supply chain as a retailer, distributor, wholesaler, and factory. A schematic of the beer game is shown in Figure 13-1. The retailer is the only one who observes customer demand. Each player fills demands from the immediate customer: the retailer fills the customer orders, the wholesaler fills the retailer's orders, the distributor fills the wholesaler's, and the factory serves the distributor. Each player carries inventory, which is represented by large shaded squares in the figure. Orders can be filled only from inventory in these boxes. The factory produces beer.

The game is played one week at a time. Each player receives orders and tries to fill as much as he or she can. If orders are not filled, they are backlogged and have to be satisfied in the future. Each player then places orders for the next week. Players possess only local information about their inventory: the demand by their immediate customer and the orders placed to their immediate supplier.

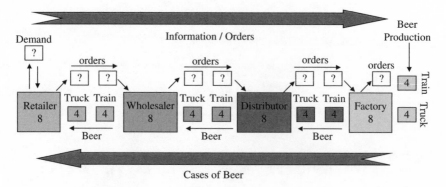

Figure 13-1. Beer game information/order flow
Source: Courtesy of Rene Caldentey, Stern School of Business, New York University.
Used with permission.

The goal for each player is to minimize the cost of holding inventory and of backlogged orders. Holding inventory costs $1 per unit per week, whereas backlogged orders cost $2 per unit per week. The team with the smallest sum of the costs of the four players wins.

The time to receive orders from the immediate supplier is two weeks. So it takes two weeks for orders shipped by the distributor to reach the wholesaler. Similarly, the delay in shipping is two weeks between the wholesaler and the retailer and between the factory and the distributor. The factory receives orders two weeks after they are planned for production. The small square shaded boxes represent these delays. Figure 13-1 shows that there are 8 units en route to each player, 4 being one week away (on truck) and 4 more being two weeks away (on train). The game is played one week at a time.

Order processing delays are two weeks between players—for example, the order placed by the retailer one week reaches the wholesaler two weeks later. These delays are designated in the illustration by the small square boxes with question marks in them. The question marks indicate that the data are revealed only to the player and only when they are needed. To reiterate, the information delays between stages are two weeks each, and the shipping delay between stages is two weeks each.

The instructions given to players are as follows:

- The purpose of this game is to experience firsthand the flow of materials through a distribution system. Teams of four people will work to minimize the total cost (both carrying costs and stockout costs) of the distribution network. The four positions of the team members are retailers, wholesalers, distributors, and factory inventory managers. Each person fills one position. There will be no collusion (i.e., talking) among team members.

■ Players will be moving two things through the network: orders (on index cards, placed facedown) and cases of beer (poker chips). They will keep track of each event on the form supplied. The holding costs are $1 per case in current inventory. The stockout cost is $2 per case on backlog (basically, negative inventory). The players must pay attention to follow along with the group. The team that achieves the lowest total cost will win the pot of money.

■ Even though the game sounds complex, the play is relatively simple. Each player executes five steps every week in synchronization. The game is supposed to start in steady state—that is, each player begins with 8 units of inventory, 4 units arriving one week later and another 4 units arriving two weeks later. In the game, those units are called "units on the truck" and "units on the train," respectively. Each player has incoming orders and outgoing orders written out for the first week and placed facedown. Those orders are 4 units each. The incoming orders for the retailer (i.e., customer demand) are written out in advance and placed facedown. Figure 13-1 shows the state of the game.

The five steps are as follows (described for the retailer and factory). All other groups operate in a similar manner. Every week the following happens:

1. The retailer receives delivery of the units on the truck. The retailer records the units that are just received and adds those to his inventory. The units on the train are then shifted to the truck (and so are now one week away from the retailer). Likewise, the factory gets shipments from a truck and takes those into inventory. The shipments on the train are moved to the truck.

2. The retailer then reads the current week's demand from the incoming orders. The demand slips for the retailer are made ready in advance and kept facedown. The retailer fills the demand by counting that number of units from his inventory and removing them from inventory. The factory reads the demand from the distributor (in the incoming orders) and fills that many units from inventory by placing them on the train going to the wholesaler. In such a case, demand cannot be satisfied from inventory. It is backlogged and must be filled eventually.

3. The retailer moves the order that was placed facedown (as the outgoing order) to the incoming order of the wholesaler. The factory reads the outgoing order from the distributor and places that number of units on

the train going to the distributor. The outgoing order for the factory represents the production planned by the factory.

4. The retailer decides how much to order, writes down that number on a piece of paper, and places it facedown in the outgoing order. The factory likewise plans how much to produce and writes that amount on a piece of paper and places it facedown in the outgoing orders.

5. Only the very last step, placing an order, requires a decision. The rest of the steps are meant to simulate movement of material and information in a supply chain: getting a shipment, taking it into inventory, filling demand during the week, and placing an order with the supplier. Those are routine tasks that every real-life retailer, wholesaler, distributor, or factory does week in and week out.

A key constraint in the game is that players are not allowed to speak to each other about their orders. They can see the supply chain and orders that are coming to them, but they cannot see the orders placed by other players. To some extent they are "forced" to work using local information, that is, information available only to each person. A version of the game is described later in the section Understanding the Results Using the Standard Inventory Management Method.

The Typical Outcome

Typically, the game is played for 20 to 40 weeks. The original aim of the game was to show that even a small change in customer demand from 4 units a week to 8 units a week could create exceedingly large variations in the orders placed by the players. The customer demand is predetermined and is 4 cases each week for the first four weeks. Thereafter, the demand jumps to 8 cases per week and stays at that level for the rest of the game. The retailer who watches the demand unfold week by week sees a level demand first. Typically, the retailer tries to work down the starting inventory by ordering less than the demand. For example, the retailer might order 2 or 3 units each week for the first four weeks. In the fifth week suddenly the demand increases to 8. The retailer reacts and orders 8 or more units. Possibly, the retailer has run short of inventory and orders, say, 12 units. The wholesaler views the small demand for 2s and 3s in the first four weeks, then the order jumps to 12 or more units. The wholesaler also has run down the inventory, probably even more than the retailer has because the orders receipts have been 2s and 3s (against the retailer demand of 4 units per week), and in turn reacts and orders more. Possibly, the wholesaler has only 4 units on hand and so orders 8 units that are backordered this week and 12 for the next, for a total of 20 units. Following a similar reasoning, the distributor in turn reacts and orders even more, and eventually the factory sees a spike of orders that can be as large as 40 units!

The factory might even produce as many as 60 units in response. Notice also that the reaction is not simultaneous because of the delay in orders reaching each player. That sequence of overreacting stuffs the supply chain with unwanted material. Eventually, the players realize that they have overreacted, but it is too late. It takes quite a while (maybe even a year) to work down the surplus inventory. The game is played for at least 20 weeks to demonstrate the buildup of inventory and its gradual builddown. This phenomenon, in which each stage in the supply chain overreacts to changes in customer demand, has been termed the "bullwhip effect." This phenomenon has been widely documented and studied. See, for example, the article on this subject by Lee, Padmanabhan, and Whang (1997),[1] which is one of the top 10 most cited papers in supply chain management.[2]

A plot of orders placed at different stages of the game in a typical experiment is provided in Figure 13-2. Notice the growth of spikes as orders are tracked from the customer to the retailer, then to the wholesaler, then to the distributor, and then to the factory.

The beer game has been played internationally in management schools with students drawn from different programs: undergraduate, graduate, executive education, and short programs. The results are always the same: The costs incurred by different players are very different from the "optimal" cost. The deviation in costs and the deviation in ordering and stocking pattern from the optimal are systematic, thus illustrating the bullwhip effect. John Sterman, in his 1989 article on the subject,[3] analyzes the outcome as follows: he first suggests a heuristic (trial and error) to order cases in each week because the optimal rule can be quite complicated. The heuristic performs quite well for the parameters of the game discussed above. It essentially involves making a correction for the desired stocking level and a correction for the supply coming to the player. The player orders the expected demand, plus a correction for the deviation in the stock from its ideal value and a correction for the deviation from the actual to the ideal supply line (the supply coming to the player). In Sterman's experiments, the optimal heuristic (the one with the best parameter values chosen by trial and error) has costs that are 10 times smaller than the costs reported by the players. The same can be said about games that were played under our supervision at different places and with different audiences.

How Would Toyota Play the Beer Game?

This section describes how the beer game might be played at Toyota. First, we provide a benchmark of how a "standard" inventory management method applies to the beer game; then we will provide the Toyota approach. The examples used in the following paragraphs are very complex and beyond the scope of

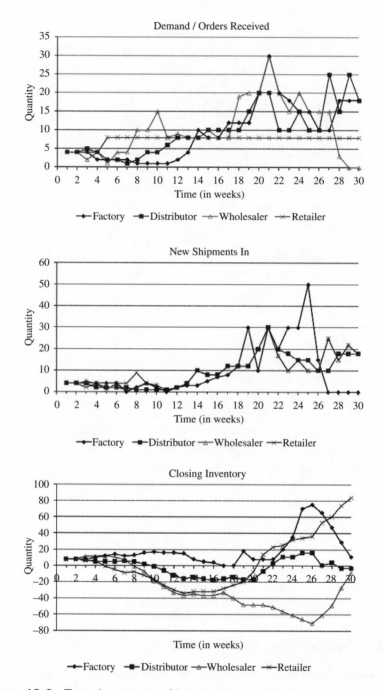

Figure 13-2. Typical outcome of beer game

Note: Plots are from a beer game played during the summer of 2008 by undergraduate students at New York University, New York, NY. Graphs designed by Vishal Gaur.

this book. We will briefly highlight some key figures in each example to examine Toyota's approach to the standard method; however, if you want to understand the logic behind the two approaches, you will need to analyze the logic of each example.

Understanding the Results Using the Standard Inventory Management Method

Figure 13-3, which details the standard inventory management method, shows that each player operates individually. Because the positions are symmetric, only the actions of the retailer are described; keep in mind that the rest of the players act in a similar manner. The shaded line of the illustration shows the periods. The demand is seen two lines below. It starts out at 4 per period until period 10 and then jumps to 8 and stays at 8 for the rest of the game. The retailer uses an "order-up-to" policy. He assumes that the lead time (LT) is four periods (a delay of two for the information to propagate and two for the physical supply). He adds a safety stock (SS) of two weeks to that and computes that his pipeline inventory (on hand plus on order) should be (LT + SS + 1), or seven weeks of supply. Each week he revises his demand forecast using a simple exponential smoothing formula with a weight of (for example) 0.8:

$$\text{The forecast for next week} = 0.8 \times \text{the forecast made last week} \\ + 0.2 \times \text{this week's demand}$$

The retailer observes demand, adjusts next week's forecast, uses the forecast value to compute the required pipeline inventory, and orders a quantity that raises the end stock to the required value. For example, in period 11, the demand forecast equals $(0.8 \times 4) + (0.2 \times 8) = 4.8$. The pipeline inventory desired equals 7 weeks of supply (7×4.8), which equals 33.6. The end stock equals 20. Therefore, the retailer orders 13.6 units. Observe that this order raises the pipeline inventory to 33.6. Figure 13-3 reveals that this order reaches the wholesaler only in period 13 due to the communication delay. The wholesaler reacts with an order of 27.04. The distributor reacts in week 15 with an order of 59.30 and the factory reacts with an order of 114.59 in week 17!

Note that the result of using the standard inventory management method produces the outcomes observed when the game is played.

At this stage, you might want to try to determine whether the simple but powerful concept of learning through scientific experimentation can be replicated in a supply chain. Is it possible to learn Plan, Do, Check, and Act in a system? What might be some of the prerequisites? The next section explains briefly how a supply chain leader achieves learning. We shall also see how Toyota's learning principles work when the beer game is played.

Figure 13-3. Beer game played the traditional way

Group	Description	Note	P 00	P 03	P 09	P 10	P 11	P 12	P 13	P 14	P 15	P 16	P 17	P 18	P 19	P 20	P 21	P 22	P 23
Retailer	Pipeline Inventory	Includes on hand and on order		28.00	28.00	28.00	28.00	33.60	38.08	41.66	44.53	46.82	48.66	50.13	51.30	52.24	52.99	53.59	54.08
	Demand			4.00	4.00	4.00	8.00	8.00	8.00	8.00	8.00	8.00	8.00	8.00	8.00	8.00	8.00	8.00	8.00
	End Stock			24.00	24.00	24.00	20.00	25.60	30.08	33.66	36.53	38.82	40.66	42.13	43.30	44.24	44.99	45.59	46.08
	Demand Forecast	Uses exponential smoothing	4.00	4.00	4.00	4.00	4.80	5.44	5.95	6.36	6.69	6.95	7.16	7.33	7.46	7.57	7.66	7.73	7.78
	Lead Time			4.00	4.00	4.00	4.00	4.00	4.00	4.00	4.00	4.00	4.00	4.00	4.00	4.00	4.00	4.00	4.00
	Plus 1			1.00	1.00	1.00	1.00	1.00	1.00	1.00	1.00	1.00	1.00	1.00	1.00	1.00	1.00	1.00	1.00
	No. of Periods Safety Stock			2.00	2.00	2.00	2.00	2.00	2.00	2.00	2.00	2.00	2.00	2.00	2.00	2.00	2.00	2.00	2.00
	Total Periods			7.00	7.00	7.00	7.00	7.00	7.00	7.00	7.00	7.00	7.00	7.00	7.00	7.00	7.00	7.00	7.00
	Base Stock	Total periods × demand forecast	28.00	28.00	28.00	28.00	33.60	38.08	41.66	44.53	46.82	48.66	50.13	51.30	52.24	52.99	53.59	54.08	54.46
	Order Quantity	Base Stock - End Stock		4.00	4.00	4.00	13.60	12.48	11.58	10.87	10.29	9.84	9.47	9.17	8.94	8.75	8.60	8.48	8.38
Wholesaler	Pipeline Inventory	Includes on hand and on order		28.00	28.00	28.00	28.00	28.00	28.00	41.44	50.62	56.72	60.59	62.88	64.07	64.51	64.46	64.08	63.52
	Demand			4.00	4.00	4.00	4.00	4.00	13.60	12.48	11.58	10.87	10.29	9.84	9.47	9.17	8.94	8.75	8.60
	End Stock			24.00	24.00	24.00	24.00	24.00	14.40	28.96	39.04	45.85	50.29	53.05	54.61	55.34	55.52	55.33	54.91
	Demand Forecast	Uses exponential smoothing	4.00	4.00	4.00	4.00	4.00	4.00	5.92	7.23	8.10	8.66	8.98	9.15	9.22	9.21	9.15	9.07	8.98
	Lead Time			4.00	4.00	4.00	4.00	4.00	4.00	4.00	4.00	4.00	4.00	4.00	4.00	4.00	4.00	4.00	4.00
	Plus 1			1.00	1.00	1.00	1.00	1.00	1.00	1.00	1.00	1.00	1.00	1.00	1.00	1.00	1.00	1.00	1.00
	No. of Periods Safety Stock			2.00	2.00	2.00	2.00	2.00	2.00	2.00	2.00	2.00	2.00	2.00	2.00	2.00	2.00	2.00	2.00
	Total Periods			7.00	7.00	7.00	7.00	7.00	7.00	7.00	7.00	7.00	7.00	7.00	7.00	7.00	7.00	7.00	7.00
	Base Stock	Total periods × demand forecast	28.00	28.00	28.00	28.00	28.00	28.00	41.44	50.62	56.72	60.59	62.88	64.07	64.51	64.46	64.08	63.52	62.85
	Order Quantity	Base Stock - End Stock		4.00	4.00	4.00	4.00	4.00	27.04	21.66	17.68	14.74	12.59	11.03	9.91	9.12	8.56	8.19	7.94
Distributor	Pipeline Inventory	Includes on hand and on order		28.00	28.00	28.00	28.00	28.00	28.00	28.00	28.00	60.26	78.53	87.58	90.69	90.18	87.58	83.94	79.91
	Demand			4.00	4.00	4.00	4.00	4.00	4.00	4.00	27.04	21.66	17.68	14.74	12.59	11.03	9.91	9.12	8.56
	End Stock			24.00	24.00	24.00	24.00	24.00	24.00	24.00	0.96	38.59	60.86	72.84	78.11	79.15	77.67	74.82	71.35
	Demand Forecast	Uses exponential smoothing	4.00	4.00	4.00	4.00	4.00	4.00	4.00	4.00	8.61	11.22	12.51	12.96	12.88	12.51	11.99	11.42	10.85
	Lead Time			4.00	4.00	4.00	4.00	4.00	4.00	4.00	4.00	4.00	4.00	4.00	4.00	4.00	4.00	4.00	4.00
	Plus 1			1.00	1.00	1.00	1.00	1.00	1.00	1.00	1.00	1.00	1.00	1.00	1.00	1.00	1.00	1.00	1.00
	No. of Periods Safety Stock			2.00	2.00	2.00	2.00	2.00	2.00	2.00	2.00	2.00	2.00	2.00	2.00	2.00	2.00	2.00	2.00
	Total Periods			7.00	7.00	7.00	7.00	7.00	7.00	7.00	7.00	7.00	7.00	7.00	7.00	7.00	7.00	7.00	7.00
	Base Stock	Total periods × demand forecast	28.00	28.00	28.00	28.00	28.00	28.00	28.00	28.00	60.26	78.53	87.58	90.69	90.18	87.58	83.94	79.91	75.92
	Order Quantity	Base Stock - End Stock		4.00	4.00	4.00	4.00	4.00	4.00	4.00	59.30	39.94	26.72	17.86	12.07	8.43	6.26	5.09	4.57
Factory	Pipeline Inventory	Includes on hand and on order		20.00	20.00	20.00	20.00	20.00	20.00	20.00	20.00	20.00	20.00	75.30	100.18	106.86	103.34	94.75	84.23
	Demand			4.00	4.00	4.00	4.00	4.00	4.00	4.00	4.00	4.00	59.30	39.94	26.72	17.86	12.07	8.43	6.26
	End Stock			16.00	16.00	16.00	16.00	16.00	16.00	16.00	16.00	16.00	-39.30	35.35	73.46	89.00	91.27	86.32	77.96
	Demand Forecast	Uses exponential smoothing	4.00	4.00	4.00	4.00	4.00	4.00	4.00	4.00	4.00	4.00	15.06	20.04	21.37	20.67	18.95	16.85	14.73
	Lead Time			2.00	2.00	2.00	2.00	2.00	2.00	2.00	2.00	2.00	2.00	2.00	2.00	2.00	2.00	2.00	2.00
	Plus 1			1.00	1.00	1.00	1.00	1.00	1.00	1.00	1.00	1.00	1.00	1.00	1.00	1.00	1.00	1.00	1.00
	No. of Periods Safety Stock			2.00	2.00	2.00	2.00	2.00	2.00	2.00	2.00	2.00	2.00	2.00	2.00	2.00	2.00	2.00	2.00
	Total Periods			5.00	5.00	5.00	5.00	5.00	5.00	5.00	5.00	5.00	5.00	5.00	5.00	5.00	5.00	5.00	5.00
	Base Stock	Total periods × demand forecast	20.00	20.00	20.00	20.00	20.00	20.00	20.00	20.00	20.00	20.00	75.30	100.18	106.86	103.34	94.75	84.23	73.65
	Order Quantity	Base Stock - End Stock		4.00	4.00	4.00	4.00	4.00	4.00	4.00	4.00	4.00	114.59	64.83	33.40	14.34	3.47	0.00	0.00
	Total Inventory			104.00	104.00	104.00	104.00	109.60	114.08	131.10	143.16	183.80	207.78	275.88	306.25	313.79	308.37	296.36	281.73

Periods 1, 2, 4 to 8 hidden

Toyota Method

If Toyota were to play the game, the game would be played from a top-down point of view. The following are some of the rules of the game played the Toyota Way:

- Production is planned once every four weeks and kept stable for the next four weeks. At each four-week planning session the retailer and factory would collaborate to forecast demand. They would enter into a dialogue to consider recent trends, stock adjustments, and back-order condition. Retail demand changes between four-week planning cycles, adjustments to safety stock, and current back orders are all evaluated to determine new production level.
- Dealers or retailers are provided some level of safety stock (inventory) to fulfill expected demand (usually about one month's, or four weeks' worth). Any additional spike in demand is placed on back order to be filled at the next planning cycle. Toyota wants to make sure that the demand change is going to be persistent so as to not to overreact to spikes that occur on a week-to-week basis.
- The cycle starts at the factory, and production is based on the latest four-week forecast.
- The two intermediaries (i.e., the distributor and wholesaler) do not carry inventory but just pass shipments through from factory to retailer.
- The retailer attempts to fulfill demand, and if any safety stock is used, the retailer sends a weekly adjustment order to recover the used up safety stock during the next production cycle. Orders that cannot be filled from safety stock are scheduled for production at the next four-week planning cycle.

Toyota's approach would result in minimal inventory buildup at each level and provide a consistent four-week production and distribution plan. The trade-off would be a delay in filling the back orders. In that situation, it is assumed that a certain fraction of the customers would wait while some others might walk away, which would result in loss sales.

Figure 13-4 shows the impact of these rules. The major assumptions are listed at the top of the table. Interestingly, the process begins with the factory plan instead of the retailer's orders! That arrangement emphasizes the supply chain view when planning. The planning is done in four-week intervals. These are labeled 1st, 2nd, and so forth. The real demand increases to 8 in week 11 as before. Until then, it is constant at 4, thereafter it is 8. The factory produces at a level base rate that is established for each interval. Added to that are the stock adjustment and backlog recovery. They create some fluctuations, but those are known well in advance and controlled to minimize the spike at the factory, as

Assumptions:

1) Every 4 periods, all agree on demand forecast. Factory builds to forecast for 4 periods starting from current period + 2 (factory lead time). Changes in safety stock & back orders planned for production during the next cycle.

2) Since production is stable and equal to demand, the wholesaler and distributor will not store inventory (Just-in-time).

3) The retailer will be provided some allowance to meet variation in demand. This will be the state as a % Flex

4) The retailer will stock Safety-stock (SS) inventory as follows: SS equal to % flex times lead time to replenish

5) Retailer SS adjustment orders will be shipped from factory and arrive in 8 weeks 2 weeks for order + 6 weeks transportation

6) Wholesaler/Distributor pipeline inventory is equal to last 6 weeks of production. Wholesaler and Distributor act as pass-through only

7) Demand forecast is changed at next planning period after real demand shows increase (Note: in real world some seasonal demand changes are forecasted in advance)

		P 00	P.03	P-09	P 10	P 11	P 12	P 13	P 14	P 15	P 16	P 17	P 18	P 19	P 20	P 21	P 22	P 23
Assumptions Planning Periods	1 every 4th period	1st		4.00	4.00	4.00	4th 4.00	4.00	4.00	4.00	5th 8.00	8.00	8.00	8.00	6th 8.00	8.00	8.00	8.00
Factory																		
% Flex	Factory allowance			10%	10%	10%	10%	10%	10%	10%	10%	10%	10%	10%	10%	10%	10%	10%
Order Lead Time (R-F)	Time to reorder Safety Stock			2	2	2	2	2	2	2	2	2	2	2	2	2	2	2
Delivery Lead Time(F-W-D-R)	Transportation Time			6	6	6	6	6	6	6	6	6	6	6	6	6	6	6
Total Lead Time for Safety Stock				8	8	8	8	8	8	8	8	8	8	8	8	8	8	8
Demand Forecast	Based on latest real demand	4.00	4.00	4.00	4.00	4.00	4.00	4.00	8.00	8.00	8.00	8.00	8.00	8.00	8.00	8.00	8.00	8.00
Base Production	Equal to Demand Forecast	4.00	4.00	4.00	4.00	4.00	4.00	4.00	8.00	8.00	8.00	8.00	8.00	8.00	8.00	8.00	8.00	8.00
Safety Stock production	Equal to SS orders placed order LT away	0.00		0.00	0.00	0.00	0.00	0.00	1.20	1.20	1.20	1.20	0.40	0.40	0.40	0.00	0.00	0.00
Recovery of backlog	Smoothed over a quarter	0.00		0.00	0.00	0.00	0.00	0.00	0.20	0.20	0.20	0.20	0.20	0.20	0.20	0.20	0.20	0.20
Total Production		4.00		4.00	4.00	4.00	4.00	4.00	9.40	9.40	9.40	9.40	12.40	12.40	12.40	12.40	12.00	12.00
Distributor/Wholesaler (can be ignored because in/out is accomplished without any extra delay)																		
Pipeline Inventory				24.00	24.00	24.00	24.00	24.00	24.00	29.40	34.80	40.20	45.60	54.00	62.40	65.40	68.40	71.00
Retailer																		
Receipts	Delay equal to prod -LT + shipping			4.00	4.00	4.00	4.00	4.00	4.00	4.00	4.00	4.00	4.00	4.00	9.40	9.40	9.40	9.40
Safety Stock	(Lead Time)x%Flex*PlanDemand			3.20	3.20	3.20	0.00	0.00	0.00	0.00	0.00	0.00	0.00	0.00	0.00	0.00	0.00	0.00
Total Inventory	Receipes +SS			7.20	7.20	7.20	4.00	4.00	4.00	4.00	4.00	4.00	4.00	4.00	9.40	9.40	9.40	9.40
Inventory used for current demand				4.00	4.00	4.00	4.00	4.00	4.00	4.00	4.00	4.00	4.00	4.00	4.00	4.00	4.00	4.00
Backlog cleared				0.00	0.00	0.00	0.00	0.00	0.00	0.00	0.00	0.00	0.20	0.20	1.40	1.40	1.40	1.40
Ending Inventory				3.20	3.20	3.20	0.00	0.00	0.00	0.00	0.00	0.00	0.00	0.00	0.00	0.00	0.00	0.00
Planned Demand				4.00	4.00	4.00	4.00	4.00	4.00	4.00	4.00	4.00	4.00	4.00	4.00	4.00	4.00	4.00
Real Demand				4.00	4.00	4.00	8.00	8.00	8.00	8.00	8.00	8.00	8.00	8.00	8.00	8.00	8.00	8.00
Fulfilled Demand				4.00	4.00	4.00	4.00	4.00	4.00	4.00	4.00	4.00	4.00	4.00	9.20	9.20	8.00	8.00
SS Order Needed	Max (Fulfilled demand-Planned, 0)			4.00	8.00	3.20			7.20						7.20		8.00	8.00
Safety Stock reorder	Reorder is smoothed over next cycle			0.00			3.20			0.80	0.80			0.40				0.60
SS Adjustment for new demand level							0.40	0.40	0.40	0.40	0.40	0.40	0.40	0.40				
SS adj smoothed over 8 periods				0.00														
Total SS order				0.00	0.00	0.00	1.20	1.20	1.20	1.20	0.40	0.40	0.40	0.40	0.00	0.00	0.60	0.60
Recovery of backlog				3.20			0.20	0.20	0.20	0.20	0.00	0.00	0.00	0.00	0.00	0.00	4.00	4.00
Financial Impact																		
Backlog this period				0.00	0.00	0.80	0.80	0.80	4.00	4.00	4.00	4.00	4.00	4.00	4.00	4.00	4.00	4.00
Cum Backlog	After accounting for backlog cleared			0.00	0.00	0.80	4.80	8.80	12.80	16.80	20.80	24.80	28.80	32.60	32.40	31.00	29.60	28.20
Backlog net	After accounting for planned recovery			0.00	0.80	3.20	4.60	8.40	12.20	16.00	16.80	16.00	16.00	16.00	12.00	8.00	4.00	0.00
Total Inventory				27.20	27.20	27.20	24.00	24.00	24.00	29.40	34.80	40.20	45.60	54.00	62.40	65.40	68.40	71.00
Benefit	Profit Margin is higher due to stable supply chain times total sales, inventory reduction times cost of inventory																	
Cost	Lost Sales times profit margin, Deferred Sales times discount given as incentive to wait																	
	Periods 1, 2, 4 to 8 hidden																	

Figure 13-4. Beer game played the Toyota way

we shall see below. Also interesting is the fact that Toyota treats the wholesaler and distributor as pass-through participants that account for six weeks of inventory. That arrangement is consistent with the way the game is set up, but it avoids the forecasting and overreaction at the two intermediate stages.

In the Toyota version of the game, the safety stock is decreased to 3.2 so that the starting inventory is 7.2 units. Safety stock that is used up is replenished by being smoothed out over four periods. In addition, an increase to accommodate the new demand levels is smoothed out over eight periods. Thus, there is a constant attempt to smooth out order changes when they are placed upstream. That effort automatically guarantees that the rest of the supply chain does not face violent demand swings.

For the retailer, observe that some complex calculations are involved. First, the retailer receives shipments after eight weeks from the factory. Second, if the retailer cannot fulfill the demand from available stock, then a back order is sent to the factory to be filled during the next planning cycle. The system manages the demand increase in week 11 with the following steps:

1. The demand is for 8 units, but planned demand is 4. Retailer stock is 7.2.

2. The retailer sells 7.2 units, and now the stock is 0. The dealer stock is exhausted, and 0.8 orders will be on back order.

3. The extra 3.2 units sold from safety stock are reordered from the factory to be produced during the next production cycle in a weekly quantity of 0.8—that is, production is smoothed out over four weeks.

4. For the next planning period beginning in week 12, adjustments are made for the recovery of the backlog smoothed out over four weeks (0.2 each for four weeks). Another adjustment is made for the new demand level of 8, which is communicated with a delay of two weeks. That takes effect for the fifth interval starting in week 14. A third adjustment is made so that the increase in production is smoothed out over eight weeks to avoid placing an unnecessary burden on the factory. All these adjustments are sent to the factory with a delay of two weeks. You can check that similar calculations are made at the end of each interval in order to propagate back orders or stock adjustments.

The results are evident. The system recovers by week 23 compared to the huge inventories in the same week in the benchmark case. The Toyota Way has smaller inventory. It is willing to backlog demand in a planned manner—an outcome that happens *unplanned* in the benchmark case if there is too little starting inventory. The Toyota system has not only lower inventory but also lower supply chain costs that are not accounted for in the game (e.g., less overtime, less costly transportation due to a level distribution activity, better quality and lower management cost due to sticking with an accepted bandwidth of operation, and fewer stockouts due to unavailable parts). The outcome is commendable because the Toyota Way, which was not designed to play the beer game, nevertheless intuitively aims to uncover the rules proposed by Sterman to play the beer game.

Interpreting the Outcome

One way to interpret the outcome of the game is to insist that there is a systematic flavor to the results. The results are due to the structure of the game, namely, the long lead times for supply, the delay in communicating orders, and the lack of communication between stages. But that is not the only way to interpret the outcome. There are many other ways of explaining the outcome of the beer game. We classify them as follows:

- *Drawback due to the system.* During the debrief session, players often tend to blame the system. They point out that if they had known the real demand, the situation would not have happened; thus information availability is said to be a constraint. Similarly, it takes two weeks for an order to go from one stage to another; thus, information propagation delay is another problem. Players also say that it takes two weeks at least to get supplies—even longer if the immediate supplier is backlogged. Rush orders might solve the problem. Thus, supply lead time or delay is a problem. Finally, they say that it is difficult to visualize the supply line— that is, to see how many units are in the pipeline headed toward them to fulfill past orders.

- *Use of heuristics.* Sterman suggests that players fall victim to "misperceptions of feedback"; for example, the players do not account for actions that they have already taken, such as the impact of placing a huge order, when viewing the response of the system. In other words, they fail to see that the system can handle regular-sized orders within the regular time but that large orders need more time. Sterman also finds that players assume that the initial stock level of 8 in stock and 8 in the pipeline is optimal. That assumption is probably due to the lack of time for optimizing these values. Similarly, players tend to underestimate the time to get deliveries.

- *Inability to learn.* When asked how to improve the system, many players first say that they feel helpless. They mention their inability to control the system. Many attribute the cause of the dynamics (e.g., huge swings resulting in excess shortages followed by excess inventory) to external factors. As Sterman puts it: "These explanations reflect an 'open loop' conception of the origin of dynamics as opposed to a mode of explanation in which change is seen as arising from the endogenous interactions of decision makers with their environment." Or, bluntly put, they have a collective inability to develop a policy to manage the system.

Here we can borrow from Peter Senge's five disciplines of a learning organization—systems thinking, personal mastery, mental models, building shared vision, and team learning—to explain the inability to learn. Let us consider the five disciplines. Clearly, the beer game participants lack personal mastery because they are somewhat at the novice level, even if they are supply chain managers in real life. They have probably never been exposed to such rapid evolution in the systems they manage. Players have a mental model of how the supply chain functions. Whether right or wrong, these ideas are not shared with others due to the rules of the game. For example, players might expect immediate delivery of orders. They may not realize that information delays create a lag in the last player (i.e., the factory) recognizing that the demand has increased. The lack of synchronous flow of information and material is not obvious, and probably its effect is difficult to imagine!

The goal is to maximize supply chain profit, because the team with the lowest cost wins. In the game, the lack of principles and practices that are necessary to translate goals into action leads to the disorderly outcome.

Finally, by focusing on being a retailer or distributor, the players fail to see how playing their position can adversely affect others. In other words, by playing their position they fail to think of the supply chain as a system. They probably might not even learn that through repeated play, especially if the game were played over long distances. Players believe that the enemy is "out there" by simply blaming everything and everyone else but their own selves for the results. They say things like "the demand was random," "we never got supply," and "we were not allowed to talk." The players additionally get trapped into the illusion of taking charge, preferring action to thought. In the beer game there is a lot of frantic calculation done with the focus on placing an order rather than trying to learn. Moreover, fixing attention on the ordering event prevents the players from taking a long-term view, such as contemplating the impact of placing a very large order on the entire supply chain.

Technology Helps Mitigate the Bullwhip Effect in the Supply Chain[4]

Mitigating the bullwhip effect in the supply chain requires coordination, and manufacturing on JIT principles requires precise timing between the manufacturer and the supplier. Looking to increase its business with Toyota, Dana Corp. has relied on technology to help it manage timing and coordination in its plant in Owensboro, Kentucky, for manufacturing truck frames.

Using a sequencing system based on Internet FTP (File Transfer Protocol) communication, Dana receives orders hourly from Toyota and uploads them into a "production instruction system." That information is fed to all the component cells, where it is displayed on bulletin boards to let the cell know which model is currently being produced. Instantaneous order delivery from Toyota means that lot sizes can be as small as one to five. The result is that the plant is extremely lean, yet flexible enough to produce 14 models for two unique platforms on a single assembly line.

As the plant completely relies on the order system to keep producing, multiple standbys have been built in. The communication relies on a cluster of servers with "hot failover" so that backup systems always track the state and can take over from the primary system at any time. If everything shuts down, the manual alternative is to print order sheets and use those instead. In another use of technology, the plant's team modified a machine that was meant to apply model numbers to verify that the right type of frame had been assembled by scanning key parts of the frame.

Always an extremely lean plant, Dana has reaped benefits from this technology. In 2002, it reduced costs by US$1.8 million, while over a three-year period it reduced the in-plant defect rate by 29 percent, raw materials inventory by 65 percent, and finished goods inventory by 29.6 percent.

As a tier 1 supplier, Dana also manages its own tier 2 suppliers who deliver parts just-in-time. A system of kanban cards and scheduled routes is used to deliver supplies to the floor, and drivers pick up cards for the next round as they drop off supplies. On the outbound side, a trigger board of 25 lights (the size of each shipment) tracks each frame rolling off the assembly line at Toyota's plant. A driver knows that when 25 lights are on, it's time for the next delivery.

Reflection Points

The manner in which the beer game is played can be related, at a somewhat deep level, to the two main themes in the book. We summarize these below. The following learning methods are systematically used in stages in every process and by every one of the participants in the Toyota version of the game:

- *Create awareness.* In the game, limits are placed so that once demand fluctuates beyond the stock level, it becomes noticed.
- *Establish capability.* Collaboration between the retailer and the factory to establish a new production plan empowers the team to take concerted action.
- *Make action protocols.* The reaction is constrained so that gradual changes are made to accommodate demand, adjust safety stock, and recover

backlog. The constraints are placed to help identify cause and effect. Clearly, the planner knows when the smoothed orders will arrive at the plant, when they will arrive at the distributor and wholesaler, and so on. Those events can be tracked and planned in advance. Notice too the similar way of reacting to changes, whether it be demand, safety stock, or back-order recovery.

- *Generate system-level awareness.* The factory is placed at the forefront. The wholesaler's and distributor's roles are subsumed into a pass-through. The entire supply chain becomes visible, with cause and effect of actions at every stage becoming clearer as one moves up the chain. Notice that what occurs is exactly the reverse of what happens in many supply chains, where the sales group is often unaware of the rest of the roles in the supply chain. In the beer game scenario, the main burden of calculation of changes is placed on the retailer. A reader well versed in the theory of incentives might spot the necessity for centralizing the planning. That step would be made because of the need for complex calculations, which would require system-level considerations by the retailer.

Link to the v4L:

- *Variety* is not explicitly considered in the beer game. But if an uncertainty related to the product mix were added to the game, the impact of Toyota's approaches would be even more significant than in the typical game.
- *Velocity.* Toyota's approach to the game begins with the factory and its production rate adjustments as a mechanism to regulate product flow in response to demand data.
- *Variability.* New adjustments related to the data about demand are smoothed over time to reduce the impact on order variability. That reduction in variability lowers inventory while lowering back-order levels in a period. In other words, the responses to new data are distributed throughout the system and over time.
- *Visibility* (or lack of it) is a key component of the game. The lack of visibility of underlying demand and absence of collaborative planning create most of the problems in the standard game. Notice that the Toyota approach to the game provides room for collaboration—and thus a smoother response to new demand level information.

Endnotes

1. Hau L. Lee, V. Padmanabhan, and Seungjin Whang, "Information Distortion in a Supply Chain: Bullwhip Effects," *Management Science* 43, no. 4 (1997): 546–558.

2. The beer game is clearly an abstraction of a real supply chain: real supply chains carry multiple products; the four players might work for the same firm and thus have the ability to coordinate; some amount of information sharing might be possible; and so on. Thus, the tendency might be to dismiss the simulation as being of low value. In fact, the beer game is introduced as the first example in the compilations of problems in industrial dynamics (W. E. Jarmain, *Problems in Industrial Dynamics*. Cambridge, MA: MIT Press, 1963).

   In the study of problems in industrial dynamics, no solution to and no explanation of the phenomenon are offered simply because to anyone familiar with Jay Forrester's book on industrial dynamics (Jay W. Forrester, *Industrial Dynamics*. Cambridge, MA: MIT Press, 1961), the outcome is obvious. Notably, even though many other examples are rarely mentioned in a core course in an MBA school, the beer game has captured the fancy of the academic and practitioner world. It probably displays a combination of what can go wrong with systems, decision making, and learning (too slowly) over time.

3. John D. Sterman, "Modeling Managerial Behavior: Misperceptions of Feedback in a Dynamic Decision Making Experiment," *Management Science* 35 (1989): 321–339.

4. Tonya Vinas, "In Sync with the Customer: Dana Plant Built for TPS Rewarded with More and More Business for Toyota's Growing Truck Line," *IndustryWeek* (October 1, 2003).

Chapter 14

Reflections of Supply Chain Participants

The following are summaries of the interviews that we conducted with Toyota executives as well as executives of the extended supply chain. Some of these comments were included throughout the book; however, we thought that including the summaries would be interesting to the reader because they bring many different viewpoints together in one place.

Interview on August 21, 2008, with Gene Tabor, General Manager, Purchasing-Supplier Relations, Supplier Diversity, and Risk Management

The purpose of the interview was to discuss how Toyota works with its suppliers and to better understand Toyota's working relationship with suppliers.

Gene Tabor believes that Toyota starts with a foundation that assumes that supplier relationships focus on the long term. Toyota also focuses on clarity of expectations with written annual expectations and mechanisms to measure, provide feedback, monitor, and improve. The goal is predictability so that the behavior of the supplier and Toyota, when an issue arises, can be forecasted by both parties. Communications with suppliers happen at the two annual supplier meetings as well as at ongoing meetings to enhance communications, expectations, and implementation.

Gene tells suppliers, "No surprises are preferred. Call even if it is 5 p.m. on a Friday afternoon instead of waiting until Monday and try to resolve it over the weekend." He reiterated that the preferred mode at Toyota is "bad news first" so that the supplier and Toyota can solve the problem. The supplier may seek help by contacting Toyota directly, a Toyota manager visiting the supplier may see a problem, or the supplier may seek help after a problem is discovered.

Supplier support is not limited to purchasing. Several possible groups may talk to the supplier. They include procurement, quality control, supply chain, and others. The relationship is in the form of a matrix with several possible contacts with Toyota interacting across the organization. The matrix has to "tighten up" to prevent problems from falling through the gaps. The most difficult issue is finding the most efficient and effective approach for sorting, sifting, directing, and coordinating help to the suppliers; Toyota considers the process to be a work in progress.

Gene says that "every supplier will have a problem of some type; the question is not if, but when it happens, how is it handled?" There are no extra resources to help suppliers; everyone, from purchasing to the line team members, may be used to solve a problem. If a supplier has a financial issue and is winding down, a team from Toyota will go to the supplier location and help to wind things down by working with the customer group to ensure a fair share of product. Many times the subsuppliers may continue to work with another supplier to ship to Toyota.

How does Toyota ensure that supplier assistance is separated from purchasing negotiations? Toyota starts with "respect for people," so that even if the supplier and Toyota do not agree, the supplier understands that the buyer is ready to listen and has the data to support a given case.

Interview on August 21, 2008, with Jamey Lykins, Toyota Purchasing General Manager

The purpose of the interview was to understand how Toyota selects and develops suppliers.

Jamey Lykins says that Toyota's view of procurement is to "cultivate the market and farm it" rather than "hunt for suppliers and use." He also says that Toyota's view is that the concept of the market producing a continuous stream of innovations at ever-decreasing prices is a myth—the market has to be fostered and harnessed to generate competitive offerings. That effort requires patience and development of suppliers, among other things. Toyota accomplishes its objectives in many ways.

Toyota developed the idea of supplier pods, which reduce the frictional costs of doing business. These pods are focused on tier 1 suppliers with whom the firm has long-term business relationships. The synergy within each pod is not orchestrated by Toyota; instead, it is nurtured. In addition, Toyota carefully selects suppliers at different tiers that have to be cultivated. In some cases, specific tier 3 or tier 4 suppliers are directly engaged by Toyota to ensure that innovative ideas are nurtured. In return for guaranteed markets for innovations, these smaller companies provide unique research and development capabilities (e.g., tool and die companies or plastic injection molding companies). The need to retain connections even with these small firms is to ensure that the know-how from 30- to 40-year industry veterans is not lost.

Not all suppliers are treated equally. Some companies that are closely tied to Toyota face greater-than-market pressures to outperform the market. Jamey cited examples where Toyota engineers and supplier engineers have committed to reducing costs by over 50 percent for some critical parts.

The purchasing manager continuously evaluates suppliers based on the flexibility of the plant to reallocate resources, the capability of the company (i.e., the skill set of the organization), and the competitiveness of the company as a whole. A supplier can be evaluated by Toyota managers who tour the shop floor to examine how it manages tasks, accommodates variability, standardizes work, maintains rhythm on the floor, solves problems, and so on. By watching tasks being performed, observing the layout of parts and steps, reviewing instructions regarding task performance, and so on, evaluators will think of potential outcomes. The "red rabbit" test is also sometimes used to check how long it takes to identify a defect. In this test, a red part is added to the mix and the time until it is discovered is identified. Toyota believes that if all of these issues are managed well, then quality will be improved and costs will be lowered.

If costs remain higher than deemed competitive, Toyota sends a team to work with the supplier to lower costs. In addition, Toyota also provides assistance to suppliers to improve performance. But the group that provides the assistance shares no information with the purchasing group.

Interview on August 21, 2008, with David Burbidge, Vice President of Production Control, Toyota

The purpose of the interview was to discuss the role of production control regarding production planning and scheduling.

David Burbidge described how the production plans are adjusted to accommodate both minor hiccups in the production process as well as a major shift in demand. When a minor hiccup happens, the selectivity lanes at the paint shop and some inventory at the assembly line play a role to recover the schedule. At the paint shops, the mix of vehicles is adjusted to restore a smooth sequence. In order to do that effectively, the Yamazumi charts for each variant (i.e., charts that show the planned cycle times for each process) are used to ensure that associates do not get overburdened and thus guarantee quality. In addition, assembly buffers at the end of each line enable production smoothing.

David then discussed the major rescheduling that took place in the case of the Toyota sports utility vehicle, the Sequoia. This SUV was launched with an annual volume estimate of 103,000. Most people at Toyota felt that the demand for the first year would be very high, but soon this volume was cut to 78,000 then 72,000. Sales revised it again to 66,000 before launch. The actual looked to be closer to 35,000, thus leaving 175 days of supply for the vehicle. As David described the situation, it appeared to be the perfect storm. Just as Toyota launched the new SUV, consumer sentiment for these larger cars had turned, and the SUV was viewed as disreputable—shunned by the public (like, say, a fur coat) as an inappropriate purchase during a period of high fuel prices and global warming.

A decision was made to stop production of the Sequoia for three months. When such a determination is made, the recent suppliers are compensated financially. Strategic suppliers help out Toyota by sharing the pain. Sequence suppliers also get some help. The system has to plan both shutdown and start-up to ensure that quality is maintained. Some of the employees are shuttled to other Toyota plants around the country to replace temporary workers. David remarked that this was new territory for Toyota—it had seen a growing market in the United States for 20 years and North America used the capacity in Japan as a buffer to ensure stable U.S. production.

Phone Interview on September 25, 2008, with Mike Botkin, General Manager of Logistics, Toyota

The purpose of the interview was to discuss the logistics operation at Toyota in North America.

Mike Botkin is general manager of the North American Logistics division. The two departments that comprise this division are Logistics and Parts Distribution. Logistics, is responsible for route planning, operations of over-the-road logistics (inbound), cross-dock management, and initial planning for new projects or model change. Outbound logistics of finished vehicles are the responsibility of Toyota Motor Sales. Parts Distribution manages the supply of service parts from the plant to the service center. It supports service parts production and shipping preparation. This group is also responsible for quality, technical support, and overseas logistics and customs.

Describing the logistics, Mike mentioned that the preferred method of routing is from supplier to cross-dock to plant. The milk run is used when demand is not satisfied from cross-dock and is not the norm. In case of milk runs, Toyota generates the routes and passes them on to a third-party logistics company. That arrangement was not always in place. In Japan, the supplier is responsible for delivering to the plant. When Toyota came to the United States, two logistics partners were charged with doing the routing. They were provided with such information as the delivery frequency and time windows. Over the

20 years that Toyota has been operating in the United States, they have developed the expertise to do the routing themselves. Routes from the supplier directly to the plant are planned at the plant. Routes integrated with other North American plants are determined by the logistics organization.

If weather delays or supplier issues occur, ordering is still based on the old timeline but a new transportation plan is manually generated. For example, if an 8-hour route is delayed to 10 hours, a one-way move may be used to recover the timeline. Such planning is done on a case-by-case basis. Some automation is utilized for communication and control of trucks. Lead time for each part and supplier is synchronized with the route and assembly requirement.

Mike described heijunka at the plant as focused on smoothing of lineside workload requirements (e.g., wire harness adjustments take more time on a vehicle with a sunroof assembly than on one that does not have that need). As a result, other considerations such as the lot size and delivery sequence determine the loading and smoothness of the logistics, handling, and transportation.

Service parts demand comes from dealers and repair shops, but demand for service parts is erratic, as it is based on need. The parts depot, in the early days of Toyota, had some buffers because of fewer models and parts. The only issue was seasonality, but that could be planned for. As the number of models increased, the parts count increased. The company is working through the process to smooth the flow.

Lead time is higher for international shipments, as they are shipped in sea containers. Transportation costs are also large. The planners first try to determine the number of containers per day required at a facility and build the containers for one production day. So when a container is unloaded at an assembly plant, it may contain all parts for 150 vehicles that are planned to be made during part of a day. If there are options, there may be inventory at the plant to handle variations at the plant.

Variation is also created because of product mix. Consider the difference between a Camry and a Sequoia—the Camry is 10 cubic meters while the Sequoia is closer to 20. The smaller vehicle has a better chance for trailer efficiency. The packaging and lot sizes are thus impacted by the product. The other issue in North America is that the vehicle is produced at the assembly plant. However, the supplier base is spread out in North America—perhaps over 300 miles from the plant, unlike in Japan where the distance from plant to supplier is less than 50 miles. Each plant manages logistics, but there is an attempt to standardize processes; thus, logistics at plants is decentralized. The expectation is that the planning will be centralized in a few years, while deployment remains decentralized.

For example, in concept, it is expected that a delivery of a pallet is one for one with a returnable container. However, with variance in orders and in scheduling the completion of vehicles, such synchronization is a challenge.

Toyota uses a core carrier program to pick up loads directly from supplier locations. The transportation partner is expected to be safe, confirm parts counts at the order level, inform about short shipments, and deliver on time. Toyota measures instances where the shipment error should have been caught, as well as in and out time. In some cases, company observers ride along to confirm drive times. The trucking company manages the route—the expectation is that it can confirm progress of the driver with a global positioning system or may contract the monitoring to another company.

Interview on September 3, 2008, with Steve Gates, Toyota Dealer

The purpose of the interview was to discuss how Toyota dealers interact with Toyota and to better understand the dealer's role in the supply chain.

Steve Gates started by explaining the Toyota car allocation system to dealers. The allocation follows a "turn and earn" model where specific vehicles are allocated by region. One of the tasks of the dealer is to explain to customers the value proposition offered by Toyota. Most repeat customers who have owned Toyota cars earlier or are familiar with other Japanese manufacturers understand the concept that variety will be limited to maintain quality and value. The remaining customers require salesperson assistance to walk them through the value proposition of the increased features that accompany the limited variety, thus providing the "added value" for the cars offered. Steve did not feel that variety limitations were a deterrent. He did highlight the fact that dealers have a voice in Toyota's product planning and their perceptions regarding customer needs were considered when allocations were made.

Some regions such as Florida usually sell cars with no cold weather kits. But other regions such as Kentucky and Indiana cannot sell cars without cold weather kits. Likewise, dealers in Cincinnati, Kentucky, and Michigan decided that an antilock brake system (ABS) would be an option most customers would not be willing to pay for; thus, vehicles with these systems would not be stocked. So customers in these areas wanting antilock brake systems in their cars would get a car from Chicago that had to be traded for a car in the region. In the Toyota system, there is a limited ability to do such trades.

Every quarter, the sales managers in each region meet with dealers to decide which cars should be built. This process is guided by Toyota Motor Sales (TMS), so dealers may not get exactly what they want. However, dealers get to influence product configuration (e.g., dealers in the Kentucky region pushed for the new Tundra truck to be sold with a big V8 engine and TMS acquiesced). Dealers get quick access to the highest levels at Toyota sales executives to provide feedback regarding customer preferences.

While most vehicles are sold as carefully planned variants, the Scion is sold differently. It continues to be allocated using the "turn-and-earn" model. The car is manufactured in Japan and shipped to the United States to the ports around the country nearest to the dealers. But the product is held at the port and then released to dealers against orders. The dealers have the choice of customizing the product at the port or at the dealership. Each customer is encouraged to customize his or her car through choice of decals, crests, and other accessories. The car and its accessories are presented to customers with fixed prices, so pricing is transparent with no negotiation. The customer waits for 7 to 10 days to get the car.

Dealerships that are allocated cars have the option to decline to take possession, but that decision will affect future allocation preferences. The allocation is based on the dealers' share of the region sales. Each line is allocated separately so that sales of one type of car (e.g., Prius) do not affect allocations of another (e.g., Camry).

The Lexus dealers use a sales approach like Toyota's. Lexus cars are usually offered fully loaded with few options. Toyota Motor Sales knows the percentage of vehicles each dealer will sell, and it allocates accordingly. The Lexus approach to allocating cars is different from that of Audi or BMW which prefer to offer more flexibility to customize the cars.

Toyota's relationship with dealers is like a partnership. The National Dealer Council consists of 10 to 12 dealers, including Steve Gates. It provides a lot of input to Toyota regarding customer preferences. For example, the dealer council pushed for a large truck and got Toyota to produce the Tundra. They have also proposed a smaller truck, which Steve referred to as a Home Depot truck that customers would use to take things home from the Home Depot. There are 1,200 Toyota dealerships across 12 regions that are represented by the dealer council.

Steve provided an anecdote regarding the collaboration between the National Dealer Council and Toyota. Two years ago, the dealer council urged TMC to increase Prius production from 125,000 to 150,000 cars. TMC asked the dealers to target 225,000 cars. But a year later, in February 2007, the dealer council found it had too many cars and requested a $500-per-car incentive to reduce inventory. But in 2008, there was again a shortage of Prius, with most dealers having a one-day supply (if all inventories in the pipeline were included). This collaboration between the dealers and Toyota is, in Steve's words, a rarity in the auto industry.

Steve mentioned that the dealers adopt Toyota's approaches toward kaizen and expect to increase their productivity. Sales associates who provide ideas for improvement are rewarded individually. The goal is to decrease expenses without affecting the customer.

Interview on August 20, 2008, with Gary Dodd, Former President of Tire & Wheel Assembly and Former Executive with Toyota

The purpose of the interview was to discuss how Toyota suppliers interact with Toyota and to understand Toyota's supply chain management from the supplier's viewpoint.

Gary was one of the first general managers hired by Toyota. He worked in a matrix structure within Toyota from the very beginning, from the construction of a project to the coordination of ongoing production operations. He was with Toyota for 12 years. He was interested in starting a company and had conversations with Toyota Chairman Fujio Cho regarding this goal. Gary left Toyota and started a supplier company, Tire & Wheel Assembly (T&WA), which delivers tire and wheel assembly—a sequence part. The supplier built a facility in Indiana and supplied the Toyota plant in Princeton, Indiana. The company mounted tires on wheels with the variety suggested by Toyota. There was no room for downtime; modest inventory was on hand to ensure enough parts to match takt time or line speed. T&WA has a record with Toyota of never creating a downtime.

When asked about the specific actions Toyota took to make life better for the suppliers, Gary mentioned that there are huge differences between supplying to Toyota and supplying to other automakers. The main differences are the high level of support Toyota provides to suppliers, the high level of collaboration, and, when good things are done and all key performance indicators (KPIs) are in alignment, there is a lot of recognition and celebration. Toyota takes its key suppliers to a resort and they all have an annual meet to play golf or tennis. In contrast, many other OEMs have a demanding approach with a lot of confrontation. Most other OEMs leave it to the supplier to fix problems, but Toyota assists with fixing problems, and suppliers are comfortable with Toyota's assistance in fixing problems.

When Gary was in the original management team with Fujio Cho, they used to have meetings twice a week. During the original period, management team members presented their accomplishments against goals. Mr. Cho told them they were selected because they were good, so he would assume that everything was fine but wanted to hear problems first so that they could be fixed. That approach was carried forward to suppliers; as they came onboard, they were also told to talk about problems—problems were expected, and suppliers would get Toyota's assistance to fix them.

How else does Toyota keep the pressure on suppliers to be competitive? The other OEMs demand output. At Toyota too the pressure is maintained—every supplier understands that Toyota want costs to decrease. But at Toyota the question is how to squeeze the waste by removing unnecessary costs. Several times a year there is an exercise between the supplier and Toyota to reduce costs and thus reduce costs to Toyota and the supplier. It is very effective because everyone is pulling in the same direction.

Usually the group that helps decrease costs is different from the purchasing group. Sometimes, even after a lot of effort, there may not be any cost savings. If so, Toyota would be willing to let the costs stay as is. There is a lot of open book reconciliation—for example, Toyota might accept a 1 percent cost reduction one year and expect to do better another year.

The KPIs that Toyota uses to evaluate suppliers are on-time delivery, quality, and cost targets. The same KPIs are used internally to be compatible with Toyota's expectations. These KPIs are looked at daily at the supplier organization and shared. In the beginning, suppliers were anxious about doing that and sharing a lot of information. Over a period of time, a level of mutual respect developed, and suppliers realized that that involvement was beneficial.

Toyota provides a great deal of visibility to the supplier for planning purposes. The annual supplier meeting provides a feel for Toyota's plans for the upcoming year. After that, for all suppliers, there are individual meetings to relate the overall plan to the supplier's volumes. The meeting is the time for such handoff discussions—to analyze the plans and understand their impact.

The supplier also gets a good sense of the volume and mix. If there are market changes, Toyota does some modest adjustments. There have been no instances where major changes were made that could cause havoc with the supplier. When asked if this process would work now when there are large product mix changes, decreases in volumes, and the like, Gary replied that he did not expect a change. He anticipates a shortening of time frames and expects Toyota to be working much harder to communicate with suppliers, working more closely with them. On a day-to-day basis, all of the Toyota data are received electronically and there are meetings to discuss the plans and operations. If there are any issues—for example, if the plans are more aggressive than can be accommodated due to equipment changes—the supplier is compensated. At the operational level, based on the T&WA takt time, the supplier gets a two-hour advance notice. An electronic order is sent to the supplier by Toyota when the vehicle body leaves the paint department. T&WA has to assemble and supply the tire and wheel assembly just-in-time for it to be mounted onto the correct car.

Gary believes that the way Toyota deals with suppliers needs to be examined more closely to understand what leadership in a supply chain really means.

Interview on September 23, 2008, with Jeffrey Smith, Vice President and General Manager, Toyota Business Unit, Johnson Controls

The purpose of the interview was to discuss how Toyota and suppliers work together as partners.

Jeffrey Smith described the forecasts shared by Toyota with Johnson Controls Inc. (JCI), a primary seat supplier, to enable stable orders and thus financial planning and budgeting. The company gets a yearly forecast broken down by months. Every week it also receives a rolling horizon 10-week forecast. Each time, the forecast for the next two weeks is firm, but the following weeks the variation is under 5 percent. Forecasts provided to JCI then cascade to forecasts to their subsuppliers and others. Heijunka at Toyota translates into a mix of seat types such as leather and cloth. That in turn creates smoother workload (due to differing work content of seat types) at JCI.

The role of design leadership for seats varies by model. In the past, JCI has been responsible for rear seats while Toyota has had leadership for front seats for several models. The rear seats vary by automobile model and design choices, but the front seat is quite independent of the rest of the car design. In the future, Jeff hoped that the roles would flip, with JCI taking leadership for front seats and Toyota leading design for the rear seats.

Toyota collaborates to obtain efficiency improvements and provides direct assistance when necessary. Jeff shared a description of what would happen if there were a problem with JCI's seats with other OEMs. The general manager would be invited into the customer's plant and subjected to an uncomfortable interrogation. Jeff contrasted that situation with what would happen if Toyota were the OEM. Toyota would send the particular specific plant person who dealt with the problem or, if the problem were more complicated, a team. In Toyota's case, the team would come to JCI's plant to assist in determining the root cause and identifying potential countermeasures.

Jeff also described the negotiation process with Toyota's purchasing managers. A seat would be broken down into specific commodities such as steel, foam, plastics, trim, and assembly. A cost index method benchmark would be used to identify a globally competitive cost point for each commodity. Likewise, details such as welding cost, injection molding cost, and assembly costs would all be considered. At Toyota, the formula is Price − Cost = Profit; compare that with the traditional formula: Cost + Profit = Price. Given a target price from Toyota, JCI would have a profit that would be the difference between the price and the cost. JCI's focus then is how to decrease costs and thus increase profit. JCI has participated with Toyota with some initiatives in this regard, such as CCC21, Value Innovation, Mass Innovation, and Gentani (i.e., recent initiative focused on efficiency improvements, lowest cost sourcing, and flexibility).

Jeff described the recent issues of coordinating with Toyota during a 14-week plant shutdown in San Antonio. JCI has five other supplier locations including plants in the United States and Mexico that will be affected by the shutdown. However, because JCI has been a partner with Toyota for over 25 years and has shared in its growth, he expected that Toyota would end up sharing the pain.

Jeff provided a current example of coordination with Toyota. JCI is scheduled to deliver rear-seat frames for the new Toyota vehicle, the Venza. The seats were to be made at a plant in Cadiz, Kentucky, an old plant built in the 1960s. From December 2007 through July 2008, Toyota's Quality Development worked with JCI to bring the Cadiz plant welding capability up to Toyota's latest standards, including a rating of over 90 percent on its prescribed welding audit. The Cadiz plant had initially achieved a welding rating of 44 percent that had improved to 83 percent by June 2008. JCI then decided it would restructure its operations and shut down the Cadiz operation. That announcement resulted in the necessity to move the Venza rear-seat frame manufacturing to its facility in Athens, Tennessee.

Before the move started, Toyota was informed that the new seat frames would be made at a plant that had never supplied to Toyota. The move was scheduled to happen over a one-week period. Toyota immediately sent its team to Athens and observed a weld rating of 23 percent that increased to 75 percent in two weeks and reached 95 percent within five weeks of the move (before the start of the full-scale manufacturing). The Toyota visits to Athens focused on "cut-and-etch" weld dissections and microscopic analysis. The Toyota team also invited JCI to Toyota's Georgetown plant to understand its systems. So Toyota went into overdrive and provided intense support for Athens.

Jeff also described the process a while ago when JCI decided to consolidate two plants in Georgetown, Kentucky, into one facility. The move involved sharing with Toyota a "high-level" plan/image six months prior to the move followed by a process change request including plans for human resources, IT, production control, equipment moves, building renovations, quality, and plant operations. JCI set up a project room, or *Obeya*, to manage the effort. The relocation was completed during a one-week July shutdown. Because JCI supplied many of the seats for the biggest-selling car in North America, the Camry, the relocation of the seating operation had to be orchestrated flawlessly and start-up had to mirror Toyota Georgetown's start-up. JCI was able to execute that risky move due to a good and very detailed plan as well as constant management attention and focus. The trust between Toyota and JCI was key to the seamless transition. Jeff's perspective was that good planning and attention to every detail is something JCI continues to learn from Toyota and practice in many situations.

Interview on August 15, 2008, with Achim Paechtner, Former Senior Manager at Toyota of Europe

The purpose of the interview was to understand the differences of the automobile supply chain in Europe versus North America. Achim Paechtner identified four major differences in Europe:

1. With retailers, the major challenge Toyota faces is the heterogeneous environment: 27 countries, different practices, and history. In addition, exclusive and selective distribution was allowed in the past, but now OEMs have to choose one or another distribution agreement. Toyota chose exclusive distribution under which retailers are given a sales territory but retailers can sell to third parties like supermarkets.

2. Retailers are reluctant to share data; for example, they do not share actual sales data with Toyota. That reluctance creates a challenge for sales forecasting. Toyota is working to improve the forecasting process. In Spain, retailers send forecasts at $N - 3$ months, the retailer's forecast is used, and that is what Toyota can expect. In Germany, retailers forecast. If retailers are keen to get cars, they provide more accurate forecasts.

3. The car has a unique social status in Europe. The retailers are smaller than elsewhere, so the available choice from the retailer's lot is limited. However, there is great demand for individualized cars, driven by domestic manufacturers that offer many million combinations. Other manufacturers (e.g., BMW and Mercedes) have many options. Toyota is implementing the "Feature Model" strategy as a marketing and sales strategy to accelerate vehicle turns. The concept is to identify the most popular mix—for example, with the Yaris, the goal would be to identify the combinations that represent 80 percent of sales—then advertise, keep the car in the showroom, and ensure that the retailer has demo cars and the vehicles in stock. That objective is a challenge in Europe because the habit of people is to have a dream car with full spec. As the car becomes a status symbol with individualization, delivery time increases. Toyota has tried to offer packages of options to counteract this impact on lead time and to streamline the mix. The hub also does some accessory installation, which is termed "post-production options" (PPOs). The hub may change the car to generate a source of profit. So the hub manager may order a car with no radio or CD

player, and use a cheaper or better source to install the item. The retailer may do the same to generate an additional source of profit.

4. The wait to get a car is longer. How long does a customer wait to get a Toyota? That depends on the model involved, where the car is manufactured, and where it is sold. Certain models of Corollas are made in South Africa, others in the United Kingdom. The time varies depending on where the car is built—six to eight weeks to ship from South Africa, but only three days from the United Kingdom. Toyota tries to centralize stock so that asset swapping reduces time. (When a car is at the hub, it may or may not be allocated to a dealer, depending on what country is involved. The central stock is owned by Toyota, not allocated to the dealer. Though cars would be allocated to dealer orders, there are dummy orders placed so that there is adequate stock.) Delivery time for special orders varies from 10 days to five to six months. The general plan is to supply 50 percent from the hub within one week to 10 days, 30 percent from the pipeline, and the rest individualized—for the minicar and small car segment. One of the causes for long lead times might be Toyota's global sourcing strategy. The decision to source parts and vehicles everywhere in the world, where prices are the lowest and quality fits, leads indeed to very long lead times (e.g., with parts from Turkey, South Africa, and Thailand for European production or South African vehicle production).

Reflection Points

The Toyota supply chain is complex and evolving. That fact is a reminder that the company faces the same set of business issues as many other firms that operate in the same environment. Nevertheless, the leadership provided by Toyota has resulted in a tremendous alignment of supply chain participants excelling at the task of creating value. That feat is in no small measure due to the fact that the supply chain participants feel a sense of identity with the Toyota Way and the v4L principles.

Chapter 15

Reflections

Now that you have read about how Toyota manages its supply chain and also how some other companies have implemented some of these principles, it is important to reflect on the Toyota experience and also look forward to the potential future innovations in the automotive supply chain.

Our hope is that you have been able to clearly understand how Toyota's emphasis on organizational learning processes creates a careful balance of variety, velocity, variability, and visibility across the supply chain and that the summary of the v4Ls at the end of many chapters was helpful to highlight the benefits of implementing Toyota's processes. However, it should be noted that Toyota has not perfected supply chain processes, and by its emphasis on continuous improvement, these processes will evolve over time. In fact, that is one of Toyota's strengths; Toyota does not rest on successes.

Reflection

In this closing chapter, we would like to highlight Toyota's strategic approach to the principles of supply chain management. The following is a summary.

- Take a holistic view of the comprehensive structure of the supply chain, which includes the following:
  - Supply chain–oriented design of products, plants, and packaging
  - Streamlined inbound and outbound logistics
  - Limited number of suppliers that are in close proximity to the plant or cross-dock
  - Integrated supply chain and kaizen processes across the extended enterprise
- Consider having suppliers and dealers as partners. Work closely with them to operate the supply chain effectively and efficiently. Strive to ensure that Toyota partners share in profits during good times and experience some

of the pain during challenging times. Diligently pursue corporate responsibility of the supply chain to the society.

- Ensure stability throughout the supply chain by managing mix and seeing to it that the production rates are synchronized with the use of heijunka.
- Break down the walls between functional groups within the supply chain to guarantee that overall supply chain efficiency takes precedence over local efficiencies; in other words, the whole is greater than the sum of the parts.
- Provide leadership and direction for development, experimentation, and growth to the extended enterprise.

Future

A useful exercise is to look toward the future and consider some potential changes to the supply chain. Among them are the following:

- *Software-based design.* Look for more use of software-controlled functions in products. One of the ways to reduce the number of parts that vary with changes in options is to install the same set of equipment in every vehicle and turn selected optional functions on and off with software controls via telematics similar to GM Onstar.[1] For example, the same instrument panel could be installed on all vehicles that included the equipment for premium radio, a navigation system, and the like. Then, when the customer purchased the vehicle, the features and functions could be selected from a menu on the screen in the dash. These features could be sold at the time of purchase and upgraded anytime after. In addition, these features and functions could be marketed to subsequent owners after the vehicle was resold.
- *Target marketing using the Web.* Use the Internet to manage demand for selected models and/or options that are experiencing an imbalance in the supply chain. That could be done on both a regional level and a national level by publishing the "special of the week," much like the airlines send out weekly specials for flights that are undersold. To make it fair for all dealers and customers, the offer could be constructed so that the special offer is available to the first "n" number of customers to sign up. For example: "the first 1,000 customers to place an order for a new Camry with V6 engine will receive a $500 rebate." The advantage of such an approach is that it could be targeted to selected options and turned on and off very quickly.
- *Changing nature of work.* Consider the use of team-based collaboration within and across the supply chain using modern collaboration technology.

Foster team building across units of the same as well as different organizations that will challenge and explore ideas that span the supply chain.

- *Improve logistics flexibility.* Consider use of adaptive merge-in-transit and reroute-in-transit capability to better match customer preferences to availability. Perhaps a greater variety can be offered without an increase in costs due to flexible logistics.

- *Changing nature of learning and knowledge creation.* The digital revolution has enabled sharing of information as well as preferences. Develop methods and systems to explore this information as it relates to the supply chain; for example, for creating new products, new ordering systems, suggesting changes to existing customer service processes, experimenting with new products and supply chain processes, and learning about new developments in vehicle and related technologies. Develop learning systems that can cater to a worldwide audience of employees and supply chain partners.

We hope that you will find *Toyota Supply Chain Management* useful in improving your business supply chain processes!

Endnote

1. Trademark of General Motors Corporation.

Appendix

Example of Why the 80/20 Rule Is Valid

W̲e will use a set of specific numbers to highlight the 80/20 rule used in the Mix Planning discussion in Chapter 3 and described in detail in the section "A Simulation Model." Consider a sample auto company that sells products in two different markets. The company is considering (1) whether to offer two products in each of two markets or (2) whether to offer one product in each market. We would like to consider conditions under which option 1 or option 2 would be the profitable choice.

Assume that an average of 100 customers represent demand each period and thus potential purchasers in each region. Also assume that the variance of the number of potential customers in a period is also 100. Suppose stockkeeping units (SKUs) 1 and 2 are offered in each of two separate regions, A and B. Suppose in region A, the demand in any week could be driven by two different customer populations. Customer population 1 would have 47 percent of customers purchasing product 1 and 20 percent purchasing product 2, with the remaining customers purchasing nothing. Customer population 2 would have 20 percent purchasing SKU 1, 20 percent purchasing SKU 2, and the remaining customers purchasing nothing. Suppose that in any week the probability that customers could come from either population (one or the other, not both) is 50 percent.

Note that given these numbers, the average demand for SKUs 1 and 2 consist of the probability that the customers belong to populations 1 or 2 and the conditional probability that they purchase an SKU given they belong to a population. Thus, the average demand for SKU 1 is as follows:

$$(0.5 \times 100 \times 0.47) + (0.5 \times 100 \times 0.2) = 33.5$$

The variance in demand for this SKU arises out of two possible reasons: (1) the variance associated with each separate population's purchase of the SKU and

(2) the mean demand that varies by population type. Using standard statistical approaches, we obtain the variance for SKU 1 as follows:

$$\{0.5 \times [(100 \times 0.47) + (100 \times 0.47)^2]\} +$$
$$\{0.5 \times [(100 \times 0.2) + (100 \times 0.2)^2]\} - (33.5)^2$$
$$= 235.75$$

A similar set of calculations generates a mean of 20 and a variance of 20 for SKU 2.

Suppose region 2 has the same set of populations but with SKU 1 and SKU 2 swapping parameters. The corresponding mean for SKU 1 in region 2 would be 20, and the corresponding variance for SKU 1 would be 20. The mean for SKU 2 in region 2 would be 33.5 and the variance would be 235.75.

Across both regions, the overall mean demand for SKUs 1 and 2 would be 53.5, and the overall standard deviation would be 15.35 for a coefficient of variation of 28.6 percent. (The coefficient of variation is the ratio of the standard deviation and the mean demand.) Intuitively, the higher the coefficient of variation, the higher the quantity of stock carried to meet unexpected demand.

Could reducing variety while increasing value through synchronized selling, improved quality, and improved features reduce the variation while maintaining the mean demand? Assume that SKU 1 is offered in region 1 and attracts 50 percent of the market. Similarly, suppose offering only SKU 2 in region 2 generates 50 percent of the market. The corresponding mean demand is 50 units, and the standard deviation is 7.07 for a coefficient of variation of 14.14 percent. These parameters correspond to a more stable overall demand! In turn, this means that the plant and suppliers experience lower forecast error and thus can focus their attention on quality improvement and value generation. Safety stocks can be low across the supply chain, thus lowering inventory costs. All of this can assist in improving supply chain profitability.

Index

About the Authors

Ananth V. Iyer is the Susan Bulkeley Butler Chair in operations management at the Krannert School of Management, Purdue University. He has supply chain expertise in a wide range of industries, from groceries and apparel to garbage pickup and automobiles.

Sridhar Seshadri is a professor of operations management in the IROM Department at the McCombs School of Business, University of Texas at Austin. He has done extensive research on supply chain contracts and risk management.

Roy Vasher is a former Toyota senior executive. Vasher played a leading role in Toyota's North American and European initiatives to streamline the supply chain to reduce order-to-delivery lead time. Currently he is president of RPV Consulting, LLC.